Economics
Sourcebook
of Government
Statistics

Economics Sourcebook of Government Statistics

Arline Alchian Hoel
Kenneth W. Clarkson
Roger LeRoy Miller
Law and Economics Center,
University of Miami

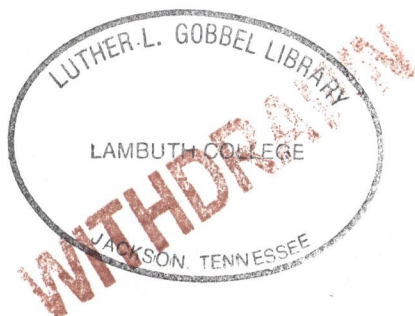

LexingtonBooks
D.C. Heath and Company
Lexington, Massachusetts
Toronto

Library of Congress Cataloging in Publication Data

Hoel, Arline Alchian.
  Economics sourcebook of government statistics.

    1. United States—Economic conditions—1981-   —Statistics—
Handbooks, manuals, etc. 2. Economic indicators—United States—
Handbooks, manuals, etc. I. Clarkson, Kenneth W. II. Miller,
Roger LeRoy. III. Title.
HC106.8.H63   1983   330.973′00212   82-49324
ISBN 0-669-06579-X

Second printing, June 1984

Published simultaneously in Canada

Printed in the United States of America on acid-free paper

International Standard Book Number: 0-669-06579-X

Library of Congress Catalog Card Number: 82-49324

Contents

Figures and Tables

Foreword

It was once said of a former chairman of the President's Council of Economic Advisers that "he never met a statistic he didn't like." The joke derived from the habit of this chairman—who served during troublesome times when the basic inflation and unemployment numbers more often provided bad news than good news for his administration—of supplying instant commentary and interpretation of most of the major statistical indicators soon after they were released. It seemed that he could always find a few among the bewildering array of numbers that pointed toward cheerier times to come or showed that things were not as bad as they seemed.

This anecdote is recited not to discredit the particular chairman of the council but to illustrate the exceptional political sensitivity of the official federal government statistics in modern times. There is no escaping this. It is a standard witticism among economists that Britain lived in happy ignorance of its balance-of-payments problem for centuries until statistics were developed showing that there was something dreadful going on. At present, there is no doubt that the upward and downward jiggles of some of the main numbers cause more headlines and front-page stories than they properly should. For example, back in the economic salad days of the early 1960s, when inflation was averaging about 1.5 percent a year, *The New York Times* regularly reported on page one each month that the consumer price index had risen to a "record high," when the real news was that the country was experiencing virtual price stability.

But like it or not, we cannot revert to earlier and simpler times when statistics, if they existed at all, were the province only of specialists. The main monthly and quarterly indicators of the economy are destined to remain major news stories and to concern presidents as much as, or more than, economists.

This being so, a serious responsibility arises for journalists, and also for their editors, in both print and broadcast media. There are not many areas of the news where biased reporting—or simply misinformed reporting—is easier. Just as a politician may seek to interpret the numbers in a favorable way, a reporter can readily do the opposite if he is so inclined. In that most sensitive of indicators, the monthly report on employment and unemployment, for example, the entire focus of the story (and the headline) can be shifted in some months depending upon whether the story emphasizes what has happened to the unemployment rate or what is happening in each of the two measures of total employment. The news can be bad or good according to the eye of the beholding journalist. Economists eagerly await the data in this same report on payroll employment and hours worked as reliable indicators of which way total production in the economy is moving, and yet

I have read column-long stories on this series that did not even mention either one, instead reciting endless detail of unemployment rates among subclasses of the labor force.

All of which brings us to this book. It is best described as a reference book, and it should have a place next to the dictionary on the bookshelf of a working reporter on the economic beat. This is not a book to be read through from cover to cover, but rather a book in which to look things up. It tells in considerable detail how the main statistical series are compiled, their strengths and weaknesses, what they describe and—equally important—what they do not describe. For new and experienced reporters alike, there are numerous warnings of the pitfalls in the statistics—too subtle for the ordinary editor and reader, perhaps, and not often possible to include in a spot news story, but most useful in helping to shape a story in the direction of accuracy. To give a new reader an idea of the nuggets to be found, I would suggest that he or she turn right away to the section in chapter 4 describing why, when actual family earnings go up, the published figures on average weekly earnings are likely to be dragged down.

As far as I know, the material in this handbook is not to be found in one place anywhere else. A serious reporter trying to look the statistics in the eye and know both their warts and their beauties should find it invaluable.

Edwin L. Dale, Jr.
Assistant Director for Public Affairs,
U.S. Office of Management and Budget

Preface: How to Use the Economics Sourcebook of Government Statistics

Government agencies turn out hundreds of different statistics on a regular basis. Among the most widely used statistics are the many economic indicators of business and financial conditions. Information that describes these statistics—what they are, what they are based on, their potential limitations, when they are released, where timely estimates can be obtained—are scattered throughout many different publications. In this book, such information is drawn together for more than fifty widely used economic statistics and explained in nontechnical terms (technical information is explained in the notes or in cited articles).

The indicators are categorized by type into six chapters:[1] (1) measures of inflation, (2) profits: indicators of general business conditions, (3) interest rates and other financial indicators, (4) measures of employment, unemployment, and earnings, (5) indicators of international finance and trade, and (6) indicators of government influence.

Each indicator in a chapter is covered in a separate section (denoted by the series name) that describes the statistic, its limitations and biases, specifies when it becomes available, where to obtain current and historical data, and who to contact with questions. Each section is broken down according to the following general format:

Series name: Name of statistic or economic indicator

Issuing agency: Name of agency and, when possible, subdivision of agency that compiles statistics

Coverage: Describes the indicator

Data available: Indicates type of data available for statistic; for example, major categories of industries or markets for which data may be available; whether statistic is available on a national, regional, or local level; whether data are available weekly, monthly, or quarterly

Related series: Specifies series that are somewhat similar to indicator described

Source of data: Describes in nontechnical terms samples or surveys on which estimates are based and time frame on which data are based

When series become available: Indicates lag with which data become available and specifies approximate release date

Limitations: Describes some shortcomings and/or potential misuses of indicator

Publications: Indicates primary source of current and historical data; statistics that appear in secondary sources—*Economic Indicators* or *Economic Report of the President*—are also specified.[2]

References: Lists selected publications that can be helpful in providing more information about series

Mail and Telephone Reference: Address and telephone number of agency to contact for questions about statistic.[3]

For some of the indicators, a modified form of the format is used: some subheadings are either dropped or combined.

Finally, a glossary is provided at the end of the book. The definitions are usually briefer, and thus less precise, than the descriptions provided in the text.

Notes

1. The *Media Economics Source Book* (MESB) by Roger LeRoy Miller and Arline Alchian Hoel, a 169 page paperback nontechnical companion to this book, briefly describes the analytical tools useful in interpreting the economic implications of issues and events that affect every segment of American life. This book is more technical and contains comprehensive information on more than fifty specific economic indicators. The chapters in this book parallel the chapters in the MESB. For example, the first chapter in the MESB deals with inflation, and the first chapter in this book describes different measures of inflation. The second chapter in the MESB deals with profits, and the second chapter in this book describes profits and indicators of business conditions that directly or indirectly affect profits.

2. We think two publications put out by the Council of Economic Advisers—*Economic Indicators* (published monthly) and *Economic Report of the President* (published annually)—are, for their price, worth purchasing as sources of current and historical data. The statistics can also be found in many other sources that we do not list. For example the Board of Governors of the Federal Reserve System compiles an *Annual Statistical Digest* which is a compact source of economic—and especially financial—data. One problem users of data—particularly historical data—face is obtaining series that incorporate the most-recent revisions. Thus we have indicated, when possible, how to obtain the data that incorporate the most-recent revisions.

A very useful source of many different historical statistics is U.S. Department of Commerce, U.S. Bureau of the Census, *Historical Statistics of the United States: Colonial Times to 1970, Bicentennial Edition, Part 1* and *Part 2*, Washington, D.C.: U.S. Government Printing Office, 1975.

3. For most statistics, we provide the address and telephone number of the public-information office of the agency responsible for the statistic. Typically the public-information office refers the caller to a person capable of answering the question. We did not provide names or direct numbers for several reasons, among them the following: the caller may be referred to a different person depending on the nature of the question (for example, one person may specialize in providing current data on a statistic and a different person may specialize in answering technical questions about the same statistic); the telephone number of the person to call for a particular statistic can change, and the person responsible for the statistic can change frequently. In order to be referred as quickly as possible to the person capable of answering a question, we recommend specifying the name of the statistic and also the subdivision of the agency (as listed under "Issuing Agency") that compiles the statistic.

1 Measures of Inflation

Consumer Price Index for All Urban Consumers (CPI-U), Consumer Price Index for Urban Wage Earners and Clerical Workers (CPI-W)

Issuing Agency: U.S. Department of Labor, Bureau of Labor Statistics, Office of Prices and Living Conditions.

Coverage: The Consumer Price Index (CPI) is a measure of the average level of prices over time in a fixed market basket of goods and services. The index represents prices of everything people buy for day-to-day living—food, clothing, automobiles, homes, house furnishings, household supplies, fuel, drugs, and recreational goods; fees to doctors, lawyers, and beauty shops; and rent, repair costs, transportation fares, and public utility rates, among others. All taxes (sales, excise, and real estate, for example) directly associated with the purchase and continued ownership of an item are included in the price. Income and other personal taxes not associated with the prices of specific goods are excluded.[1]

Effective with the January 1978 index, the Bureau of Labor Statistics began publishing CPIs for two population groups: a new CPI for All Urban Consumers (CPI-U), which covers approximately 80 percent of the total noninstitutional civilian population, and a revised CPI for Urban Wage Earners and Clerical Workers (CPI-W), which represents about half of the population covered by the CPI-U. The CPI-U includes, in addition to wage earners and clerical workers, groups that historically have been excluded from CPI coverage, such as professional, managerial, and technical workers, the self-employed, short-term workers, the unemployed, and retirees and others not in the labor force.

Data Available: The CPI is available nationally for the United States and for some major cities by expenditure category and commodity and service group. Detailed components of each of the major groupings are published as well. In addition, some special indexes are also published. The major groupings are shown in table 1-1.

Related Series and Cost-of-Living Comparisions:

Separate CPIs. Separate indexes are published by size of city, by region of the country, for cross-classifications of regions and population-size classes, and for twenty-eight local areas. Area indexes do not measure differences in the level of prices among cities; they measure only the average change in prices for each area since the base period (1977).[2]

Table 1-1
Major Groupings of Consumer Price Index

All items:

Food and beverages
Housing
Apparel and upkeep
Transportation
Medical care
Entertainment
Other goods and services

Commodities
  Commodities less food and beverages
  Nondurables less food and beverages
  Durables

Services
  Rent, residential
  Household services less rent
  Transportation services
  Medical care services
  Other services

Special indexes
  All items less food
  All items less mortgage interest costs
  Commodities less food
  Nondurables less food
  Nondurables less food and apparel
  Nondurables
  Services less rent
  Services less medical care
  Domestically produced farm foods
  Selected beef cuts
  Energy
  All items less energy
    All items less food and energy
      Commodities less food and energy
      Energy commodities
      Services less energy

American Chamber of Commerce Researchers Association (ACCRA) Inner-City Cost-of-Living Indicators. These indicators are produced quarterly for a wide variety of cities of various sizes; 237 communities participated in the third-quarter 1981 survey. City chambers of commerce participated in the survey on a voluntary basis.

The Inner-City Cost-of-Living Indicators show price levels as index numbers for an all-items index and the major components of the index grocery items, housing, utilities, transportation, health care, and miscellaneous good and services. Although the indicators are subject to a variety of shortcomings,[3] they do provide a source of current living cost for a large sample of cities. The ACCRA data should be available at local chamber of commerce offices.[4]

Personal Consumption Expenditures Deflators. Another index that measures the price of consumer expenditures on final goods and services, the Personal Consumption Expenditures Deflators, is published by the Bureau of Economic Analysis as a by-product of the National Income and Product Accounts.[5]

Source of Data: For a number of years, the CPI was based on a 1960-1961 survey of a market basket of goods and services purchased by individuals. Since 1978, it has reflected a spending pattern of a fixed market basket of goods and services based on a 1972-1973 survey.[6]

Prices are collected regularly in eighty-five urban areas across the country from about 18,000 tenants, 18,000 housing units for property taxes, and about 24,000 establishments—grocery and department stores, hospitals, filling stations, and other types of stores and service establishments. Prices of food, fuels, and a few other items are obtained every month in all eighty-five locations. Prices of most other commodities and services are collected every month in the five largest geographic areas and every other month in other areas. Prices of most goods and services are obtained by personal visits of the bureau's trained representatives. Mail questionnaires are used to obtain public-utility rates, some fuel prices, and certain other items.[7]

When Series Become Available: The release date is published in the U.S. Department of Labor, Bureau of Labor Statistics, *Monthly Labor Review* near the beginning of the "Current Labor Statistics." The CPI is usually released around the beginning of the fourth week of each month for the preceding month. For example, data released around April 23 cover March.

Limitations: The CPI is not an exact measure of price change. No price index, however constructed, can be completely accurate. It is subject to sampling errors that may cause it to deviate somewhat from the results that would be obtained if actual records of all retail purchases by urban consumers could be used to compile the index. These estimating or sampling errors are limitations on the accuracy of the index rather than mistakes in the index calculation. The accuracy could be increased by using much larger samples, but the cost is prohibitive.[8]

Users of the indexes should be aware of some of the limitations in order to interpret the data correctly.[9] The CPI, for example, is not an index of the cost of living, as the Bureau of Labor Statistics constantly points out. It is a measure of the change in prices of a market basket of goods and services purchased by a typical urban worker's family in 1972 and 1973.

In practice, consumers do not actually purchase the same products and services in fixed quantities because prices, tastes, and incomes change over time. For example, since 1972 and 1973, consumers have reacted to changes in relative prices of housing, energy, and food by purchasing proportionately smaller amounts of those products. Therefore too much weight is given to those goods whose prices have risen since the base year relative to other goods. (The problem exists with all other price indexes using base-year quantities.)[10] The government, however, cannot revise the CPI yearly to reflect the different proportions of goods purchased with current-year quantities because of cost.

The CPI may be biased because of improper accounting for changes in quality. For example, at the same nominal price a product is actually cheaper if its quality has been improved. Conversely a product is more expensive if, at the same price, its quality has fallen. In many instances, changes in quoted prices are accompanied by changes in the quality of consumer goods and services. Also new products are introduced frequently that bear little resemblance to products previously on the market; hence, direct price comparisons cannot be made. Quoted prices are adjusted for changes in quality whenever necessary data are available. (In practice, these adjustments are difficult to make.)

Another kind of error occurs because people who give information do not always report accurately. The bureau makes every effort to keep these errors to a minimum, obtaining prices wherever possible by personal observation, and corrects errors whenever they are discovered subsequently.

The CPI represents the average movement of prices for urban consumers as a broad group but not the change in prices paid by any one family or small group of families. The index is not directly applicable to any other occupational group. Some families, for example, may find their outlays changing because of changes in factors other than prices, such as family composition. The index measures only the change in prices and none of the other factors that affect family living expenses.

Another important limitation of the index is that it measures only time-to-time price change in a given area. City indexes do not show intercity differences in either prices or living costs. They show only differences in rates of price change from one time to another.

Publications: Current Data:

Council of Economic Advisers, *Economic Indicators*, Washington, D.C.:
    U.S. Government Printing Office. Monthly.
U.S. Department of Labor, Bureau of Labor Statistics, "CPI Detailed
    Report." Monthly.
U.S. Department of Labor, Bureau of Labor Statistics, *Monthly Labor
    Review*. Monthly.
U.S. Department of Labor, Bureau of Labor Statistics, *News: Consumer
    Price Indexes*. Monthly statistical release.

Publications: Historical Data:

Council of Economic Advisers, *Economic Report of the President*, Washington, D.C.: U.S. Government Printing Office. Annual. See statistical appendix.

For the most complete and up-to-date historical data, write to the U.S. Department of Labor, Bureau of Labor Statistics, Washington, D.C., 20212 and request the historical tables for the "Consumer Price Index for All Consumers, U.S. City Average All Items" (if that is the relevant series desired).

References:

The Consumer Price Index: Concepts and Content over the Years, Report 517, Revised Edition, U.S. Department of Labor, Bureau of Labor Statistics, May 1978.

Ginsbury, Daniel H., "Revisions in the Medical Care Service Component of the Consumer Price Index," *Monthly Labor Review*, August 1978; and *CPI Issues*, Report 593, U.S. Department of Labor, Bureau of Labor Statistics, February 1980.

Layng, John W., "The Revision of the Consumer Price Index," reprinted from *Statistical Reporter*, February 1978, No. 78-5, U.S. Department of Commerce.

U.S. Comptroller General, General Accounting Office, *Measurement of Homeownership Costs in the Consumer Price Index Should Be Changed*, April 1981.

U.S. Department of Labor, U.S. Bureau of Labor Statistics, *BLS Handbook of Methods for Surveys and Studies*, Bulletin 1910, 1976.

Mail and Telephone Reference:

U.S. Department of Labor,
Bureau of Labor Statistics
Publications Department
441 G Street, N.W.
Washington, D.C.　20212
(202) 523-1913

Gross National Product Implicit Price Deflators

Issuing Agency: U.S. Department of Commerce, Bureau of Economic Analysis, National Income and Wealth Division.

Coverage: The gross national product (GNP) implicit price deflator is an index of the average price level of all final goods and services. It is called a deflator because if the nominal or current-dollar GNP is divided by the GNP implicit price deflator, a measure of real-, or constant-, dollar GNP is obtained. That is, final output is evaluated in terms of base-year prices.[11]

The GNP deflator is often called an implicit price deflator because it is calculated after current and real GNP are calculated. Today's GNP is obtained by adding up the current market value of all final goods and services. Then the dollar value of current output of final goods and services is evaluated at prices prevailing in the base year, which is currently 1972. In practice, this is done by deflating the current market value of groups of products and services by appropriate price indexes. Most of these indexes are obtained from various government agencies. For example, expenditures on men's and boys' clothing are deflated by a price index for clothing. The implicit price deflator is then obtained by dividing current-year quantities at current-year prices by current-year quantities evaluated at base-year prices.

Since the quantities of final goods and services that constitute GNP change from year to year, the quantity weights used to construct GNP change as well. For example, the quantities of goods and services produced in 1980 differ from the quantities of goods and services produced in 1979, and so on for other years, including the base year 1972. Thus, the change in the deflator reflects not only changes in prices but changes in quantities (the mix of products and services) as well. The GNP deflator therefore differs from the conventional price indexes that use fixed weights in the base period (such as the CPI) that measure price changes for fixed quantities of goods.[12]

Data Available: In addition to the GNP deflator, implicit price deflators are available:

By major type of product.

By sector.

For the relation of GNP, net national product, and national income.

For auto output.

For truck output.

For personal-consumption expenditures by major type of product.[13]

8

For government purchases of goods and services by type.

For exports and imports of goods and services.

For merchandise exports and imports by type of product and end-use category.

For inventories and final sales of business.

Related Series: The Bureau of Economic Analysis publishes a fixed-weight deflator (conceptually similar to the CPI), which is calculated by comparing base-year quantities of final goods and services at current prices with base-year quantities at base-year prices.

The Bureau of Economic Analysis also publishes a chain index, which attempts to minimize the disadvantage of the implicit price deflator of mixing together price and quantity changes and the substitution bias of fixed-quantity-weight indexes. The chain index averages together changes in individual prices between periods rather than computing an index level, such as the implicit price deflator. Then the price changes are averaged together using the average share of expenditures for each category in adjacent periods.[14]

Source of Data: The Bureau of Economic Analysis constructs the indexes with data collected from different government agencies and private groups. For example, the components of several price indexes (the CPI and the Producer Price Index) are collected from the Bureau of Labor Statistics; the U.S. Department of Agriculture provides data on prices paid by farmers; the Census Bureau provides unit-value index for imports and exports. In some cases, direct physical-volume measures are used as proxies for changes in costs.

Some price indexes are based on a common set of underlying price data. They differ, however, because of differences in coverage and the different sets of procedures used to calculate them.

When Series Become Available: The best estimate of the actual release data is published on the last page of the December issue of the U.S. Department of Commerce, Bureau of Economic Analysis, *Survey of Current Business* for the preceding year. Thus, the December 1981 issue provides the estimated release date for quarterly GNP data released in 1982. In general, quarterly GNP and GNP-related data, including the implicit price indexes, are released as follows: preliminary estimates appear about three weeks after the end of the quarter to which the data refer; the first revision appears about one and a half months after the end of the quarter; the second revision appears about two and a half months after the end of the quarter.

Limitations: First, there are coverage problems.[15] A large number of important products—mainly capital goods but some soft goods and services too—are not priced at all. For many other products, price indexes are available but are based on very small samples. Further, within the Producer Price Index (PPI) system, some prices that are components of the PPI are not available for different markets; for example, prices paid by the government, which are not available, may differ from prices paid by private consumers. In addition, the CPI currently covers purchases by only a portion of the total consumer market; therefore if prices move differently in the other portion, there is no satisfactory mechanism for reflecting that disparity.

Second, some of the prices are list prices rather than transaction prices. This means that the price indexes tend to be sticky, and when they do change, the change may be too abrupt because the list prices that are measured do not reflect the smoother transition that gradually moves the transaction price from the old list price to the new list price.

Third, the available price indexes are faulty to varying degrees because they are not fully corrected for changes in product quality; that is, some quality changes erroneously appear as price changes rather than as output changes. This problem occurs because the specifications of the product monitored by the pricing agencies are not precise or because they do not cover all of the relevant characteristics. Furthermore, even for characteristics that agencies do monitor, the information on the costs of the quality change is not sufficient to allow an accurate adjustment to be made for the change in specifications.

A related and fourth problem is that some indexes are derived from unit values rather than from price observations. Unit values are usually computed for heterogeneous mixes of products. In such cases, variations over time in the product mix will be read as changes in prices.

The fifth shortcoming affects construction and some services, where proper price indexes are almost nonexistent. Instead the Bureau of Economic Analysis must use indexes of the cost of inputs as poor substitutes.

Publications: Current Data:

Council of Economic Advisers, *Economic Indicators*, Washington, D.C.: U.S. Government Printing Office. Monthly.

U.S. Department of Commerce, Bureau of Economic Analysis, *Survey of Current Business*. Monthly.

Publications: Historical Data:

Council of Economic Advisers, *Economic Report of the President*, Washington, D.C.: U.S. Government Printing Office. Annual. See statistical appendix.

U.S. Department of Commerce, Bureau of Economic Analysis, *National Income and Product Accounts, 1976-79*, 1981.

U.S. Department of Commerce, Bureau of Economic Analysis, *The National Income and Product Accounts of the United States, 1929-76: Statistical Tables*, 1981.

References:

Marimont, Martin L., "Deflating Quarterly GNP," U.S. Department of Commerce, Bureau of Economic Analysis, Staff Paper 25, "Quarterly GNP Estimates Revisited in a Double-Digit Inflationary Economy," 1980, pp. 23-28.

"Reconciliation of Quarterly Changes in Measures of Prices Paid by Consumers," *Survey of Current Business*, March 1978, U.S. Department of Commerce, Bureau of Economic Analysis, pp. 6-9, 24.

Mail and Telephone Reference:

U.S. Department of Commerce
Bureau of Economic Analysis
1401 K Street, N.W.
Washington, D.C.   20230
(202) 523-0777

The Bureau of Economic Analysis also provides on request a list, "BEA Contacts for Data Users." The list provides the names and telephone numbers of people to contact by subject. The list is updated periodically.

Producer Price Indexes (PPIs)

Issuing Agency: U.S. Department of Labor, Bureau of Labor Statistics.

Coverage: The Producer Price Indexes are currently undergoing a comprehensive revision that is scheduled for completion in the mid-1980s. At that time all indexes will be calculated under the new methodology. Until the revision is completed, some of the PPIs are being compiled under the new methodology and some under the old. A more precise account of the dual methodologies used to calculate the PPIs until the revision has been completed is available elsewhere.[16]

The long-term objective of the program is to produce output price indexes for every industry in the private economy. The first stage, which is well under way, will include all production of both goods and services in the mining and manufacturing sectors. The next phase will cover output of agriculture and contract construction. Finally, some work has begun on calculating service-sector price indexes.

PPIs can be organized by stage of production, industry, or commodity:

The stage-of-processing structure organizes products by degree of fabrication (finished goods, intermediate or semifinished goods, and crude materials). Finished goods are commodities that will not undergo further processing and are ready for sale to the ultimate user, either an individual consumer or a business firm. Examples are machine tools, fresh vegetables, automobiles, and apparel. Intermediate materials, supplies, and components are commodities that have been processed but require further processing before they become finished goods; examples include flour, cotton, and steel-mill products. Crude materials for further processing include products entering the market for the first time that have not been manufactured or fabricated but will be processed before becoming finished goods; examples include grains, livestock, raw cotton, and crude petroleum.

The industry structure organizes products by producing industry as defined in the Standard Industrial Classification system.[17] Industries may be represented by one to three kinds of product indexes. Every industry has primary-product indexes to show changes in prices received by establishments classified in the industry for products made primarily, but not exclusively, within that industry. Some industries also may have secondary product indexes to show changes in prices received by establishments classified in the industry for products primary to some other industry. Finally, some industries have miscellaneous receipts indexes to show price changes in other sources of revenue received by establishments within the industry that are not derived from the sale of their products.

The commodity structure organizes products by similarity of end use or material composition.

Data Available: When the revision of the PPI is completed in the mid-1980s, all 493 mining and manufacturing industries in the Standard Industrial Classification are expected to be covered by approximately 90,000 price quotations and 6,000 published product indexes each month.[18] As of 1982, monthly prices and indexes are published for some 3,000 products and groupings by commodity line (end use) and stage of processing (degree of fabrication and class of buyer).

Indexes are available for fifty groupings by stage of processing, all commodities combined, two major commodity categories (industrial commodities, farm products, processed foods, and feeds), fifteen major product groupings, eight groupings by durability of product, and about 2,800 detailed commodities.

Annual average indexes are published for all groupings and items.

Regional indexes for refined petroleum products, electric power, and bituminous coal are also published.

Source of Data: The PPI revision aims to produce output price indexes and detailed product indexes for each of the 493 Standard Industrial Classification industries in mining and manufacturing. Each industry has an individually designed sample. In constructing a list of establishments for an industry, the primary source of data is the Unemployment Insurance System. Supplementary information is obtained from other publicly available lists. Companies are selected to participate in the survey on the basis of stratified probability sampling techniques. Participation is voluntary. The companies that cooperate with the program agree to one interview-and-disaggregation process that averages about two hours. Every month they also supply prices for the items selected. Respondents are asked to provide transactions prices—net prices or prices that include all applicable discounts. The terms of sale are reported effective for the Tuesday of the week that includes the thirteenth. These data are combined with data from other reporters in the same industry to produce the PPIs.

The respondent also provides descriptions of changes that may occur in the physical specification or terms of sale. The information is used to evaluate these changes so that comparisons are made only between comparable items and transactions terms.

When Series Become Available: PPIs are published monthly. The release date is published in the U.S. Department of Labor, Bureau of Labor Statistics, *Monthly Labor Review* near the beginning of the "Current Labor

Statistics.'' The PPI is usually released on the first (or second) Friday of each month for the preceding month. For example, a release date around April 3 covers March.

Limitations: Under the new methodology, the PPIs are based on a theoretical model of a fixed-input output price index. Indexes based on this model avoid one of the chief defects of indexes constructed by traditional methods—multiple counting of price changes.[19] The theoretically ideal output price index would show all firms adjusting their outputs in response to relative price changes. The PPIs use a fixed-weight (Laspeyres) index that approximates the ideal. Both measure the change in revenue from the base period in response to a price change. Under the ideal, however, the firm is permitted to change its output in response to price changes in order to maximize its profits. Thus it will show a revenue at least as large (and probably larger) as the one shown in the fixed-output Laspeyres index (in which firms are constrained to maintain fixed proportions in their outputs). The Laspeyres index is the lower bound of the ideal output price index.

The theoretical model for a fixed-input output price index assumes no technological change; however, such change does occur and new products are frequently introduced into the marketplace. As a result, it is impossible to obtain prices for identical items over long periods of time. Moreover the bureau is primarily interested in obtaining price changes that are representative of current production. Although it is impossible to maintain the assumption of no technological change over time, three procedures are being used to deal with these problems.[20]

When the bureau prices the output of the production unit, it needs the transaction price—the price the producer actually received for the item. Under the traditional methodology, this involves including discounts, extras, and surcharges. The price is f.o.b. (free on board) and excludes all direct excise taxes and transportation charges. To overcome some of the difficulties involved in obtaining or estimating these prices, there is additional emphasis, under the new procedures, on pricing all of the different types of transactions in which a particular item may be sold. In addition, the bureau tries to avoid using the average realized price approach.

Publications: Current Data:

Council of Economic Advisers, *Economic Indicators*, Washington, D.C.: U.S. Government Printing Office. Monthly.
U.S. Department of Commerce, Bureau of Labor Statistics, *Producer Prices and Price Indexes*. Monthly and annual supplement.
U.S. Department of Labor, Bureau of Labor Statistics, *Monthly Labor Review*. Monthly.

Publications: Historical Data:

Council of Economic Advisers, *Economic Report of the President*, Washington, D.C.: U.S. Government Printing Office. Annual. See statistical appendix.

The most-complete set of historical data can be obtained by writing to the U.S. Department of Labor, Bureau of Labor Statistics, Washington, D.C., 20212 and requesting the desired components of the PPIs from the "Producer Price Index Historical Subfile."

References:

Early, John F., "Improving the Measurement of Producer Price Change," *Monthly Labor Review*, April 1978, U.S. Department of Labor, Bureau of Labor Statistics.

Early, John F., "The Producer Price Index Revision: Overview and Pilot Survey Results," *Monthly Labor Review*, December 1979, U.S. Department of Labor, Bureau of Labor Statistics.

U.S. Department of Commerce, Office of Federal Statistical Policy and Standards, *A Framework for Planning U.S. Federal Statistics in the 1980's*, 1978.

U.S. Department of Labor, Bureau of Labor Statistics, *BLS Handbook of Methods for Surveys and Studies*, Bulletin 1910, 1976.

U.S. Department of Labor, Bureau of Labor Statistics, *BLS Handbook of Methods, Vol. 1*, Bulletin 2134-1, 1982.

Mail and Telephone Reference:

U.S. Department of Labor
Bureau of Labor Statistics
Publications Department
441 G Street, N.W.
Washington, D.C.   20212
(202) 523-1913

Notes

1. On October 27, 1981, the commissioner of labor statistics announced that the method used to calculate the home-ownership component in the CPI would be changed to a more-appropriate basis.

The Bureau of Labor Statistics is scheduled to make the change in two steps. It shifted the Index for All Urban Consumers (CPI-U) as of January 1983 but will not change the Index for Wage Earners and Clerical Workers (CPI-W) until January 1985. Since the CPI-W is used more extensively than the CPI-U in escalation agreements in both private and public sectors, the bureau felt it necessary to notify all users far in advance of the actual change.

The CPI, as a buyers' price index, reflects the purchase price of goods and services in a fixed market basket of goods and services. Many of the goods and services are consumed in the period in which they are purchased. In effect, the cost of consuming these goods is equivalent to the cost of purchasing these products.

Durable goods such as houses, cars, and appliances, however, are not completely used up in the period in which they are purchased. As a result, the cost of consuming a durable good (since only part of the services are consumed in the current period) differs from the purchase price. The CPI, however, is supposed to measure changes in the cost of consuming services over any given time period. Consequently the method used to calculate changes in the cost of home ownership is being changed to reflect the cost of consuming services over a given time period. This means a change to a rental-equivalence measure of housing instead of the approach which relies on estimates of new home prices and current mortgage costs.

For some time, the Bureau of Labor Statistics published five alternative measures of home-ownership costs and finally adopted the rental-equivalence method of measuring the cost of the flow of services from home ownership.

Both durable goods and nondurable goods are treated the same way in the CPI: changes in the cost of consuming services from the products in any given period are based on differences in the purchase price. In the case of home ownership, however, the distinction between the purchase price and consumption costs became extremely pronounced and led to the change in the method of calculating home-ownership costs in the CPI.

Significant discussion of the shortcomings of the asset-price approach to measuring home-ownership costs in the CPI and the possibility of adopting other measures dates back to the 1960s. In fact, alternative measures of home-ownership costs were proposed for the 1978 revision of the CPI but were rejected because of lack of support from labor and business advisory groups. For a detailed discussion, see Comptroller General, Government Accounting Office, "Measurement of Homeownership Costs in the Consumer Price Index Should Be Changed," April 1981.

2. When cost-of-living comparisons are made between different areas, conceptually one is looking for estimates of income required to maintain equal states of satisfaction, comfort, and well-being in each location. The measure should reflect both differences in prices of goods and services and amounts of goods and services required to maintain a specified standard of living. Thus, a cost-of-living index must include geographically determined (location-specific) influences on living standards and exclude all demographically determined (consumer-specific) variations.

The major shortcoming in comparing CPIs from city to city is that each area-price index is based on the 1977 price level, the base period. Thus, equal index values for two cities indicate only that prices in the two cities rose at the same rate. For example, a rise from 100 to 120 between 1977 and 1980 indicates prices rose by 20 percent over the three-year interval. This would be true even if the price level were substantially higher in one of the cities than the other.

Other drawbacks in using the CPI as a cost-of-living index are that it omits income and personal-property taxes; the market basket of goods and services in each area is purposely held constant (except for infrequent revisions); the CPI market baskets are not identical for all U.S. cities (they are based on urban consumers' actual consumption patterns in the area) and to that extent do reflect geographic differences but may also reflect demographic differences.

For a more-complete discussion, see James T. Fergus, "Cost-of-Living Comparisons: Oasis or Mirage?" *Economic Review*, July-August 1977, Federal Reserve Bank of Atlanta, pp. 92-100.

For a more-complete description of some statistics used to compare living costs, see Leigh Watson Healy and William N. Cox III, "Cost of Living Data: A Guide to Sources," *Economic Review*, March 1982, Federal Reserve Bank of Atlanta, pp. 44-50.

In 1982 the Bureau of Labor Statistics eliminated the Family Budget Program. The program provided annual estimates of the cost of purchasing hypothetical market baskets of goods that represent three standards of living: lower, intermediate, and higher. The budgets were designed for a traditional four-person family and for a retired couple. The budgets represented costs that were specified in the mid-1960s to portray three relative levels of living. The budgets were replicated for twenty-five major cities and for regional areas.

For other problems with the budgets methodology and applicability, see Fergus, "Cost-of-Living Comparisons," pp. 92-100. Several considerations limited application of the data. One was the specific definition of the characteristics of the family. The bureau's equivalence factors that were used to adjust family size and characteristics (from the standard) resulted in alterations that sometimes appeared to be unreasonable. Two, value judgments crept into the budget specifications so that measurements were based on desirable, rather than actual, consumption patterns. For example, all tobacco products were excluded. Third, some problems arise from revisions of budget data. For example, occasional changes in living standards interrupted the continuity of the data series and impaired its comparability over time.

3. See Healy and Cox, "Cost-of-Living Data," p. 46. Briefly, the manner in which ACCRA conducts the survey introduces a number of potential problems or errors; each ACCRA component consists of a very small market basket, and the ACCRA survey does not include taxes.

4. For additional references, see the publications by the American Chamber of Commerce Research Associations: "Inner-City Cost-of-Living Instruction Manual for Participating Cities," revised January 1981, and *Inner-City Cost-of-Living Indicators, Third Quarter 1981*.

5. For an explanation of the two indexes and reconciliation, see Jack E. Triplett, "Reconciling the CPI and the CPE Deflator," *Monthly Labor Review*, September 1981, U.S. Department of Labor, Bureau of Labor Statistics, pp. 3-15.

6. A CPI revision has three elements: determining what people buy, determining where they buy it, and improving statistical techniques. In determining what people buy, a series of extensive sample surveys were undertaken. The most important was the Consumer Expenditure Survey, which provided the basis for selecting and weighting items in the fixed market basket of goods and services on which the CPI is based. The Bureau of Labor Statistics developed the questionnaire, and the Bureau of the Census selected a sample of households and conducted interviews. The household sample was spread throughout 216 areas of the country, representing rural and urban areas. Most of the information was obtained in a series of quarterly interviews involving about 20,000 families. The data collected covered the calendar years 1972 and 1973.

7. In calculating the index, price changes for the various items in each location are averaged together with weights that represent their importance in the spending of the appropriate population group. Local data are then combined to obtain a U.S. city average.

8. The index is believed to be sufficiently accurate for most of the practical uses made of it.

9. Much of the following section is adapted from *BLS Handbook of Methods for Surveys and Studies*, Bulletin 1910, U.S. Department of Labor, Bureau of Labor Statistics, 1976, pp. 105, 106.

10. The market basket is deliberately kept constant because the CPI measures price changes, not changes that may occur in living standards. Most research also indicates that these shifts in consumer purchases have not created the large differences in price indexes that have been observed in the past.

11. The GNP implicit price deflator measures the general price level of the economy. It is more broadly based than the CPI and the PPIs. The deflator takes into account prices of final goods and services paid by consumers, business, the government, and the foreign sector.

12. Since the GNP deflator does not measure price changes alone, as does the CPI, but quantity changes as well, some people express confusion over the purpose of the implicit price deflator. For many purposes, it is important to know how the physical volume of output has changed. A major use of the GNP deflator is to obtain a measure of changes in the physical volume of current output.

One way of estimating how real GNP or the physical output of final goods and services has changed over time is to deflate current GNP by the GNP deflator. The result is real GNP or current-year output (that is, final output for 1980, 1979, 1978, and so on) expressed in terms of base-year (1972) prices. Thus, changes in real GNP reflect the changes in the physical volume of physical output from one period to the next—for example, from quarter to quarter or from year to year.

13. The U.S. Department of Commerce, Bureau of Economic Analysis, publishes quarterly in the *Survey of Current Business* a reconciliation of changes in the implicit price deflator for Personal Consumption Expenditures and the Consumer Price Index for All Urban Consumers. For an explanation of the reconciliation, see "Reconciliation of Quarterly Changes in Measures of Prices Paid by Consumers," *Survey of Current Business*, March 1978, U.S. Department of Commerce, Bureau of Economic Analysis; Triplett, "Reconciling the CPI," pp. 3-14; Julie A. Bunn and Jack E. Triplett, "Reconciling the CPI and the PCE Deflator: An Update," *Monthly Labor Review*, January 1982, U.S. Department of Labor, Bureau of Labor Statistics, pp. 43, 44.

14. "Reconciliation of Quarterly Changes," pp. 6-9, 24, and Triplett, "Reconciling the CPI," pp. 3-15, describe the chain index, as well as the reconciliation between the CPI and PCE.

15. This section is taken largely from Martin L. Marimont, "Deflating Quarterly GNP," U.S. Department of Commerce, Bureau of Economic Analysis Staff Paper No. 25, "Quarterly GNP Estimates Revisited in a Double-Digit Inflationary Economy," 1980, pp. 23, 24.

16. The description of the PPI is based on U.S. Department of Labor, Bureau of Labor Statistics, *BLS Handbook of Methods, vol. 1,* Bulletin 2134-1, 1982, pp. 43-61; John F. Early, "Improving the Measurement of Producer Price Change," *Monthly Labor Review*, April 1978, U.S. Department of Labor, Bureau of Labor Statistics; and Early, "The Producer Price Revision: Overview and Pilot Survey Results," *Monthly Labor Review*, December 1979, U.S. Department of Labor, Bureau of Labor Statistics.

The new methodology used in the PPI revision is designed to reduce many of the limitations of the PPIs as calculated under traditional procedures. The following are the differences between the traditional and new methodology used in computing the PPIs. Probability sampling instead of judgment sampling is being used to select reporting companies, products, and the price-determining transaction terms. Companies of all sizes (not just the larger ones) are being asked to report prices and transactions on all types of output (not just volume-selling items). Thus precise statistical measures will be available for the first time.

Coverage is being expanded to include all 493 Standard Industrial Classification industries in the mining and manufacturing sectors. Before the revision began, indexes representing only half of the total value of mining and manufacturing output were incorporated into the PPI system. Expanded coverage also lessens the importance of imputations of unpriced goods.

Under the revision, indexes are industry oriented rather than commodity oriented. The traditional indexes were based on prices received by producers without regard to industry classification. The entire output of each industry is sampled, including primary and secondary production and miscellaneous receipts. The traditional indexes were based on prices received by producers without regard to industry classification.

PPIs classified according to industry thus will be compatible with other industry-oriented economic data such as employment and wages.

Imports will not be priced under the revision, since the PPI are designed to measure changes in prices of output of domestic industries. Exports, however, will be incorporated into the revision. Under traditional methods, the PPIs were intended to measure changes in prices received in the first commercial transaction in this country, including imports and exports.

Specifications for the commodities under the revisions are broader than under traditional methods. The averages of a company price index in the PPI revision are weighted by the company's relative size instead of giving equal weight to each reporter.

Indexes calculated under the revision emphasize actual transaction prices at the time of shipment to minimize the use of list and order prices.

17. See appendix C.

18. See appendix C.

19. For example, suppose that a price rise for steel scrap results in an increase in the price of steel sheet and then an advance in prices of automobiles produced from that steel. Under the traditional methodology, the All Commodities Price Index and the Industrial Commodities Price Index would reflect the same price movement three times: once for the steel scrap, once for the steel sheet, and once for the automobiles. This multiple counting occurs because the weighting structure for the All Commodities Index uses the total shipment values for all commodities at all stages of processing. The Finished Goods Price Index would reflect the change in automobile prices, the Intermediate Materials Price Index would reflect the steel sheet price change, and the Crude Materials Price Index would reflect the rise in the price of steel scrap.

20. U.S. Department of Labor, Bureau of Labor Statistics, *BLS Handbook of Methods, vol. 1*, Bulletin 2134-1, 1982, p. 52.

2 Profits: Indicators of General Business Conditions

Capacity Utilization

Issuing Agency: Board of Governors of the Federal Reserve System, Business Conditions Section.

Coverage: Industrial capacity-utilization rates are designed to measure the extent to which a firm is realizing its potential output rate with the existing stock of capital in a given time frame. The capacity-utilization rate is expressed as a percentage of the actual output to the potential output.

Capacity utilization is not an easy concept. There is considerable difference in opinion about how it should be constructed. There are, in fact, seven different series that measure capacity utilization; six of the estimates cover all manufacturing, and one covers industrial materials.

The seven capacity-utilization series are: the materials series published by the Board of Governors of the Federal Reserve System; and the six manufacturing or total industrial series published by the Bureau of the Census; Bureau of Economic Analysis; the McGraw-Hill Publications Company; Wharton Econometric Forecasting; the Federal Reserve; and Rinfret Associates, Inc. (New York City). All six maintain current measures.[1] In general, the different measures of capacity utilization move up and down together; however, there are differences in the amplitude and timing of these movements.[2] The way in which these different measures of capacity utilization are constructed differ as well. Consequently it is not appropriate to make direct comparisons among these different measures.

Data Available: The most widely used measures of capacity utilization probably are the rates published by the Federal Reserve; consequently the data available for that series are described in this section.[3]

Capacity-utilization rates, published by the Board of Governors of the Federal Reserve System, are available by stage of processing in manufacturing: advanced processing and primary processing. The categorization of all manufacturing capacity-utilization rates into primary and advanced processing approximates the split of industrial-production groupings into materials and products.[4]

The Federal Reserve's measures of capacity and capacity utilization in the production of industrial materials cover the same ninety-six series as the Federal Reserve's index of industrial production. The materials group covers industrial goods such as raw steel that are generally used in manufacturing, mining establishments, and utilities. An example of the type of data available is shown in table 2-1.

Source of Data: There are two ways of coming up with estimates of capacity-utilization rates. Some, such as the series published by the Bureau

Table 2-1
Output, Capacity, and Capacity Utilization

Series	Output (1967 = 100)				Capacity (percent of 1967 output)				Utilization Rate (percent)			
	1981				1981				1981			
	Q1	Q2	Q3	Q4r	Q1	Q2	Q3	Q4	Q1	Q2	Q3	Q4r
Manufacturing	151.3	152.4	152.5	144.9	189.4	190.9	192.4	193.9	79.9	79.8	79.3	74.7
Primary processing	157.5	156.5	155.8	143.5	193.8	195.0	196.3	197.5	81.3	80.3	79.4	72.7
Advanced processing	148.1	150.2	150.7	145.6	187.1	188.7	190.4	192.0	79.1	79.6	79.2	75.9
Materials	154.2	153.4	154.3	144.1	187.6	189.0	190.3r	191.5r	82.2	81.2	81.1	75.2
Durable goods	150.9	152.3	152.8	140.2	191.8	192.9	194.2	195.3	78.7	78.9	78.7	71.8
Metal materials	117.5	112.8	114.2	99.5	141.5	141.7	141.9	142.1	83.0	79.6	80.5	70.0
Nondurable goods	179.2	178.4	175.8	164.4	207.3	209.2	211.2	213.1	86.5	85.3	83.3	77.3
Textile, paper, and chemical	186.7	185.9	182.8	169.7	217.1	219.4	221.7	223.9	86.0	84.8	82.5	75.8
Textile	114.8	114.5	115.5	106.8	140.1	140.6	141.0	141.6	81.9	81.4	81.8	75.4
Paper	151.4	151.0	152.2	148.1	159.7	160.7	161.9	162.8	94.8	93.9	94.1	91.0
Chemical	232.7	231.6	224.9	206.2	274.1	277.5	281.0	284.4	84.9	83.5	80.0	72.5
Energy materials	130.9	125.1	131.6	127.8	153.5	154.3r	155.0	155.8r	85.3	81.1	84.9	82.0

Source: Board of Governors of the Federal Reserve System, *Federal Reserve Bulletin*, March 1982, p. A46.

Note: This table shows the type of data available for the Federal Reserve series on capacity utilization. The superscript *r* indicates revised information. Although the figures shown are quarterly (Q) for 1981, capacity-utilization rates are also available monthly. The utilization rate is output as a percentage of capacity. For example, the utilization rate for manufacturing for the first quarter of 1981 is 79.9 percent (or 151.3/189.4).

of Economic Analysis, send questionnaires to companies and ask business persons to provide estimates of their operating rates as a percentage of capacity. The second method, which is used by the Federal Reserve, is based almost entirely on Federal Reserve estimates of industrial production.

When Series Become Available: Federal Reserve estimates of capacity utilization are released monthly. Estimates are available around the middle of each month. For example, in mid-April, estimates are released for March.[5] For the estimated release dates also see, each year, the June issue of the Board of Governors of the Federal Reserve System, *Federal Reserve Bulletin.*

Limitations: Two types of limitations or criticisms of capacity-utilization measures should be pointed out: one is conceptual, the second empirical. First, probably the most widely used concept of capacity is based on the maximum output that can be produced during a given time period using existing plant and equipment and under normal operating schedules. Although this concept is vague, it seems to be based on the idea of producing an average output mix under average or typical operating conditions—in contrast to operating with a full staff twenty-four hours a day, seven days a week. Maximum capacity under this concept would differ among different producers according to their technological requirements or customs.

The concept of normal capacity, as well as average output mix, can change over time. For example, it is possible that price controls, devaluation of the dollar, and worldwide hoarding, which led to shortages of many materials, influenced businesses to reduce their estimates of practical capacity during the 1973-1974 boom. With more-normal price relationships and with more-adequate availability of materials, overall capacity might appear to grow more rapidly in the next expansion.[6]

Second, the widely used Federal Reserve Index of Capacity Utilization relies on empirical or historic relationships, which may change substantially over time. As a result, these relationships need to be reestimated frequently, or else a bias may develop. The Federal Reserve closely monitors the index to ensure the possible bias is minimal.

Publications: Current Data:

Council of Economic Advisers, *Economic Indicators,* Washington, D.C.: U.S. Government Printing Office. Monthly.[7]

Board of Governors of the Federal Reserve System, *Capacity Utilization: Manufacturing and Materials,* G.3 (402), statistical release. Monthly.

Publications: Historical Data:

Council of Economic Advisers, *Economic Report of the President,* Washinton, D.C.: U.S. Government Printing Office. Annual. See statistical appendix.[8]

Board of Governors of the Federal Reserve System, *Federal Reserve Measures of Capacity and Capacity Utilization,* 1978.

References:

Board of Governors of the Federal Reserve System, *Federal Reserve Measures of Capacity and Capacity Utilization,* February 1978, p. 39.

de Leeuw, Frank, "Why Capacity Utilization Estimates Differ," *Survey of Current Business,* May 1979, U.S. Department of Commerce, Bureau of Economic Analysis, pp. 45-55.

de Leeuw, Frank, Lawrence R. Forest, Jr., Zoltan E. Kenessey, and Richard D. Raddock, *Measurement of Capacity Utilization: Problems and Tasks,* Board of Governors of the Federal Reserve System, July 1979, pp. 259.

Hertzberg, Marie P., Alfred I. Jacobs, and Jon E. Trevathan, "The Utilization of Manufacturing Capacity, 1965-73," *Survey of Current Business,* July 1974, U.S. Department of Commerce, Bureau of Economic Analysis, pp. 47-57.

Ragan, James F., "Measuring Capacity Utilization in Manufacturing," *Quarterly Review,* Winter 1976, Federal Reserve Bank of New York, pp. 13-20.

Mail and Telephone Reference:

Board of Governors of the Federal Reserve System
Division of Research and Statistics
20th and Constitution Ave., N.W.
Washington, D.C. 20551
(202) 452-3000

Construction Cost Indexes

Issuing Agency: U.S. Department of Commerce and various private organizations.

Coverage, Source, and Frequency of Publication: The U.S. Department of Commerce consolidates and publishes ten indexes of construction costs, which it acquires from various sources. These indexes are published by the U.S. Department of Commerce in *Construction Review.* The ten indexes are listed in table 2-2 along with the source, a brief description, the frequency of publication, and the historical data available.

Limitations: Analyses suggest that many of the construction statistics listed in table 2-2 (which are also used to deflate most construction expenditures) are not representative of actual material, labor, and overhead costs.[9] The indexes tend to overstate the increase in construction costs due to inflation, leading to an understatement of the estimated volume of construction in constant dollars. The main reason for the upward bias in the indexes is that many of the deflators are based on privately compiled cost indexes that measure the prices of inputs to construction (such as labor and materials) rather than the prices of construction output. Since the input-cost indexes do not take account of productivity changes, they cannot adequately measure the price trends of construction.[10]

Publications: Current Data:

U.S. Department of Commerce, Bureau of Industrial Economics, *Construction Review.* Bimonthly.

Publications: Historical Data:

Levy, Elliot, "Construction Cost Indexes 1915-76," *Construction Review,* June-July 1977, U.S. Department of Commerce, Domestic and International Business Administration, Bureau of Domestic Commerce, pp. 4-17.

References:

U.S. Department of Commerce, Bureau of the Census, *Construction Statistics Data Finder,* Washington, D.C., 20233.

This thirteen-page publication is useful in locating different construction statistics and can be obtained by writing to Subscriber Services, Bureau of the Census.

Table 2-2
Construction Cost Indexes

Index Name and Source	Frequency	Description	Historical Data Available on Annual Basis to
Department of Commerce, Composite Cost Index (Bureau of the Census, U.S. Department of Commerce, Washington, D.C.)	Monthly	The Composite Cost Index is weighted and reflects implicit changes since the 1972 base period in the cost of all types of construction combined.	1915
American Appraisal Company Indexes, also known as "Boeckh Indexes" (Milwaukee, Wisc.)	Monthly	The company publishes separate indexes for: total construction costs; residence; apartments, hotels, and office buildings; commercial and factory buildings. The indexes are based on a detailed bill of quantities of materials and labor entering into the structural portion of four representative types of buildings—frame, brick, concrete, and steel—in 30 cities throughout the United States, with allowance for contractor overhead and profits.	1915
Engineering News-Record Indexes (McGraw-Hill Publishing Co., New York)	Monthly	National cost indexes are available for total construction and for building. Both indexes have four components—three material items plus labor. The component series are weighted according to their relative importance as determined by their compilers.	1915
Environmental Protection Agency (EPA) Sewer and Sewage Treatment Plant Indexes (EPA, Washington, D.C.)	Monthly to 1974 and quarterly thereafter	Indexes represent construction costs of municipal sewers and of sewage-treatment plants assisted by the EPA, and are based on weighted averages of detailed labor and materials costs in 20 cities.	1957

Federal Highway Administration Indexes (Federal Highway Administration, Department of Transportation, Washington, D.C.)	Quarterly	Two indexes are available. The Composite Index is a price index measuring price changes for fixed amounts of the following items put in place: common excavation, surfacing, and structures. The Structures Index is derived from the average unit bid prices and base quantities of reinforcing steel for structural concrete.	1922
Index of New One-Family Houses Sold Excluding Census Lot Value (Bureau of the Census, U.S. Department of Commerce, Washington, D.C.)	Quarterly	Measures the change in sales price of new one-family houses that are the same with respect to 10 characteristics.	1963
Water and Power Resources Service Composite Index (Bureau of Reclamation, U.S. Department of Interior, Washington, D.C.)	Quarterly	Reflects the costs of constructing dams and reclamation projects sponsored by the Water and Power Resources Service in 11 western states. The index is a weighted average of the costs of labor, materials and equipment furnished by contractors and the government.	1940
Turner Construction Company Index (New York)	Quarterly	Represents a measure of building construction costs in eastern cities and is derived from the firm's cost experience.	1915
Handy-Whitman Indexes (computed by Bureau of the Census from data compiled by Whitman, Requardt and Assoc., Baltimore, Md.)	Semiannual	These indexes (for building and for electric light and power) are compiled individually for various elements for 3 types of construction—utility buildings, gas plants, and electric light and power plants—within 6 geographic regions.	1915
Bell System Telephone Plant Indexes (American Telephone and Telegraph Co. New York)	Annual	The American Telephone and Telegraph Company compiles indexes for construction of telephone company buildings and of outside plant (such as poles, cable, aerial wire and underground conduits).	1930
Federal Energy Regulatory Commission (FERC) Pipeline Index (FERC, U.S. Department of Energy, Washington, D.C.)	Annual	Derived from expenditure and volume data reported to FERC by commission-regulated pipeline companies.	1949

Adapted from: Elliot Levy, "Construction Cost Indexes 1915-76," *Construction Review*, June-July 1977, U.S. Department of Commerce, pp. 4-17.

Mail and Telephone Reference:

U.S. Bureau of the Census
Economic Census Staff
Suitland, MD   20233
(301) 763-4040

Value of New Construction Put in Place

Issuing Agency: U.S. Department of Commerce, Bureau of the Census, Construction and Statistics Division.

Coverage and Data Available: The value of new construction put in place is available for both public and private construction in current and constant (or real) dollars. Value of construction is further categorized by type of construction (table 2-3). The bulk of the data is available monthly.

The annual value of new privately owned nonresidential buildings by geographic area is also available.[11]

Source of Data: Estimates of the value of new construction put in place are calculated from data obtained from a variety of governmental and private sources.[12]

When Series Become Available: Most of the data become available one month after the period to which the data refer.

Table 2-3
Categories of Data Available for Value of New Construction Put in Place

Private Construction	*Public Construction*
Residential buildings	Buildings
New housing units	Housing and redevelopment
1 unit	Industrial
2 or more units	Educational
Nonhousekeeping	Hospital
Additions and alterations	Other
Nonresidential buildings	Highways and streets
Industrial	Military facilities
Office	Conservation and development
Other commercial	Other public construction
Religious	Sewer systems
Educational	Water-supply facilities
Hospital and institutional	Miscellaneous public
Miscellaneous	
Farm nonresidential	
Public utilities	
Telephone and telegraph	
Other public utilities	
Gas	
Electric light and power	
Railroads	
Petroleum pipelines	
All other private	

Limitations: Construction-cost indexes tend to result in an understatement of construction costs in constant dollars. Analyses have shown that the bulk of the construction-cost indexes statistics used to deflate most construction expenditures are not representative of actual material, labor, and overhead costs.[13] The main reason for the upward bias is that many of the deflators are based on privately compiled cost indexes that measure the prices of inputs to construction (such as labor and materials) rather than the prices of construction output. Since the input cost indexes do not take account of productivity changes, they cannot adequately measure the price trends of construction.[14]

Publications: Current Data:

Council of Economic Advisers, *Economic Indicators,* Washington, D.C.: U.S. Government Printing Office. Monthly.

U.S. Department of Commerce, Bureau of the Census, *Construction Reports: Value of New Construction Put in Place,* Series C30. Monthly.

U.S. Department of Commerce, Bureau of Industrial Economics, *Construction Review.* Bimonthly.

Publications: Historical Data:

Council of Economic Advisers, *Economic Report of the President,* Washington, D.C.: U.S. Government Printing Office. Annual. See statistical appendix.

U.S. Department of Commerce, Bureau of the Census, *Construction Reports: Value of New Construction Put in Place 1980,* Series C30-81-5, 1981.

U.S. Department of Commerce, Bureau of the Census, *Construction Reports: Value of New Construction Put in Place 1979,* Series C30-80-5, 1980.

U.S. Department of Commerce, Bureau of the Census, *Construction Reports: Value of New Construction Put in Place, 1976-1978,* Series C30-79-5.

U.S. Department of Commerce, Bureau of the Census, *Construction Reports: Value of New Construction Put in Place, 1970 to 1977,* Series C30-78-5.

References:

U.S. Department of Commerce, Bureau of the Census, *Construction Statistics Data Finder,* Washington, D.C.

Mail and Telephone Reference:

U.S. Bureau of the Census
Economic Census Staff
Suitland, MD   20233
(301) 763-4040

Actual Expenditures for New Plant and Equipment [and] Planned Expenditures for New Plant and Equipment.

Issuing Agency: U.S. Department of Commerce, Bureau of Economic Analysis, Business Outlook Division.

Coverage: Expenditures for new plant and equipment cover all domestic private business except farming, real estate, the professions (medical, legal, educational, and cultural), and nonprofit membership institutions.[15] New plant and equipment expenditures refer to all costs (both replacement and expansion) chargeable to fixed-asset accounts and for which depreciation accounts are ordinarily maintained. The estimates cover expenditures to replace or to add to existing facilities and to provide new facilities and for exploration and development of properties. Included in the totals are expenditures for new construction, machinery, and equipment (automobiles, trucks, and other transportation equipment). The figures do not include expenditures for land and mineral rights, maintenance and repair, used plant and equipment, residential construction, and expenditures made in foreign countries.

Data Available: In each quarterly survey, the following data for expenditures on new plant and equipment are collected: actual expenditures for the previous quarter and planned expenditures one quarter ahead (the current quarter), two quarters ahead, and three quarters ahead. Expenditures for each quarter therefore are estimated four times in successive surveys: as planned expenditures three quarters ahead, two-quarters ahead, one quarter ahead, and as actual expenditures.

The estimates are available for major categories of manufacturing (durables, nondurables and subcategories) and nonmanufacturing industries (mining, transportation, public utilities, trade and services, communication and other) as shown in table 2-4.[16] (More-detailed categories are also available.)

Total expenditures for new plant and equipment, both actual and planned, have been collected quarterly since the survey began in 1947. Expenditures for plant and equipment separately have been collected annually since 1947 and quarterly since 1972.

Related Series: A series on carry-over of investment projects in manufacturing and public utilities measures the expenditures to be incurred on projects underway at the end of each quarter. Quarterly collection of the carry-over of investment projects for manufacturers and utilities and of manufacturers' evaluation of their capital equipment began late in 1962 and 1963, respectively.

Starts of new projects are derived by adding expenditures for the quarter to the charge in carry-over during the quarter. A project is defined to be started when the first charge is made to the capital account or when firm contracts or orders for all or part of the project are placed.

Manufacturing survey respondents are also requested to report on the adequacy of capital facilities. They are asked to characterize the facilities, taking into account their current and prospective sales over the next year: "more plant and equipment needed," "about adequate," and "existing plants and equipment exceeds needs." The responses are weighted, and the percentage distributions are computed for the three categories for each industry and for total manufacturing.

Source of Data: Estimates are based on reports submitted by a sample of about 15,000 companies reporting to the Bureau of Economic Analysis and by transportation companies reporting to the Interstate Commerce Commission. The sample, established in 1972, accounted for about 53 percent of the nonfarm business expenditures in the United States; the corresponding percentages were 68 percent manufacturing and 47 percent for nonmanufacturing companies.

Table 2-4
Expenditures for New Plant and Equipment by U.S. Nonfarm Business
(billions of dollars, seasonally adjusted)

	1981			
Expenditures	*QI*[a]	*QII*[a]	*QIII*[a]	*QIV*[a]
Total nonfarm business	312.24	311.87	322.88	333.09
Manufacturing	124.50	121.99	130.46	133.45
Durable goods	61.24	60.28	64.90	68.65
Nondurable goods	63.27	61.71	65.56	64.80
Nonmanufacturing	187.74	189.88	192.42	199.64
Mining	16.20	15.93	17.51	17.87
Transportation	11.74	11.48	11.58	13.71
Public utilities	36.05	37.39	38.23	37.31
Trade and services	83.43	84.55	84.12	88.33
Communication and other	40.32	40.54	40.97	42.43

Source: U.S. Department of Commerce, Bureau of Economic Analysis, *Survey of Current Business,* June 1981, p. 30.

Note: In this example, the estimates are based on planned capital expenditures reported by business in late April and May. Thus, figures for the first quarter of 1981 are estimates of actual expenditures, and figures, for the second, third, and fourth quarters of 1981 are estimates of planned expenditures for new plant and equipment.

[a]Q = quarter.

When Series Become Available: Estimates of actual and planned expenditures on new plant and equipment are available quarterly. The best estimate of the approximate release dates can be found on the back page of the December issue of the U.S. Department of Commerce, Bureau of Economic Analysis, *Survey of Current Business.* Quarterly estimates of actual and planned expenditures on plant and equipment are released with a lag of about two and a half months (with respect to the quarter for actual expenditures). For example, in mid-June, estimates of actual expenditures for the first quarter and of planned expenditures for the second, third, and fourth quarters of the year are released.

Limitations: Planned or anticipated expenditures on new plant and equipment have long been used as indicators of actual future expenditures. Examination of the relation between planned and actual expenditures shows systematic bias, reflecting the time of year at which the survey is taken, the size of the firm, and the planning horizon. A comprehensive analysis of the errors between actual and planned investment expenditures and an examination of the variables that may influence the realization of investment plans is available.[17]

Publications: Current Data:

Council of Economic Advisers, *Economic Indicators,* Washington, D.C.: U.S. Government Printing Office. Monthly.
U.S. Department of Commerce, Bureau of Economic Analysis, *Survey of Current Business.* Monthly.

Publications: Historical Data:

Green, George R., and Marie P. Hertzberg, "Revised Estimates of New Plant and Equipment Expenditures in the United States, 1947-77," *Survey of Current Business,* October 1980, U.S. Department of Commerce, Bureau of Economic Analysis, pp. 24-59.
McKelvey, Michael J., "Constant Dollar Estimates of New Plant and Equipment Expenditures in the United States 1947-80," *Survey of Current Business,* September 1981, pp. 26-41.

References:

de Leeuw, Frank, and Michael J. McKelvey, "The Realization of Plans Reported in the BEA Plant and Equipment Survey," *Survey of Current Business,* October 1981, U.S. Department of Commerce, Bureau of Economic Analysis, pp. 28-37.

Green, George R., and Marie P. Hertzberg, "Revised Estimates of New Plant and Equipment Expenditures in the United States, 1947-77," *Survey of Current Business,* October 1980, U.S. Department of Commerce, Bureau of Economic Analysis, pp. 24-59.

Mail and Telephone Reference:

U.S. Department of Commerce
Bureau of Economic Analysis
1401 K Street, N.W.
Washington, D.C.   20230
(202) 523-0777

The Bureau of Economic Analysis also provides on request a list, "BEA Contacts for Data Users." The list provides the names and telephone numbers of people to contact, by subject. The list is updated periodically.

Financial Statements: Components and Ratios—Where to Find Them for Industries and Companies

Issuing Agency: U.S. Treasury Department, Internal Revenue Service; Federal Trade Commission; Standard & Poor's Corporation; Moody's Investors Service.

Coverage, Data Available, Source, and When Available: The question frequently arises of where to look to obtain balance-sheet and income-statement information for an individual firm or for an industry. This section tells how to find such information. We indicate where to find specified items, totals, and financial ratios for individual firms and for industry groups.[18] Appendix A provides an excellent list of sources of industry and company information, including: general information on business and financial developments; industry information; company information; securities-market information (such as investment advice); security-price quotations; security-price indexes and averages; data on foreign companies; data on money markets; and data on mutual funds.[19]

Much has been written about the problems using balance-sheet and income-statement data. These issues are not treated here, for these issues are beyond the scope of this book.

In appendix B, the main items that appear on the balance sheet and income statements are defined, and some of the problems in measuring balance-sheet items are indicated.

Industry Financial Data: The Federal Trade Commission (FTC) in the *Quarterly Financial Report of: Manufacturing, Mining and Trade Corporations (QFR)* publishes timely aggregate statistics on the financial positions of U.S. corporations. The data are based on an extensive sample survey and are available quarterly. In each calendar quarter, the *QFR* presents estimates of the major components of the income statement classified, for example, as sales and expenses; estimates of the major items on the balance sheet categorized as assets, liabilities, and stockholder equity; and related financial and operating ratios for all manufacturing corporations and for mining and trade corporations. The statistical data are classified by industry and (for manufacturing) by asset size. Industry groups for which the financial data are available are shown in table 2-5. The *QFR* is published approximately seventy-five days after the end of the first, second, and third calendar quarters and approximately ninety-five days after the end of the fourth calendar quarter.

A major advantage in using the *QFR* is that the published data are well documented. The basis for the different classifications are explained; the

38

Table 2-5
Industry Groups for Which Financial Information Is Available
from Federal Trade Commission

All manufacturing corporations
  Nondurable manufacturing corporations
    Food and kindred products
    Tobacco manufactures
    Textile-mill products
    Paper and allied products
    Printing and publishing
    Chemicals and allied products
      Industrial chemicals and synthetics[a]
      Drugs[a]
    Petroleum and coal products
    Rubber and miscellaneous plastics products
    Other nondurable manufacturing corporations
  Durable manufacturing corporations
    Stone, clay, and glass products
    Primary metal industries
      Iron and steel[a]
      Nonferrous metals[a]
    Fabricated metal products
    Machinery, except electrical
    Electrical and electronic equipment
    Transportation equipment
      Motor vehicles and equipment[a]
      Aircraft, guided missiles and parts[a]
    Instruments and related products
    Other durable manufacturing corporations
All mining corporations
All retail trade corporations
All wholesale trade corporations

[a]Included in major industry.

sample used to derive the estimates of financial statistics as well as the precision of those estimates is described; reasons for similarities and differences with other industrial and financial statistics are listed; and changes that have occurred in the series over time, such as changes in accounting, industry classification, sampling, and discontinuities, are explained.

Standard & Poor's *Industry Surveys* is a comprehensive two-volume reference work, which is divided into thirty-three segments covering sixty-nine major domestic industries. Coverage in each area is divided into a basic analysis and a current analysis.

Each basic analysis begins with an examination of the prospects for that particular industry as perceived by analysts at S&P's. This is followed by a description of the trends and problems in the industry presented in historical perspective. The text contains statistical tables and charts. One section, "Comparative Company Analysis," is designed to facilitate a comparison of the growth in sales and earnings of the leading companies in the industry and to track profit margins, dividends, price-earning ratios, and other data for each company over a five-year period.

The current analysis provides a description of the latest developments and available industry, market, and company statistics.

The surveys are revised three times a year, and at any given time, some are in the process of revision. The analyses that appear in each edition contain the latest data available, in the opinion of S&P's, at the time the particular survey was prepared.

For historical industry comparisons, S&P's also publishes annually *Analysts Handbook: Composite Corporate per Share Data by Industries.* This publication presents selected income-account and balance-sheet items and related ratios as applied to the S&P's group-industry stock-price indexes from 1950 to date. The data are kept up to date quarterly to the extent that quarterly information is available. Continuity is not always possible, as is pointed out.

The U.S. Department of the Treasury's Internal Revenue Service prepares a series of different statistics of income publications; some cover individual income-tax returns, some cover income-tax returns of sole proprietorships and partnerships, and so on. The data are comprehensive and well documented. A major disadvantage of this source of information is that the data become available with a lag of two or more years.

This section focuses on the annual *Statistics of Income: Corporation Income Tax Returns,* which contains a wealth of financial information. The report presents data by industry on assets, liabilities, receipts, deductions, net income, income subject to tax, credits, distributions to stockholders, additional tax for tax preferences, and book net income. The data are also classified by the size of total assets, income taxed at normal tax and surtax rates (if applicable), income tax, and size of business receipts. Data presented in the report are estimates based on stratified probability samples of corporate income-tax returns selected before audit from approximately 2 million corporations.

Individual Companies: The standard source of information on any important security is the most-recent annual Moody's Investors Service *Manual.* The *Manuals* are bound and provide data on over 20,000 corporations and institutions. The *Manuals* are divided into six areas of specialization: bank and finance, industrial, international, over-the-counter (OTC) industrials, public utility, and transportation.

Each entry contains details of the history, background, mergers and acquisitions, subsidiaries, business and products, and services. When applicable, financial statements are presented, and a description of the capitalization of each company is shown. This includes information concerning a company's long-term debt and capital stocks, as well as data on warrants and subscription rights.[20]

Standard & Poor's Corporation publishes in *Corporation Records* financial descriptions of many publicly held corporations, including those listed on the New York and American stock exchanges and the larger unlisted and regional exchange companies. S&P's also publishes an annual, *Stock Market Encyclopedia.* This volume provides a variety of pertinent information on over 1,000 companies; for each data are included on earnings, dividends, and price history, and key income-account and balance-sheet statistics are presented.[21]

A variety of financial information about individual companies can be obtained through the Securities & Exchange Commission (SEC).[22] It can also be obtained for a fee from private organizations that photocopy the documents filed with the SEC.[23] A list of the major information available follows:

Prospectus: A document filed with the SEC whenever a company makes a new issue of shares, debentures, or other securities offered to the public. The document is supposed to contain all material facts concerning a company and its operations so that a prospective investor may make an informed decision about the merit of the investment. The content of the prospectus is governed by federal securities laws and regulations.

Form 8-K: A monthly report that lists certain material events that affect the change in control of a company, such as the material acquisition of a company or a material issuance of securities.

Form 10-Q: Filed quarterly, it provides unaudited financial information about a company.

Form 10-K: The annual report filed by a company.

Forms 3 and 4: Report any change in ownership in the shares of a company by officers, directors, or shareholders who own more than 10 percent of the stock.

Forms 13-D and 14-D: Show the acquisition of large stock interests in a registered company.

Copies of proxy statements filed with the SEC can also be obtained.

Gross National Product (GNP): National Product and National Income

Issuing Agency: U.S. Department of Commerce, Bureau of Economic Analysis, National Income and Wealth Division.

Coverage: Policymakers must know how the economy is performing in order to decide when, how, and how much stimulus or constraint should be applied. Therefore policymakers need a statistical knowledge of the nation's performance. Further, a historical statistical record aids economists in testing their theories about how the economy actually works. Thus, national-income accounting is an important topic in the study of economics. It is not an exact science, although in principle national-income accounting can help us decide how best to measure the economy's performance. Two methods can be used to measure national output: expenditure approach and income approach.

In principle, GNP could be measured by government statisticians' adding up all of the purchase prices times quantities purchased of every single final product. That would mean that a very long table showing the quantity and price of each of the apples sold, stereos sold, toothpicks sold, and so on, would be used. Clearly, a shortcut method must be devised. One way of measuring aggregate economic activity is the expenditure approach. Under that approach, the estimated dollar value at current market prices of all final goods and services are added in terms of broad categories, which include consumption, investment, government purchases, and net exports (lines 26-44 of table 2-6). The alternative method of measuring GNP, the income approach, is shown in lines 1-25 of the table, where all of the national income is added up.[24]

Expenditure Approach: GNP (table 2-6, right bottom total) represents the total money value of the nation's final product or output produced during the year. More precisely, GNP is the market value of the goods and services produced by labor and property supplied by residents of the United States, before deduction of depreciation charges and other allowances for business and institutional consumption of fixed capital goods and after deduction of products charged to expense by business. GNP consists of the purchases of goods and services by persons and government, gross private domestic investment (including the change in business inventories), and net exports (exports less imports).[25]

Personal-consumption expenditures (line 26) are goods and services purchased by individuals, operating expenses of nonprofit institutions serving individuals, and the value of food, fuel, clothing, rent of dwellings, and financial services received in kind by individuals.[26] Consumption expen-

42

Table 2-6
Summary National Income and Product Accounts, 1980[1]
(billions of dollars)

Line	Income Approach		Line	Expenditure Approach	
1	Compensation of employees	1,596.7	26	Personal consumption expenditures	1,671.1
2	Wages and salaries	1,343.8	27	Durable goods	211.6
3	Disbursements	1,343.8	28	Nondurable goods	674.3
4	Wage accruals less disbursements	0	29	Services	785.3
5	Supplements to wages and salaries	252.9			
6	Employer contributions for social insurance	115.8	30	Gross private domestic investment	396.8
7	Other labor income	137.1	31	Fixed investment	399.8
			32	Nonresidential	294.7
8	Proprietors' income with inventory valuation and capital-consumption adjustments	130.6	33	Structures	108.3
			34	Producers' durable equipment	186.5
9	Rental income of persons with capital-consumption adjustment	31.9	35	Residential	105.1
			36	Change in business inventories	-3.0
10	Corporate profits with inventory-valuation and capital-consumption adjustments	182.1	37	Net exports of goods and services	26.1
11	Profits before tax	242.7	38	Exports	340.6
12	Profits tax liability	80.8	39	Imports	314.5
13	Profits after tax	161.9	40	Government purchases of goods and services	534.8
14	Dividends	56.0	41	Federal	199.2
15	Undistributed profits	105.9	42	National defense	131.9
16	Inventory-valuation adjustment	-43.3	43	Nondefense	67.3
17	Capital-consumption adjustment	-17.2	44	State and local	335.6
18	Net interest	180.1			
19	National income	2,121.4			
20	Business transfer payments	10.5			
21	Indirect business tax and nontax liability	212.2			
22	Less: Subsidies less current surplus of government enterprises	4.5			
23	Statistical discrepancy	1.7			
24	Charges against net national product	2,341.3			
25	Capital-consumption allowances with capital-consumption adjustment	287.5			
	Charges against Gross National Product	2,628.8		Gross National Product	2,628.8

Adapted from: *Survey of Current Business*, February 1981, U.S. Department of Commerce, Bureau of Economic Analysis, p. 24.
Note: Estimates are those published in the January 1981 *Survey of Current Business.*

diture falls into three categories: durable consumer goods, nondurable consumer goods, and services. Durable goods (line 27) are arbitrarily defined as items that last more than three years; these include automobiles, furniture, and household appliances. Nondurable goods (line 28) are all the rest, such as food and gasoline. Services (line 29) are just what the name suggests: medical care, education, and so on. Net purchases of used goods are also included in personal-consumption expenditures. All private purchases of residential structures are classified as gross private domestic investment.

Some goods and services do not pass through the marketplace. For example, food grown on the farm for household consumption by the farmers' families is certainly a consumption expenditure, but it does not show up in the usual way because it does not pass through an organized market. Government statisticians have to estimate it to put it into the GNP. Additionally, the implicit rental value of owner-occupied homes is also estimated and added to personal-consumption expenditures (rental payments on apartments and the like are automatically included).

Gross private domestic investment (line 30) is fixed investment (line 31) purchased by private business and nonprofit institutions and the value of the change in the physical volume of inventories held by private business (line 36). Inventories include finished goods, goods in process, and raw material that a firm has on hand for sale or use at a later date. Fixed investment includes all private purchases of residential structures, whether purchased for tenant or owner occupancy. Net purchases of used goods are also included.

Net exports of goods and services (line 37) is exports less imports of goods and services. Exports (line 38) are part of national production. Imports (line 39) are not but are included in the components of GNP and are therefore deducted. There are differences between the national income and product account (NIPA) measures of exports and imports and those in the detailed balance-of-payments accounts.

Government purchases of goods and services (line 40) is the compensation of government employees and purchases from business and from abroad. It excludes transfer payments, interest paid by government, and subsidies. It includes gross investment by government enterprises but excludes their current outlays. It includes net purchases of used goods and excludes sales and purchases of land and financial assets.

Generally goods and services are valued at the price at which they are sold, but many government goods and services are provided at no direct cost to the consumer. Therefore their market value cannot be used when computing GNP. The value of these goods is considered to be equal to their cost. For example, the value of a new road is considered to be equal to its construction cost and is included in the GNP for the year it was built.

Income Approach: Charges against GNP can be calculated in terms of the flow of costs or payments that firms make in order to produce the things they sell to households. National income can be loosely defined as the total amount of national-factor payments to the owners of the factors of production that are used. Stated in other words, national income is the total income earned by the owners of resources who put their factors of production to work.

Charges against GNP (table 2-6, left bottom total) is the costs incurred and the profits earned in the production of GNP. Accordingly, it equals GNP, except for the statistical discrepancy. These charges are arranged in two groups. The first of these—compensation of employees, proprietors' income, rental income of persons, corporate profits, and net interest—are factor charges because they represent the incomes of the factors of production (labor and property). The total of factor incomes is called the national income. The second group consists of nonfactor charges. Addition of business transfers, indirect business taxes, and current surplus of government enterprises less subsidies—which are included in this group—to national income yields charges against net national product (and net national product). Addition of capital consumption allowances—the remaining item in the nonfactor cost group—to charges against net national product yields, in principle, charges against GNP (and GNP). In practice, measurement errors result in a statistical discrepancy, which is entered between national income and charges against net national product to secure balance between GNP and the factor and nonfactor charges against it.

Compensation of employees (line 1) is the income accruing to employees as remuneration for their work. It is the sum of wages and salaries and supplements to wages and salaries.

Wages and salaries (line 2) consists of the monetary remuneration of employees, including the compensation of corporate officers; commissions, tips, and bonuses; and receipts in kind that represent income to the recipients. It consists of disbursements (line 3) and wage accruals less disbursements (line 4). Disbursements is wages and salaries as just defined except that retroactive wages are counted when paid rather than when earned.

Supplements to wages and salaries (line 5) consists of employer contributions for social insurance and of other labor income. Employer contributions for social insurance (line 6) includes employer payments under the following programs: federal old-age, survivors', disability, and hospital insurance; state unemployment insurance; railroad retirement and unemployment insurance; government retirement; and publicly administered workmen's compensation. Other labor income (line 7) includes employer contributions to private pension and welfare funds, and directors' fees.

Proprietors' income with inventory valuation and capital-consumption adjustments (line 8) is the income, including income in kind, of proprietorships and partnerships and of producers' cooperatives. Interest and dividend income received by proprietors and rental incomes received by persons who are not primarily engaged in the real-estate business are excluded. The inventory-valuation adjustment is described under corporate profits and the capital-consumption adjustment under capital-consumption allowances (line 25).

Rental income of persons with capital-consumption adjustment (line 9) is the income of persons from the rental of real property, except the income of persons primarily engaged in the real-estate business; the imputed net rental income of owner-occupants of nonfarm dwellings; and the royalties received by persons from patents, copyrighs, and rights to natural resources. The capital-consumption adjustment is described under capital-consumption allowances (line 25).

Corporate profits with inventory-valuation and capital-consumption adjustments (line 10) is the income of corporations organized for profit and of mutual financial institutions that accrues to residents, measured before-profits taxes, before deduction of depletion charges, after exclusion of capital gains and losses, and net of dividends received from domestic corporations. Corporate profits includes net inflows from abroad of dividends, reinvested earnings of incorporated foreign affiliates, and earnings of unincorporated foreign affiliates. In other major respects, profits are defined as in federal income-tax regulations. The capital-consumption adjustment is described under capital-consumption allowances (line 25).

Profits before tax (line 11) is corporate profits without inventory-valuation and capital-consumption adjustments.

Profits tax liability (line 12) is federal, state, and local taxes on corporate income.

Profits after tax (line 13) is profits before tax less profits tax liability. Dividends (line 14) is payments in cash or other assets, excluding stock, by corporations organized for profit to stockholders who are U.S. residents (including state and local social insurance funds).

Undistributed profits (line 15) is corporate profits before tax less corporate profit tax liability and less dividends. It may also be viewed as the sum of purchases of fixed capital assets, the change in the book value of corporate inventories, and the net acquisition of financial assets, less the sum of capital-consumption allowances, net borrowing, and net stock issues.

Inventory-valuation adjustment (line 16) is the change in the business-inventories component of GNP, which is measured as the change in the physical volume of inventories valued in prices of the current period, less the change in the value of inventories reported by business (book value). The inventory-valuation adjustment converts inventories at historical cost, the valuation concept generally underlying business accounting, to replacement cost, the concept underlying the NIPA's. It is required only for nonfarm inventories; the change in farm inventories is estimated directly. To make the measurement of charges against GNP consistent with GNP, an inventory-valuation adjustment must be applied to reported corporate profits and proprietors' income.

Capital-consumption adjustment (line 17) is described under capital-consumption allowances (line 25).

Net interest (line 18) is interest paid by business less interest received by it, plus net interest received from abroad. In addition to monetary interest flows, net interest includes flows of interest in kind (imputed interest). The latter have their counterparts in service charges, which are included in personal consumption expenditures and in government purchases.

National income (line 19) is the income that originates in the production of goods and services attributable to labor and property supplied by residents of the United States. Thus, it measures the factor costs of goods and services produced. Incomes are recorded in the forms in which they accrue to residents and are measured before deduction of taxes on those incomes. They consist of the compensation of employees, proprietors' income, rental income of persons, corporate profits, and net interest.

Business transfer payments (line 20) is payments to persons for which the latter do not perform current services. They include liability payments for personal injury, corporate gifts to nonprofit institutions and bad debts incurred by consumers. Most of personal-consumption expenditures is stated before deduction of consumer bad debts; corporate profits and proprietors' income are stated after allowance for bad debts. Accordingly, bad debts have to be entered explicitly among the charges against GNP, and because they are written off rather than collected, they fit into the general category of transfer payments.

Indirect business tax and nontax liability (line 21) consists of tax liabilities (except employer contributions for social insurance) chargeable to business expense in the calculation of profit-type incomes and of certain other business liabilities to government agencies (except government enterprises) that it is convenient to treat like taxes. Indirect business taxes include sales, excise, and property taxes and the windfall-profit tax on crude-oil production. Taxes on corporate income are excluded; these taxes cannot be calculated until profits are known and in that sense are not a business expense. Nontaxes includes regulatory and inspection fees, special assessments, fines and penalties, rents and royalties, and donations. Nontaxes generally excludes business purchases from government of goods and services that are similar to business purchases of intermediate products from other businesses. Government receipts from the sale of such products are netted against government purchases so that they do not appear in GNP and other measures of production.

Subsidies less current surplus of government enterprises (line 22). Subsidies is the monetary grants paid by government to business, including government enterprises at another level of government. The current surplus of government enterprises is their sales receipts less their current outlays. In the calculation of their current surplus, no deduction is made for depreciation charges and net interest paid. Subsidies and current surplus are often combined because deficits incurred by government enterprises may result from selling goods to businesses at lower than market prices in lieu of giving them subsidies. This is also the major reason for not counting the current surplus of government enterprises as a profit-type income and, accordingly, as part of factor charges.

Statistical discrepancy (line 23) is GNP less charges against GNP other than the statistical discrepancy. It arises because GNP and charges against GNP are estimated independently by methodologies that are subject to error.

Capital-consumption allowances with capital-consumption adjustment (line 25). Capital-consumption allowances consists of depreciation charges and accidental damage to fixed business capital. For nonfarm business, they are as reported on federal income-tax returns. For farms, nonprofit institutions, and owner-occupied houses, depreciation charges are not based on income-tax returns but instead are calculated to conform to NIPA definitions. Capital-consumption adjustment (line 17) for corporations is the tax return-based capital-consumption allowances less capital-consumption allowances that are based on estimates of uniform service lives, straight-line depreciation, and replacement cost. Similar adjustments are applied to proprietors' income and rental income of persons. The capital-consumption allowances with capital-consumption adjustment for nonprofit institutions serving individuals is the value of the current services of the fixed capital assets owned and used by these institutions; it is included in personal-consumption expenditures.

Data Available: Information for the figures shown in table 2-6 is available not only for years but also for quarters and, in the case of personal income and its disposition, for months. For most annual information, the period since 1929 is covered; for most quarterly and monthly information, the post-World War II period is covered.

For GNP and its product components, current-dollar measures are separated into real measures (measures from which price change has been eliminated) and measures of price change.

Finally, most of the items shown in table 2-6 are available in much greater detail. For instance, annual estimates of personal-consumption expenditures are broken down into about 100 types of expenditures, and annual and quarterly estimates of government receipts and expenditures are shown separately for the federal government and for state and local governments.

Related Series: Five widely used measures of production and income—GNP, net national product, national income, personal income, and disposable personal income—are shown in table 2-7.

Table 2-7
National Income Accounts since 1970
(billions of dollars)

Year	Sum of These Expenditures				Equals	Less	Equals	Less	Equals		Less		Plus	Equals	Less	Equals
	Personal-Consumption Expenditures	Gross Private Domestic Investment	Government Purchases of Goods and Services	Net Exports	GNP	Depreciation	NNP	Indirect Business Taxes	National Income	Undistributed Corporate Profits	Social Security	Corporate Income Taxes	Transfer Payments (includes Government and Business)	Personal Income	Personal Tax and Nontax Payments	Disposable Personal Income
1970	618.8	140.8	218.9	3.9	982.4	90.8	891.6	94.0	798.4	14.1	58.7	34.5	110.2	801.3	115.3	685.9
1971	668.2	160.0	233.7	1.6	1063.4	98.8	964.7	103.4	858.1	21.3	64.8	37.7	124.8	859.1	116.3	742.8
1972	733.0	188.3	253.1	-3.3	1171.1	105.4	1065.8	111.0	951.9	30.0	73.6	41.5	135.7	942.5	141.2	801.3
1973	809.9	220.0	269.5	7.1	1306.6	117.7	1188.9	120.2	1064.6	39.3	91.5	48.7	167.3	1052.4	150.8	901.7
1974	887.5	215.0	303.3	7.5	1413.2	137.7	1275.5	128.4	1135.7	44.4	103.4	52.4	217.8	1153.3	170.4	982.9
1975	973.2	183.7	339.0	20.5	1516.3	161.4	1355.0	138.7	1207.6	33.2	109.7	49.2	234.2	1249.7	168.8	1080.9
1976	1078.6	241.2	365.8	6.9	1692.4	179.8	1512.7	149.7	1349.4	49.0	122.8	64.7	262.5	1375.4	193.6	1181.8
1977	1211.2	294.2	395.0	-10.9	1889.5	196.9	1692.6	172.1	1520.5	58.4	139.0	76.2	289.8	1536.7	226.0	1303.0
1978	1348.7	375.3	432.6	-.6	2156.1	199.4	1956.7	211.3	1745.4	95.7	137.2	83.0	292.3	1721.8	258.8	1462.9
1979	1510.9	415.8	473.8	13.4	2413.9	217.2	2196.7	233.4	1963.3	117.6	159.0	87.6	344.7	1943.8	302.0	1641.7
1980	1672.3	395.4	534.6	24.2	2626.5	242.8	2383.7	264.2	2119.5	105.1	112.0	80.7	338.5	2160.2	338.6	1821.6

Source: Roger LeRoy Miller, *Economics Today,* 4th ed., New York: Harper & Row, 1982, p. 196.

GNP is a measure of the value of the nation's final output of goods and services produced during the year. In the course of a year, however, machines and structures wear out or are accidentally damaged as they are used. For example, houses deteriorate or are accidentally damaged, and machines need repairs, or they will stop working. Most capital, or durable goods therefore depreciate or may be accidentally damaged. An estimate of this, called capital-consumption allowances, is subtracted from GNP to arrive at net national product (NNP).[27]

NNP represents the total market value of goods and services available for both consumption, used in a broader sense here to mean "resource exhausting," and net additions to the economy's stock of capital. NNP does not, however, represent the income available to individuals within that economy because it includes indirect business taxes, such as sales taxes. We therefore deduct these indirect business taxes from NNP to arrive at the figure for all income of resource owners. The result is national income.

National income does not actually represent what is available to individuals to spend because some people obtain income for which they have provided no concurrent good or service, and others earn income but do not receive it. In the former category are mainly recipients of transfer payments from the government, such as social security, welfare, and food stamps. These payments represent shifts of funds within the economy by way of the government, where no concurrent good or service is rendered in exchange. For the other category, income earned but not received, the most-obvious examples are undistributed corporate profits that are plowed back into the business, contributions to social insurance, and corporate income taxes. When transfer payments are added and when income earned but not received is subtracted, the result is personal income.[28]

Disposable personal income is derived by subtracting all personal-income taxes from personal income. This is the income that individuals have for consumption or saving.

Source of Data: Estimates of the national income and product accounts are based on a wide range of sources obtained from both the government and private organizations.[29]

When Series Become Available: The best estimate of the release date is published on the last page of the December issue of the U.S. Department of Commerce, Bureau of Economic Analysis, *Survey of Current Business* for the preceding year. Thus, the December 1981 issue provides the release date for quarterly GNP data released in 1982. In general, quarterly GNP and GNP-related data, including the implicit price indexes, are released as follows: preliminary estimates, about three weeks after the end of the quarter to which the data refers; first revision, about one and a half months after the end of the quarter; second revision, about two and a half months after the end of the quarter.

Limitations: Consider some items that should be included in GNP but are not because of measurement problems.[30]

Do-It-Yourself Activities: When you decide to fix your own car, you engage in the production of a service that is not included in GNP because the transaction does not pass through the marketplace. Had you decided to take your car to a garage, that same service would have been included in GNP because you would have paid a mechanic. Services in the home represent the biggest category under this heading of what is left out of GNP.

Homemakers' Services: The value of the services performed by homemakers is substantial. These services range from cooking, to food buying, to being a practical nurse. In fact, if an individual marries a paid housekeeper and that housekeeper leaves the labor force, GNP will fall by the amount he or she used to be paid. The services of nonworking spouses and roommates are becoming less significant with respect to computing GNP, however. As more services are contracted for with regular businesses and with individuals selling those services, they become part of GNP (assuming that the income is reported). Cases in point are the purchases of dry-cleaning services and convenience foods. Since World War II, the market purchase of household services has increased markedly so some of the growth in measured real GNP has been exaggerated relative to previous growth before this phenomenon occurred.

Illegal Activities and Income Never Reported: For a variety of reasons, a large amount of income is generated that does not enter the national income accounts. For example, many illegal activities do not enter into our national income accounting system. These include, but are not limited to, narcotics, gambling, bootlegging, and prostitution. It is difficult to estimate their total market value, but it is probably about $150 billion per year. Other economic activities generate income but are not included. It has been estimated that nonreported cash income-producing activities, if completely taken account of, would add another 20 percent to measured GNP. Hence the measured rate of economic growth may be seriously underestimating the true rate.

Measures of Satisfaction: Assuming that we were able to include every economic activity that should be included to measure real GNP, we could come up with a perfect measure of output, or production. However, output does not necessarily equal satisfaction, and a higher level of output may not be associated with a higher level of satisfaction.

Consider an example. If output were to increase by 10 percent but population were to increase by 20 percent, the amount of output available per person would fall. We can correct for this problem by dividing real GNP by population to obtain per-capita real GNP. But even then we are faced with the problem of increased inequality of income.

What if the rich get richer and the poor get poorer as GNP grows? Has the general level of satisfaction increased? Many people would say no, because the distribution of income, even though we have no way of taking it into account, must surely play an important part in determining the level of satisfaction of society.

And what about leisure? Surely it is a scarce good. As such, it has value and generates satisfaction. Although it has recently leveled off in the United States, the amount of leisure time has been growing since World War II. The number of hours worked per week fell on average by some 18 percent from 1943 to mid-1975. This increased leisure has added to our satisfaction, but it is not included in any measure of the national income accounts.

Gross National Pollution: Environmental concern in the 1980s has focused attention on a large deficiency in our measurement of the nation's economic well-being. Numerous critics of environmental degradation maintain that the standard definition of GNP is misleading. In fact, some regard GNP as a symbol of everything that is wrong with America. Their idea is that if GNP growth were slowed or even halted, economic output would fall but so would pollution. Dr. Arthur F. Burns, former chairman of the Board of Governors of the Federal Reserve System, told Congress that he would like to see GNP adjusted to "take account of the depreciation in our environment." He indicated that there should be a "proper recording of the minuses as well as the pluses." In Burns's opinion, GNP, properly adjusted, would be a good deal lower than it now appear.

Given all the deficiencies in our national income accounts, is it possible to come up with a new measure of GNP? Yes, say two innovating experts in the field, James Tobin and William Nordhaus.

Professors Tobin and Nordhaus presented their view of what GNP would look like if it were to take account of many of the deficiencies. They called it "measure of economic welfare," or MEW. MEW is obtained by modifying GNP in three ways:

1. Subtracting certain costs or "bads," such as pollution.
2. Excluding "regrettable necessities," such as police services.
3. Adding activities that are not included in GNP, such as household services, home repairs, and leisure.

Using MEW instead of NNP is considered by many to be a step in the right direction. MEW is a good measure of consumption, but it is not a measure of economic welfare. The two concepts are related, but economic welfare depends on the amount of total satisfaction that each of us actually receives from our consumption.[31]

Publications: Current Data:

Council of Economic Advisers, *Economic Indicators,* Washington, D.C.: U.S. Government Printing Office. Monthly.

U.S. Department of Commerce, Bureau of Economic Analysis, *Survey of Current Business.* Monthly. Annual revisions appear in the July issue.

Publications: Historical Data:

Council of Economic Advisers, *Economic Report of the President,* Washington, D.C.: U.S. Government Printing Office. Annual. See statistical appendix.

U.S. Department of Commerce, Bureau of Economic Analysis, *National Income and Product Accounts of the United States, 1929-76: Statistical Tables,* 1981.

U.S. Department of Commerce, Bureau of Economic Analysis, "The U.S. National Income and Product Accounts: Revised Estimates," *Survey of Current Business,* July 1982.

References:

Carson, Carol S., and George Jaszi, "The National Income and Product Accounts of the United States: An Overview," *Survey of Current Business,* U.S. Department of Commerce, Bureau of Economic Analysis, February 1981, pp. 22-34.

Denison, Edward F., and Robert P. Parker, "The National Income and Product Accounts of the United States: An Introduction to the Revised Estimates for 1929-80," *Survey of Current Business,* December 1980, U.S. Department of Commerce, Bureau of Economic Analysis, pp. 1-26.

Nordhaus, William, and James Tobin, "Is Growth Obsolete?," *Economic Growth, Fiftieth Anniversary Colloquim, vol. 5,* New York: National Bureau of Economic Research, 1972.

Mail and Telephone Reference:

U.S. Department of Commerce
Bureau of Economic Analysis
1401 K Street, N.W.
Washington, D.C.   20230
(202) 523-0777

The Bureau of Economic Analysis also provides on request a list, ''BEA Contacts for Data Users.'' The list provides the names and telephone numbers of people to contact by subject. The list is updated periodically.

Housing Permits: New Privately Owned Housing Units Authorized, But Not Started, in Permit-Issuing Places

Issuing Agency: U.S. Department of Commerce, Bureau of the Census, Construction Statistics Division.

Coverage: This series measures the number of housing units authorized by local permit-issuing places. The data relate to the issuance of permits, not to the actual start of construction.

Data Available: Estimates of number of private housing permits authorized are categorized by number of units per structure and region of the country. Detailed estimates are available on a national basis, for each of the fifty states, regional divisions, selected Standard Metropolitan Statistical Areas, and selected permit-issuing places.[32]

Data are also available for the number of new housing units in projects (publicly owned housing units) for which public-housing agencies have given a developer notice to proceed with construction, by location and program.

Source of Data: Data are based on sample surveys of permit-issuing areas. The number of permit-issuing areas covered by the survey has increased over time. For example, data for 1963 to 1967 are based on reports from 12,000 permit-issuing places; for 1968 to 1972 on 13,000 permit-issuing places; from 1973 to 1978 on 14,000 permit-issuing places; and from 1979 to date (1982) on 16,000 permit-issuing places. Permits by these 16,000 places account for approximately 88 percent of all new residential construction in the United States (the other 12 percent occurs in areas that do not require permits). The monthly sample survey covers about half of the 16,000 permit-issuing areas. Once a year, reports are obtained from all 16,000 areas, and monthly data from the preceding year are revised accordingly.

When Data Become Available: Estimates of housing units authorized become available around the eighteenth working day of the month or, equivalently, around the fourth week of the month.

Limitations: Permits can be a misleading indicator of housing activity for several reasons. Often several months may pass between the issuance of a permit and the start of construction. In some cases permits may be allowed to lapse and construction is never started.

Housing construction also occurs in areas that do not require permits. About 12 percent of all new construction occurs in areas where permits are not issued. Housing activity in those areas is not covered by the housing permit series.[33]

Publications: Current Data:

Council of Economic Advisers, *Economic Indicators*, Washington, D.C.:
U.S. Government Printing Office. Monthly.

U.S. Department of Commerce, Bureau of the Census, *Housing Units Authorized by Building Permits and Public Contracts*, Report C40.
Monthly and annual issue (June).

U.S. Department of Commerce, Bureau of Industrial Economics, *Construction Review*. Bimonthly.

Publications: Historical Data:

Council of Economic Advisers, *Economic Report of the President,* Washington, D.C.: U.S. Government Printing Office. Annual. See statistical appendix.

Historical data can be obtained by writing to: U.S. Department of Commerce, Bureau of the Census, Chief, Construction Statistics Division, 3737 Branch Ave., Temple Hill, MD 20748. Phone (301) 763-7244.

Mail and Telephone Reference:

U.S. Bureau of the Census
Economic Census Staff
Suitland, MD　20233
(301) 763-4040

Housing Starts

Issuing Agency: U.S. Department of Commerce, Bureau of the Census, Construction Statistics Division.

Coverage: New private-housing starts measure the number of private-housing units on which construction is started each month in the United States. Included are all types of accommodations designed as family living quarters and constructed in new buildings.

A housing start consists of the start of construction on a new housing unit when located within a new building intended primarily as a housekeeping residential building designed for nontransient occupancy. Start of construction for private-housing units is defined as the beginning of excavation for the foundation of a building. Housing provided by conversion of either residential or nonresidential space to provide additional numbers of housing units and the production of mobile homes are excluded.

Data Available: Housing starts are reported for publicly owned units, as well as privately owned units. Privately owned units are available by number of units per structure and by location.

New housing starts are classified by region—Northeast, North Central, South, West—and by new homes started inside and outside Standard Metropolitan Statistical Areas.

Starts are also available by number of units per structure, for example, structures with one unit, two to four units, and five units.

Source of Data: The statistics on housing starts are estimated from sample surveys. The survey is based on two parts: a survey of permit-issuing areas (which account for about 88 percent of all residential building activity) and a survey of non-permit-issuing areas (which account for the other 12 percent of residential building activity). Of the approximately 16,000 permit-issuing areas in the United States, interviewers canvass about 850 of these areas and collect information on permits issued, starts, completions, sales, and prices. These 850 offices cover about 40 percent of the residential building activity. In areas that do not require building permits (which account for about 12 percent of all residential building), interviewers canvass prespecified areas for similar information on housing starts, completions, and so on. Information on housing starts in both permit- and nonpermit-issuing areas is combined to come up with housing starts for the country and for major regions.

When Data Become Available: Housing starts become available around the twelfth working day of the month. Typically data are published around two and one-half to three weeks into the month.

Limitations: A housing start is defined as the beginning of excavation, but some houses that are started may never be completed or may be finished only after a long time.[34] For example, during a slowdown in economic activity, builders may stop or slow construction on partially built homes.[35]

Publications: Current Data:

Council of Economic Advisers, *Economic Indicators*, Washington, D.C.: U.S. Government Printing Office. Monthly.

U.S. Department of Commerce, Bureau of the Census, *Construction Reports: Housing Starts*, Report C20. Monthly.

U.S. Department of Commerce, Bureau of Industrial Economics, *Construction Review*. Bimonthly.

Publications: Historical Data:

Council of Economic Advisers, *Economic Report of the President*, Washington, D.C.: U.S. Government Printing Office. Annual. See statistical appendix.

Historical data are available from 1959. A complete list of the historical data (or any subportion) can be obtained by writing to the U.S. Department of Commerce, Bureau of the Census, Housing Statistics Branch, Construction Statistics Division, Washington, D.C. 20233.

References:

U.S. Department of Commerce, Bureau of the Census, *Construction Reports: Housing Starts*, April 1981, appendix. Monthly.

U.S. Department of Commerce, Bureau of the Census, *Construction Statistics Data Finder*, Washington, D.C.

U.S. Department of Commerce, Bureau of Industrial Economics, *Construction Review*. Bimonthly.

Mail and Telephone Reference:

U.S. Bureau of the Census
Economic Census Staff
Suitland, MD   20233
(301) 763-4040

Price of New Houses: Median Price of New Houses Sold, Average Price of New Houses Sold, [and] Price Index of New One-Family Houses Sold

Issuing Agency: U.S. Department of Commerce, Bureau of the Census, Construction Statistics Division.

Coverage and Limitations: Prices of new homes can be measured in several ways. Two frequently used measures, issued monthly, are the median price of new homes and the average (or mean) price of new homes. Median Price is the middle price of new homes; half of the prices are above and half are below the median price of new homes sold during the period. Average (or mean) Price provides an arithmetic average obtained by summing the prices of new homes sold during the period and dividing by the number of new homes sold.

Of the two measures, the median price of new homes is more representative of the price a typical family pays for a new home. The average price of new homes tends to be higher than the median because of the nature of the distribution of home prices.

Changes in the median and average sales price reflect changing proportions of houses of different sizes, locations, and other characteristics, as well as changes in the prices of houses with identical characteristics.

A more-meaningful measure of changes in new housing prices would hold the quality of housing constant, thereby more accurately reflecting price changes alone. The Bureau of the Census publishes such a price index quarterly, the Price Index of New One-Family Houses Sold.[36] This price index is designed to measure changes in the sales price of new houses sold that are the same with respect to ten important physical characteristics as the houses sold in the base year 1977. The ten characteristics are floor area, number of stories, number of bathrooms, presence of central air-conditioning, type of parking facility, type of foundation, geographic division within the region, whether the house is inside or outside a Standard Metropolitan Statistical Area, the size of the lot, and the presence of one or more fireplaces.

Data Available: The Median Price of New Houses Sold, Average Price of New Houses Sold, and Price Index of New One-Family Houses Sold are available for the United States overall and by region of the country: Northeast, North Central, South, and West.

59

Source of Data: Median and average prices of new homes are obtained from sample survey interviews in permit- and nonpermit-issuing areas of the United States.

The Price Index of New One-Family Houses Sold is constructed by the Bureau of the Census by using information from the sample survey.

When Series Become Available: Average Price of New Houses Sold and Median Price of New Houses Sold are available monthly. The data are released around the twenty-first working day of the month, or with a lag of about one month.

The Price Index of New One-Family Houses Sold is published quarterly. It is released with a lag of about one month.

Publications: Current Data:

Median Price of New Houses Sold and Average Price of New Houses Sold: U.S. Department of Commerce, Bureau of the Census and U.S. Department of Housing and Urban Development, *Construction Reports: New One-Family Houses Sold and for Sale*, Report C25. Monthly.

U.S. Department of Commerce, Bureau of Industrial Economics, *Construction Reports*. Bimonthly.

Price Index of New One-Family Houses Sold: U.S. Department of Commerce, Bureau of the Census, *Construction Reports: Price Index of New One-Family Houses Sold*, Report C27. Quarterly.

U.S. Department of Commerce, Bureau of Industrial Economics, *Construction Reports*. Bimonthly.

Publications: Historical Data:

Selected data on new one-family houses sold and for sale, for the period 1963 to date, are available from Construction Starts Branch, Construction Statistics Division, Bureau of the Census, Washington, D.C. 20233. The telephone number is (301) 763-7842.

References:

U.S. Department of Commerce, Bureau of the Census, *Construction Statics Data Finder*, Washington, D.C.

Mail and Telephone Reference:

U.S. Bureau of the Census
Economic Census Staff
Suitland, MD   20233
(301) 763-4040

Indicators: Index of Leading Indicators, Index of Coincident Indicators, [and] Index of Lagging Indicators

Issuing Agency: U.S. Department of Commerce, Bureau of Economic Analysis, Statistical Indicators Division.

Coverage and Source: Sometimes the overall business climate is buoyant—few workers are unemployed, businesses are expanding, and not many firms are facing bankruptcy. At other times, the business situation is not so good—there are many unemployed workers, businesses are cutting back in their production, and a significant number of firms are going out of business. These ups and downs in economic activity are called business fluctuations. They used to be called business cycles. A business cycle was defined as a recurrent (but nonperiodic) fluctuation in general business and economic activity taking place over a period of years. Talk about business and general economic activity generally refers to such economy-wide variables as employment and unemployment, income, output, and the price level.

Many important individual, business, and government decisions hinge on expectations about future economic conditions. Nevertheless forecasting remains inexact. Whether the primary input is an elaborate statistical model of the economy or simply a hunch based on the weather, it is likely to be supplemented by many other pieces of information. Among the more widely used pieces are the Index of Leading Indicators, Index of Coincident Indicators, and Index of Lagging Indicators.

Hundreds of statistics about the economy are generated every month. Each gives some information about the condition of the economy. None of these statistics alone is a reliable indicator of overall economic health. Many economic statistics, though certainly not all, can be assigned to one or another of three distinct groups depending on the timing of their movements relative to changes in the national economy.[37] Some tend to turn upward on a fairly regular basis in advance of the national economy and typically turn downward before the national economy begins to weaken. These are known as *leading indicators*, and they signal the advent of recessions and recoveries several months in advance. Others perform much in step with the economy as a whole and so are known as *coincident indicators*. Finally, those whose turning points trail behind the national business cycle are known as *lagging indicators*.[38]

Many different series that fit into these three categories were examined and rated according to a set of criteria. Those that performed the best overall were selected for inclusion in each of the three indexes.[39] In brief, the individual components of each index are weighted to reflect their relative importance then added together to form the index.

The twleve series on which the Index of Leading Indicators is based are:[40]

1. Average work week for production workers in manufacturing.
2. Average weekly initial claims, state unemployment insurance.
3. Value of manufacturers' new orders for consumer goods and materials (constant dollars, 1972).
4. Vendor performance measured as a percentage of companies reporting slower deliveries.
5. Net business formation.
6. Contracts and orders for plant and equipment (constant dollars, 1972).
7. New building permits for private-housing units.
8. Net change in inventories on hand and on order (constant dollars, 1972).
9. Change in sensitive materials prices.
10. Change in credit oustanding—business and consumer borrowing.
11. Stock prices (Standard & Poor's index of 500 stocks).
12. Money supply (M2 in constant dollars, 1972).

The four series on which the Index of Coincident Indicators is based are:

1. Employees on nonagricultural payrolls.
2. Personal income minus transfer payments (constant dollars, 1972).
3. Industrial production.
4. Manufacturing and trade sales (constant dollars, 1972).

The six series on which the Index of Lagging Indicators is based are:

1. Average duration of unemployment in weeks.
2. Ratio of deflated inventories to sales in manufacturing and trade.
3. Labor cost per unit of output in manufacturing—as a percent of trend.
4. Average prime-interest rate charged by banks.
5. Commercial and industrial loans outstanding (constant dollars, 1972).
6. Ratio of consumer installment debt to personal income.

Data Available: Values of each of the series used to compile the three composite indexes, as well as the values of the indexes, are published monthly.[41]

Related Series: Some analysts contend that the ratio of the Index of Coincident to the Index of Lagging Indicators (proposed by Geoffrey Moore) produces a reasonably stable and predictively useful relationship.[42] The turning points in the ratio will lead those of the Coincident Index if the movement of the latter decelerates before its turning point while the Lagging Index continues to move at a faster rate. In addition, there are some economic reasons for expecting the ratio to have early cyclical timing. For example, a downturn in the ratio of sales (coincident indicators) to inventories (lagging indicators) should have an adverse effect on, and may anticipate the downturn in, new orders (leading indicators). Similarly, a slowdown in the rise of output (coincident indicators) combined with a continuing strong rise in unit labor cost and other costs (such as those associated with growing inventories and business indebtedness, which all lag) will depress profits and new investment commitments (leading indicators).

The advantage of the derived ratio of coincident to lagging indicators as a forecasting tool is twofold. First, it provides an additional comprehensive leading series, based on series that are entirely different from those included in the composite index of leaders. Second, if its turning points do indeed precede those in the composite leading index, the ratio has considerable supplementary forecasting value.[43]

When Series Become Available: The composite indexes become available with a lag of about one month. For example, the composite indexes of leading, coincident, and lagging indicators for March become available at the end of April. For the estimated release dates, see the last page of the December issue of the U.S. Department of Commerce, Bureau of Economic Analysis, *Survey of Current Business.*

Limitations: Two major weaknesses of the Index of Leading Indicators (the most widely publicized of the three composite cycle indexes) are the false signals and variable leads times given by it.[44] Usually two ways are used to evaluate the forecasting effectiveness of the index. One way (often called the *turning-point approach*) looks at the ability of the index to predict business-cycle turning points (peaks and troughs). The second way (often called the *whole-cycle approach*) looks at the ability of the index to predict movements of economic activity at all points of the cycle. By either method, the index is shown to give highly variable signals that are somewhat unreliable.

For example, when the index is used to forecast business-cycle peaks and troughs (under the turning-point approach) a judgment must be made about when the index is forecasting a peak or a trough. One way is to decide if an upturn (downturn) in economic activity will occur if the index has been above (below) its previous high (low) for a specified number of months. Then one must decide how many months the index should be followed before predicting an upturn or a downturn. The approach is inherently arbitrary in deciding on the number of months since it is not obvious how many months the index must move in the same direction before predicting a turning point.

If a one-month rule is used, a turning point usually will not be missed; however, the index will produce a number of false signals for peaks and troughs. Using a four- or five-month rule, at the other extreme, the predictive accuracy of the index increases, but the ability of the index to give advance notice declines. Then there is a trade-off between the accuracy of prediction and the length of advance notice. Moreover, the trade-off is not the same for peaks as it is for troughs. (For example, the Index of Leading Indicators predicts troughs more accurately than peaks under any rule.)

No index of leading indicators (or any other economic forecasting device) can perform well if used mechanically and in isolation from other informational tools. Good results can be expected only if the current behavior of such an index is interpreted with judgment and in the light of other evidence. Even then, external factors can distort the relations between the leading, coincident, and lagging indicators of business expansions and contractions. Moreover, structural change in the economy, and possibly major unanticipated shifts in the inflation rates, will affect these relationships. Continuous study of the indicators, not limited to any short list of series used in the composite index, is needed to keep track of such developments and make best use of the approach.[45]

Publications: Current Data:

U.S. Department of Commerce, Bureau of Economic Analysis, *Business Conditions Digest*. Monthly.

Publications: Historical Data:

U.S. Department of Commerce, Bureau of Economic Analysis, *Handbook of Cyclical Indicators*, Washington, D.C.: U.S. Government Printing Office, 1977.

References:

U.S. Department of Commerce, Bureau of Economic Analysis, *Handbook of Cyclical Indicators*, Washington, D.C.: U.S. Government Printing Office, 1977.
U.S. Department of Commerce, Bureau of Economic Analysis, *Business Conditions Digest*, March 1983, pp. 107-109.

Mail and Telephone Reference:

U.S. Department of Commerce
Bureau of Economic Analysis
1401 K Street, N.W.
Washington, D.C.   20230
(202) 523-0777

The Bureau of Economic Analysis also provides on request a list, "BEA
Contacts for Data Users." The list provides the names and telephone
numbers of people to contact, by subject. The list is updated periodically.

Index of Industrial Production

Issuing Agency: Board of Governors of the Federal Reserve System, Business Conditions Section.

Coverage: The Index of Industrial Production is a comprehensive measure of the physical output in the manufacturing, gas, and electric utilities of the nation. Although the index does not cover production on farms or in the construction, transportation, or trade and service industries, it does include production at government-owned and -operated plants and shipyards. For the sectors it covers, the Industrial Production Index provides an alternative measure of the nonagricultural-goods-producing part of the economy.

Data Available: The Index of Industrial Production is calculated for two different major groupings, as shown in table 2-8: one by market or product grouping and the other by industry grouping. Within each major grouping, indexes for different subgroups are calculated.

Source of Data: Overall, the index combines 235 different output series with value-added weights to create the total Index of Industrial Production. The data are supplied by various government agencies and trade associations. Similarly, appropriate series are combined to create indexes for the individual subgroups.

Table 2-8
Index of Industrial Production: Major Market and Industry Groupings

	1967 Proportion	1981 Average Level of Index
Major market grouping		
Products	60.71	150.6
Final products	47.82	149.5
Consumer goods	27.68	147.8
Equipment	20.14	151.8
Intermediate products	12.89	154.4
Materials	39.29	151.6
Major industry grouping		
Mining and utilities	12.05	154.9
Mining	6.36	142.2
Utilities	5.69	169.1
Electric	3.88	190.9
Manufacturing	87.95	150.4
Nondurable	35.97	164.7
Durable	51.98	140.5

Note: 1967 = 100 for index.

66

The first step in constructing the index is to calculate the level of output for each series relative to the level of output in the base period, 1967. (The average level of output over the twelve months in 1967, which is the base period, is set equal to 100.) Then the relative output level is weighted for each product it represented in 1967.[46] Finally, the product of the relative output levels and weights are summed to give the index level for the month.

When Series Become Available: The Index of Industrial Production is usually available about fifteen days after the month to which it refers. For example, the estimate of the Index of Industrial Production for March is released around the middle of April. For the estimate release dates see also, each year, the June issue of the Board of Governors of the Federal Reserve System, *Federal Reserve Bulletin.*

Limitations: The Index of Industrial Production measures changes in the physical volume of output that occur over time. The index is constructed by weighting the relative output level of each component by the proportion of output it represented in 1967. Major structural changes that have occurred since 1967, such as the energy situation and measures directed at reducing pollution, are not directly reflected in the weights. Consequently the index may not be representative of changes in output that are occurring in the economy. In some periods, for example, the index is felt to be subject to greater distortion than in other periods. The important point, however, is that users of the index should be aware of potential sources of distortion and use the index accordingly.

Major revisions that are necessary to incorporate the effects of such changes into the index are very costly and time-consuming; they require extensive data collection as well. Thus, they often occur with substantial time lags. Such a major revision in the Index of Industrial Production is expected to be released in 1984. The base and weights in the index will be updated from 1967 to 1977, and other improvements will be incorporated as well.[47]

Publications: Current Data:

Council of Economic Advisers, *Economic Indicators*, Washington, D.C.: U.S. Government Printing Office. Monthly.

Board of Governors of the Federal Reserve System, *Federal Reserve Bulletin*. Monthly.

Board of Governors of the Federal Reserve System, *Industrial Production*, G.12.3 (414), statistical release. Monthly.

Publications: Historical Data:

Council of Economic Advisers, *Economic Report of the President,* Washington, D.C.: U.S. Government Printing Office. Annual. See statistical appendix.

Board of Governors of the Federal Reserve System, *Industrial Production—1976 Revision*, 1977. Monthly data are generally available beginning with 1954; the total and some large aggregations go back to 1919; a few series begin in 1967.

References:

Armitage, Kenneth, and Joan D. Hosley, "Revision of Industrial Production Index," *Federal Reserve Bulletin,* August 1979, pp. 603-605.

Board of Governors of the Federal Reserve System, *Industrial Production—1971 edition*, 1972.

Board of Governors of the Federal Reserve System, *Industrial Production—1976 Revision*, 1977.

Gehman, Clayton, "Industrial Production—1976 Revision," *Federal Reserve Bulletin*, June 1976, pp. 470-478.

Mail and Telephone Reference:

Board of Governors of the Federal Reserve System
Division of Research and Statistics
20th and Constitution Ave., N.W.
Washington, D.C.   20551
(202) 452-3000

Manufacturers' Shipments, Inventories, and Orders

Issuing Agency: U.S. Department of Commerce, Bureau of the Census, Industry Division.

Coverage: The Manufacturers' Shipments, Inventories, and Orders survey provides broad-based data on economic conditions in the manufacturing sector.

Shipments.[48] Value of shipments represents net selling values, free-on-board (f.o.b.) plant, after discounts and allowances and excluding freight charges and excise taxes, where possible. Where the products of an industry are customarily delivered by the manufacturing establishment (such as in certain food industries—fluid milk, bakery products, soft drinks), the value is based on delivery price rather than the f.o.b. plant price.

The value-of-shipments figures contain some duplication since the products of some industries are used as materials by other industries within the same industry aggregate. The significance of the duplication varies depending on their industry composition. It is most pronounced in a few highly integrated industry areas, such as primary metals and motor vehicles and parts.

Inventories.[49] Inventories are reported at book values. Since different methods of inventory valuation are used, the definition of the value of aggregate inventories for all plants in an industry is not precise. (The change in the value of inventories, month to month as well as year to year, is considered to have greater significance and reliability.)

Orders. A new order is a communication of an intention to buy for immediate or future delivery. Only orders supported by binding legal documents (such as signed contracts, letters of intent, or letters of award) are included. The monthly series includes all new orders received during the month less cancellations. Unfilled orders are orders received that have not yet passed through the sales account (that is, unfilled orders at the end of the reporting period are equal to unfilled orders at the beginning of the period, plus net new orders received during the period, minus net sales).

Data Available: Manufacturers' shipments, inventories, and orders are classified according to two major categories: industry categories and market categories. Inventories are further classified by stage of fabrication. The major classifications are shown in table 2-9. (More-detailed classifications are also available.)

Table 2-9
Manufacturers' Shipments, Inventories, and Orders: Major Categories

Shipments	Inventories (Book Value, End of Period)	Net New Orders
By industry group	By industry group	By industry group
Durable goods industries, total	Durable goods industries	Durable goods industries
Stone, clay, and glass products	Stone, clay, and glass products	Primary metals
Primary metals	Primary metals	Blast furnaces, steel mills
Blast furnaces, steel mills	Blast furnaces, steel mills	Nonferrous and other
Fabricated metal products	Fabricated metal products	primary met.
Machinery, except electrical	Machinery, except electrical	Fabricated metal products
Electrical machinery	Electrical machinery	Machinery, except electrical
Transportation equipment	Transportation equipment	Electrical machinery
Motor vehicles and parts	Motor vehicles and parts	Transportation equipment
Instruments and related products	Instruments and related products	Aircraft, missiles, and parts
Nondurable goods industries, total	Nondurable goods industries	Nondurable goods industries, total
Food and kindred products	Food and kindred products	Industries with unfilled orders
Tobacco products	Tobacco products	Industries without unfilled orders
Textile mill products	Textile mill products	
Paper and allied products	Paper and allied products	
Chemical and allied products	Chemical and allied products	
Petroleum and coal products	Petroleum and coal products	
Rubber and plastics products	Rubber and plastics products	
By market category	By market category	By market category
Home goods and apparel	Home goods and apparel	Home goods and apparel
Consumer staples	Consumer staples	Consumer staples
Equipment and defense prod., excl. auto	Equip. and defense prod., excl. auto	Equip. and defense prod., excl. auto
Automotive equipment	Automotive equipment	Automotive equipment
Construction materials and supplies	Construction materials and supplies	Construction materials and supplies
Other materials and supplies	Other materials and supplies	Other materials and supplies
Supplementary series	Supplementary series	Supplementary series
Household durables	Household durables	Household durables
Capital goods industries	Capital goods industries	Capital goods industries
Nondefense	Nondefense	Nondefense
Defense	Defense	Defense
	By stage of fabrication	
	Materials and supplies	
	Work in process	
	Finished goods	

Source of Data: Monthly estimates of manufacturers' shipments, inventories, and orders are based on information obtained from approximately 4,500 reporting units and include most manufacturing companies with 1,000 or more employees. In addition, selected smaller companies are included to strengthen the sample coverage in individual industry categories.[50] Each company or reporting unit of a company in the survey is classified into one of seventy-nine industry categories for which separate estimates are made based on the major activity of the reporting unit.

The current coverage levels in the survey show that approximately 50 to 55 percent of the shipment estimates at the all-manufacturing level are based on reported data, while the individual coverage rates for the twenty two-digit major Standard Industrial Classification (SIC) industries vary from about 20 to 90 percent.[51]

When Series Become Available: Three sets of estimates are released for manufacturers' shipments, inventories, and orders: advance, preliminary, and final. Advance estimates are released with a lag of about three weeks (or the fifteenth or sixteenth working day of the month); thus about the third week of April, advance estimates are released for March. Preliminary estimates are released with a lag of about one month (or the twenty-second or twenty-third working day of the month); around the end of April, preliminary estimates are released for March. Final figures are released with a lag of around about a month and three weeks (on the fifteenth or sixteenth working day of the month); thus about the third week of April, final figures estimates are released for February.

Publications: Current Data:

Council of Economic Advisers, *Economic Indicators*, Washington D.C.: U.S. Government Printing Office. Monthly.

U.S. Department of Commerce, Bureau of the Census, Industry Division, *Current Industrial Reports: Manufacturers' Shipments, Inventories, and Orders*. Monthly.

U.S. Department of Commerce, Bureau of Economic Analysis, *Survey of Current Business*. Monthly.

Publications: Historical Data:

Council of Economic Advisers, *Economic Report of the President*, Washington, D.C.: U.S. Government Printing Office. Annual. See statistical appendix.

U.S. Department of Commerce, Bureau of the Census, Industry Division, *Current Industrial Reports: Manufacturers' Shipments, Inventories, and Orders: 1977-1982*, M3-1.12.

U.S. Department of Commerce, Bureau of the Census, Industry Division, *Current Industrial Reports: Manufacturers' Shipments, Inventories, and Orders: 1972-1980*, M3-1.10, July 1981.

U.S. Department of Commerce, Bureau of the Census, Industry Division, *Current Industrial Reports: Manufacturers' Shipments, Inventories, and Orders: 1968-1978*, M3-1.8.

U.S. Department of Commerce, Bureau of the Census, Industry Division, *Current Industrial Reports: Manufacturers' Shipments, Inventories, and Orders: 1958-77*, M3-1.7.

Mail and Telephone Reference:

U.S. Bureau of the Census
Economic Census Staff
Suitland, MD   20233
(301) 763-4040.

Personal Income and Outlays

Issuing Agency: U.S. Department of Commerce, Bureau of Economic Analysis, National Income and Wealth Division (for national data) and Regional Economic Income Division (for regional, state, and local data).

Coverage: Personal income and outlays consist of a number of components as shown in table 2-10. The right side of the account (lines 7 through 22) shows the components of personal income, and the left side of the account (lines 1 through 6) shows the disposition of personal income. Definitions for the components of personal income and outlays follow.[52]

Personal Income: Personal income (table 2-10, bottom right) is the income received by persons from all sources, that is, from participation in production, from transfer payments from government and business, and from government interest, which is treated like a transfer payment. Persons consist of individuals, nonprofit institutions, private noninsured welfare funds, and private trust funds. Proprietors' income is treated in its entirety as received by individuals. Life-insurance carriers and private noninsured pension funds are not counted as persons, but their saving is credited to persons. Personal income is the sum of wage and salary disbursements, other labor income, proprietors' income, rental income of persons, dividends, personal interest income, and transfer payments, less personal contributions for social insurance.[53]

Wage and salary disbursements (line 7) consists of the monetary remuneration of employees, including the compensation of corporate officers; commissions, tips, and bonuses; and receipts in kind that represent income to the recipients.

Other labor income (line 8) includes employer contributions to private pension and welfare funds, and directors' fees.[54]

Proprietors' income with inventory-valuation and capital-consumption adjustments (line 9) is the monetary income and income in kind of proprietorships and partnerships, including the independent professions, and of producers' cooperatives. Interest and dividend income received by proprietors and rental income received by persons who are not primarily engaged in the real-estate business are excluded.

Inventory-valuation adjustment (line 9) is the change in the business-inventories component of GNP, which is measured as the change in the physical volume of inventories valued in prices of the current period, less the change in the value of inventories reported by business (book value). Alternatively, the inventory-valuation adjustment can be defined as the excess of the replacement cost of inventories used up over their historical acquisition cost. An inventory-valuation adjustment is needed only for non-

Table 2-10
Personal Income and Outlay Account, 1978
(billions of dollars)

Line	Disposition of Personal Income		Line	Components of Personal Income	
1	Personal tax and nontax payments	259.0	7	Wage and salary disbursements	1,103.3
2	Personal outlays	1,386.4	8	Other labor income	106.5
3	Personal consumption expenditures	1,350.8	9	Proprietors' income with inventory-valuation and capital-consumption adjustments	116.8
4	Interest paid by consumers to business	34.8	10	Farm	27.7
5	Personal transfer payments to foreigners (net)	.8	11	Nonfarm	89.1
6	Personal saving	72.0	12	Rental income of persons with capital-consumption adjustment	25.9
			13	Dividends	47.2
			14	Personal interest income	163.3
			15	Net interest	109.5
			16	Interest paid by government to persons and business	49.8
			17	Less: Interest received by government	30.7
			18	Interest paid by consumers to business	34.8
			19	Transfer payments to persons	224.1
			20	From business	9.2
			21	From government	214.9
			22	Less: Personal contributions for social insurance	69.6
	Personal taxes, outlays, and saving	1,717.4		Personal income	1,717.4

Survey of Current Business, November 1979, U.S. Department of Commerce, Bureau of Economic Analysis, p. 19.

farm proprietors' income because the Department of Agriculture values inventories at replacement cost in measuring farm income.

Capital-consumption adjustment (line 9) is tax-return-based capital-consumption allowances—that is, depreciation charges and accidental damage to fixed business capital—less capital-consumption allowances based on estimates of economic service lives, straight-line depreciation, and replacement cost. This adjustment is made to proprietors' income and to rental income of persons.

Rental income of persons with capital-consumption adjustment (line 12) is the monetary income of persons from the rental of real property, except the income of persons primarily engaged in the real-estate business; the imputed net rental income of owner-occupants of nonfarm dwellings; and the royalties received by persons from patents, copyrights, and rights to natural resources.

Dividends (line 13) is payments in cash or other assets, excluding stock, by corporations organized for profit to stockholders who are U.S. persons.

Personal interest income (line 14) is the interest income of persons from all sources. In addition to monetary interest flows, personal interest income includes flows of interest in kind (imputed interest). It is calculated as net interest (a component of national income), plus interest paid by government to persons and business, less interest received by government, plus interest paid by consumers to business. The last item consists of all interest paid by individuals in their capacity as consumers and, accordingly, excludes their interest payments on mortgages and home-improvement loans because home owners are treated as businesses in the NIPAs.

Transfer payments to persons (line 19) is income payments to persons, generally in monetary form, for which they do not render current services. It consists of business-transfer payments and government-transfer payments. Business-transfer payments include corporate gifts to nonprofit institutions and bad debts incurred by consumers. Government-transfer payments include payments under the following programs: federal old-age, survivors', disability, and hospital insurance; supplementary medical insurance; state unemployment insurance; railroad retirement and unemployment insurance; government retirement; workmen's compensation; veterans, including veterans' life insurance; food stamps; black lung; supplemental security income; and direct relief. Government payments to nonprofit institutions, other than for work under research and development contracts, is also included.

Personal contributions for social insurance (line 22) includes payments by employees, self-employed, and other individuals who participate in the following programs: federal old-age survivors', disability, and hospital insurance; supplementary medical insurance; state unemployment insurance; railroad retirement insurance; government retirement; and veterans' life insurance.

Disposition of Personal Income: Personal tax and nontax payments (line 1) is tax payments (net of refunds) by persons (except personal contributions for social insurance) that are not chargeable to business expense and certain other personal payments to general government. Personal taxes include income, estate and gift, and personal-property taxes. Nontaxes include passport fees, fines and penalties, donations, and tuitions and fees paid to schools and hospitals operated mainly by government.

Personal outlays (line 2) is the sum of personal-consumption expenditures, interest paid by consumers to business, and personal transfer payments to foreigners (net).

Personal-consumption expenditures (line 3) is goods and services purchased by individuals, operating expenses of nonprofit institutions, and the value of food, fuel, clothing, rent of dwellings, and financial services received in kind by individuals. Net purchases of used goods are also included. All private purchases of dwellings are classified as gross private domestic investment.

Purchases of durable goods—goods that have an average life of at least three years—are shown monthly in three categories: motor vehicles and parts, furniture and household equipment, and other durable goods.

Purchases of nondurable goods—goods that have an average life of less than three years—are shown monthly in four categories: food, clothing and shoes, gasoline and oil, and other nondurable goods.

Interest paid by consumers to business (line 4) is described under personal interest income (line 14).

Personal transfer payments to foreigners (net) (line 5) are personal remittances of goods, services, cash, and other financial claims between U.S. private residents and foreign residents. Receipts include postal money orders received by U.S. private residents, German government pension and indemnification payments, Canadian government pension payments, and immigrants' transfers. Payments include cash and goods distributed abroad by U.S. religious, charitable, educational, scientific, and other nonprofit organizations; personal remittances by U.S. private residents through banks, communications companies, and the U.S. Postal Service; parcel-post shipments; and emigrants' transfers. In the balance-of-payment accounts, personal transfer payments to foreigners (net) are called private remittances and other transfers.

Personal saving (line 6) is disposable personal income less personal outlays. (Disposable personal income is personal income less personal tax and nontax payments.)

Data Available and Related Series: Monthly, quarterly, and annual estimates are available nationally for personal income and the components of personal income and for the disposition of personal income. The data are available in current and constant dollars.[55]

Disposable income and personal income are reported on a per-capita basis.[56] Saving is also reported as a percentage of disposable personal income.

Information on personal income for regions, states, county and metropolitan areas is available, as well as regional and state projections of income.

Projections of total personal income, earnings and employment for fifty-seven industries (nearly all two-digit industries in the Standard Industrial Classification), and population, by sex and age group, are available on computer tape for regions and states for 1985, 1990, 1995, 2000, 2010, and 2030. Projections of total personal income, earnings and employment for major industry groups, and total population are available on computer tape for Standard Metropolitan Statistical Areas (SMSAs), Bureau of Economic Analysis (BEA) economic areas, and, in cases where state boundaries divide SMSAs and/or economic areas, for state pieces of SMSAs and/or economic areas for all years listed.[57]

The Regional Economic Measurement Division of the BEA publishes annually a nine-volume set, *Local Area Personal Income*. The set presents for local areas BEA's estimates of total and per-capita personal income, as well as additional detail on the sources of personal income by type and major industry. There are six major categories of personal income payments: wage and salary disbursements; other labor income; proprietors' income; rental income of persons, dividends, and personal interest income; transfer payments; and personal contributions for social insurance. The sum of three of these categories of income payments (wage and salary disbursements, other labor income, and proprietors' income) is termed *labor and proprietors' income* and is presented for the major industry groups.[58] A sample of the available data is shown in table 2-11. Estimates are presented for the most-recent year (the calendar year ending approximately eighteen months earlier) prior to publication date and the preceding five years. For example, the nine-volume set published June 1981 covers 1974 through 1979.[59]

Volume 1 of the set is a national volume presenting estimates for the United States as a whole and for all the regions, states, SMSAs, and BEA economic areas. Each of volumes 2-9 presents estimates for one of the eight BEA regions: New England, Mideast, Great Lakes, Plains, Southeast, Southwest, Rocky Mountain, and Far West. A single regional volume includes estimates for the United States, the region, the states, SMSAs, and counties of the region, and a summary methodology.

The personal income tables contained in the nine-volume set, as well as other standard tabulations, are available on request from the BEA Regional Economic Information System (REIS). REIS is the term applied to the data

Table 2-11
Personal Income for States and Counties of the Southwest Region, 1974-1979
(thousands of dollars)

	Cochran, Texas					
Labor and Proprietors' Income by Place of Work	*1974*	*1975*	*1976*	*1977*	*1978*	*1979*
By type						
Wage and salary disbursements	7,582	8,507	9,014	10,744	11,105	13,247
Other labor income	463	570	630	838	767	912
Proprietors' income	3,113	-159	-2,913	6,095	-464	6,174
Farm	1,269	-2,220	-5,322	3,765	-3,003	3,325
Nonfarm	1,844	2,061	2,409	2,330	2,539	2,849
By industry						
Farm	3,110	-470	-3,225	6,352	-324	6,428
Nonfarm	8,048	9,388	9,956	11,325	11,732	13,905
Private	5,839	7,070	7,387	8,347	8,463	10,298
Agricultural services, forestry, fisheries, and other	(D)	(D)	(D)	649	(D)	(D)
Mining	1,293	1,343	1,235	1,597	1,004	1,401
Construction	503	608	449	379	489	557
Manufacturing	(D)	368	616	695	932	1,222
Nondurable goods	(D)	307	(D)	(D)	(D)	929
Durable goods	(D)	61	(D)	(D)	(D)	293
Transportation and public utilities	(D)	(D)	(D)	(D)	(D)	(D)
Wholesale trade	231	534	666	(D)	(D)	(D)
Retail trade	1,457	1,275	1,293	1,165	1,183	1,290
Finance, insurance, and real estate	335	317	618	1,131	329	457
Services	834	1,458	1,392	1,561	1,631	1,967
Government and government enterprises	2,209	2,318	2,569	2,978	3,269	3,607
Federal, civilian	279	288	328	355	387	412
Federal, military	(L)	(L)	(L)	(L)	(L)	(L)
State and local	1,900	1,998	2,207	2,589	2,845	3,157
Derivation of personal income by place of residence						
Total labor and proprietors' income by place of work	11,158	8,918	6,731	17,677	11,408	20,333
Less: Personal contributions for social insurance by place of work	419	500	559	662	661	750
Net labor and proprietors' income by place of work	10,739	8,418	6,172	17,055	10,747	19,583
Plus: Residence adjustment	79	75	113	128	241	246
Net labor and proprietors' income by place of residence	10,818	8,493	6,285	17,183	10,988	19,829
Plus: Dividends, interest, and rent	3,897	4,499	4,804	5,438	6,239	7,037
Plus: Transfer payments	2,212	2,622	2,854	3,090	3,312	3,731
Personal income by place of residence	16,927	15,614	13,943	25,711	20,539	30,597
Per-capita personal income (dollars)	3,428	3,153	2,781	5,302	4,297	6,276

Source: Local Area Personal Income 1974-79: Southwest Region, vol. 7, U.S. Department of Commerce, 1981, p. 65.

Note: D = not shown to avoid disclosure of confidential information, data are included in totals, L = less than $50,000, data are included in totals.

files, computer programs, and staff established for the maintenance, management, and distribution of the regional data base. This system currently contains approximately 24 million separate estimates covering 3,500 areas.[60]

Source of Data: The data underlying the estimates come from a variety of sources. Much of the information is from the Bureau of Labor Statistics (BLS), the Internal Revenue Service (IRS), or the Bureau of the Census.[61]

When Series Become Available: The best estimates of the approximate release dates are published on the last page of the December issue of the U.S. Department of Commerce, Bureau of Economic Analysis, *Survey of Current Business*. Estimates of personal income and outlays become available with a lag of about two and one-half to three weeks. For example, estimates of personal income and outlays for March are released around April 18-20.

Publications: Current Data:

Council of Economic Advisers, *Economic Indicators*, Washington, D.C.: U.S. Government Printing Office. Monthly.

U.S. Department of Commerce, Bureau of Economic Analysis, *Survey of Current Business*, Washington, D.C.: Superintendent of Documents. Monthly.

Publications: Historical Data:

Council of Economic Advisers, *Economic Report of the President*, Washington, D.C.: U.S. Government Printing Office. Annual. See statistical appendix.

Byrnes, James C., Gerald F. Donahoe, Mary W. Hook, and Robert P. Parker, "Monthly Estimates of Personal Income, Taxes, and Outlays," *Survey of Current Business*, November 1979, U.S. Department of Commerce, Bureau of Economic Analysis, pp. 18-38. Monthly since 1959.

Mail and Telephone Reference:

U.S. Department of Commerce
Bureau of Economic Analysis
1401 K Street, N.W.
Washington, D.C.   20230
(202) 523-0777

The Bureau of Economic Analysis also provides on request a list, "BEA Contacts for Data Users." The list provides the names and telephone numbers of people to contact, by subject. The list is updated periodically.

Index of Productivity: Output per Employee-Hour[62]

Issuing Agency: U.S. Department of Labor, Bureau of Labor Statistics, Office of Productivity and Technology.

Coverage: Productivity measures the constant dollar value of final goods and services produced within a given time period per hour of labor input. Changes in the index over time reflect changes in the effectiveness of combining all factors of production—capital, labor, raw materials—in producing current output. It does not reflect the effectiveness of labor alone.

Output is measured in constant 1972 dollars as gross domestic product, which is the constant dollar value of final goods and services produced by labor, capital, and property located in the United States. Labor hours used in calculating the index are based on the number of hours worked by people employed both full time and part time during an average work week; hours paid for vacation time, sick leave, and holidays are included. Wage and salary workers, the self-employed (proprietors), and unpaid family workers are covered.

Data Available: Quarterly and annual indexes of output per employee-hour and output per employee are available for the following sectors: private business, nonfarm business, nonfinancial corporations, and manufacturing (manufacturing for durable and nondurable goods).

Annual measures are also available for some seventy-five selected industries in manufacturing, mining, transportation, public utilities, trade and services.

Annual indexes of productivity are available for the federal sector.

Related Series: The bureau has developed multifactor productivity measures, output per unit of input, to supplement the labor productivity measures. The multifactor productivity measures are available for the private businesss, private nonfarm, and manufacturing sectors. Measures will also be introduced for the two-digit Standard Industrial Classification manufacturing industry groups. (See appendix C.)

Source of Data: Productivity or output per hour requires two basic sets of data: one, of domestically produced final goods and services (called real gross domestic product—real GDP), measures physical output, and the other measures number of hours worked.

Measures of physical output are derived from information obtained from the U.S. Department of Commerce used in calculating GNP, the current value of final goods and services. Since the value of final output reflects price changes as well as the changes in physical volume, the U.S.

Department of Commerce Bureau of Economic Analysis, prepares estimates of constant-dollar GDP for the private business sector and major sectors; these estimates exclude changes in the value of production resulting from price change. Therefore they reflect only changes in real product, which is basis for output-per-hour measures.

The primary source of hours and employment data is the Bureau of Labor Statistics Current Employment Statistics (CES) program, which provides monthly survey data on employment (for all employees and production or nonsupervisory workers) and average weekly hours of production workers in nonagricultural establishments. Jobs rather than persons are counted so multiple jobholders are counted more than once. Weekly hours are measured as hours paid for rather than as hours at work.

When Series Become Available: Measures of productivity become available with different lags depending on the sectors to which the data refer. Productivity measures of nonfarm business and manufacturing become available about one month after the end of each quarter (to which the data refer). Productivity measures for nonfinancial corporations become available about two months after the end of each quarter (to which the data refer).

Limitations: Measures of output to one input, specifically labor time, do not measure the specific contribution of labor to the production of output, or any other input. Instead the measures reflect the combined influence of changes in technology, capital, capacity utilization, availability of materials, skill and effort of the work force, and managerial ability.[63]

Productivity measures do not fully reflect changes in the quality of products produced.

Although efforts have been made to maintain consistency of coverage between the output and labor input, the estimates of output and labor inputs, some differences may still remain.

Production statistics do not adequately reflect changes in the extent of plant integration and specialization. This can result in the overstatement of gains in productivity in some years and understatement in other years.

Year-to-year changes in output per employee-hour are irregular and are not necessarily indicative of fundamental changes in long-term trends.

Publications: Current Data:

Council of Economic Advisers, *Economic Indicators*, Washington, D.C.:
    U.S. Government Printing Office. Monthly.
U.S. Department of Labor, Bureau of Labor Statistics, *Employment and Earnings*. Monthly.
U.S. Department of Labor, Bureau of Labor Statistics, *Monthly Labor Review*. Monthly.

Publications: Historical Data:

Council of Economic Advisers, *Economic Report of the President*, Washington, D.C.: U.S. Government Printing Office. Annual. See statistical appendix.

U.S. Department of Labor, Bureau of Labor Statistics, *Productivity Measures for Selected Industries 1954-79*, Bulletin 2093, April 1981.

References:

Adler, Paul S., "The Productivity Puzzle: Numbers Alone Won't Solve It," *Monthly Labor Review*, October 1982, U.S. Department of Labor, Bureau of Labor Statistics, pp. 15-21.

Denison, Edward F., "Explanations of Declining Productivity Growth," *Survey of Current Business*, Part II, August 1979, U.S. Department of Commerce, Bureau of Economic Analysis.

Moore, Geoffrey H., "Productivity Cloud Has a Silver Lining," *Morgan Guaranty Survey*, October 1980, pp. 4-5.

U.S. Department of Labor, Bureau of Labor Statistics, *BLS Handbook of Methods*, Bulletin 1910, 1976, pp. 219-224.

U.S. Department of Labor, Bureau of Labor Statistics, *BLS Handbook of Methods, vol. 1*, Bulletin 2134-1, 1982.

U.S. Department of Labor, Bureau of Labor Statistics, *Productivity Measures for Selected Industries 1954-79*, Bulletin 2093, April 1981.

Mail and Telephone Reference:

U.S. Department of Labor
Bureau of Labor Statistics
Publications Department
441 G Street, N.W.
Washington, D.C.   20212
(202) 523-1913

Retail Trade: Inventories and Sales

Issuing Agency: U.S. Department of Commerce, Bureau of the Census (Business Division) and Bureau of Economic Analysis.

Coverage: The retail trade report provides estimates of sales coverage and inventories of retail stores by kind of business for the United States and geographic areas. These series measure the sales and inventories of all establishments classified as retail trade according to the Standard Industrial Classification (SIC). (See appendix C.) This includes establishments engaged in selling merchandise for personal or household consumption and rendering services incidental to the sale of the goods. The term *establishment* refers to the physical location at which the retail business is conducted.

Inventories represent stocks of merchandise, valued at cost, on hand for sale by retail establishments at the end of the month. Methods of valuation may vary according to the accounting practices of the firm. Inventories are shown for retail stores and warehouses combined. Only warehouses that maintain supplies of merchandise primarily intended for distribution to retail stores within the organization are included. Inventories exclude the value fixtures, furnishings, equipment, and supplies used in store and warehouse operations and not held for resale.

Sales are net after deductions for refunds and allowances for merchandise returned by customers. Net sales include cash and credit sales but exclude discounts, returns, allowances, sales taxes, excise taxes, and finance charges. Also excluded are the retail sales of manufacturers, wholesalers, service establishments, and other businesses whose primary activity is not retail trade.

Data Available: Inventories of retail establishments are available for the major groups of business, shown in table 2-12. Unlike sales of retail establishments, inventories are not available by geographic area.

Retail sales are classified on the basis of geographic area and kind of business. The kind-of-business classification includes the major categories shown in table 2-12.

The geographic classification reports retail sales for geographic regions (table 2-13), divisions, selected states, standard consolidated areas, Standard Metropolitan Statistical Areas, and cities. (More detailed subcategories are also available.)[64]

Related Series: Inventories-sales ratios are based on the data series described in the sections on retail inventories and retail sales.[65] National ratios are published by kind of business.

Table 2-12
Retail Trade Sales and Inventories: Major Categories

Estimated sales, total
  Durable-goods stores
    Building materials, hardware, garden supply, and mobile-home dealers
    Automotive dealers
    Furniture, home furnishings, and equipment

  Nondurable-goods stores
    General merchandise, group stores
    Food stores
    Gasoline service stations
    Apparel and accessory stores
    Eating and drinking places
    Drug and proprietary stores
    Liquor stores

Estimated inventories (book value end of period)
  Durable-goods stores
    Building materials and supply stores
    Automotive dealers
    Furniture, home furnishings, and equipment

  Nondurable-goods stores
    General merchandise, group stores
    Food stores
    Apparel and accessory stores

Source of Data: Estimates of retail inventories are based on a subsample of the firms and companies included in the bureau's Annual Retail Trade Survey. The inventory samples approximately 2,700 organizations operating about 48,000 retail establishments. All firms selected in the inventory sample are requested to report their end-of-month inventory each month.

The statistics on sales of retail stores are based on estimates derived by the Census Bureau from its monthly sample survey of retail establishments of all sizes and types throughout the country.

The procedure has two components. One is based on a probability sample selected from a list of retail employers that account for about 94 percent of all retail sales. Information for this component is obtained through a mail canvass of employers. The second component involves the retailers who are not covered in the sampling list of retail employers (and account for the remaining 6 percent of retail sales). Estimates of those sales are based on a probability sample of areas. Enumeration is carried out in person.

Data are adjusted for seasonal variation, holidays, and trading-day differences.

When Series Become Available: The Bureau of Census publishes two estimates of retail inventories: preliminary and final.[66] Both estimates

Table 2-13
Retail Sales Available by Geographic Regions

New England
Middle Atlantic
South Atlantic
East North Central
East South Central
West North Central
West South Central
Mountain
Pacific

become available around the thirteenth of each month. Preliminary estimates are available about one and a half months after the reference period, and final estimates are available about two and a half months after the reference period. For example, on April 13, preliminary estimates of retail inventories are released for February, and final estimates are released for January.

Each month around the twelfth, the Census Bureau issues three sets of estimates of retail sales: advance, preliminary, and final. Advance estimates of retail sales become available about two weeks after the reference period; preliminary estimates are released about one and one-half months after the reference period; and final estimates are published about two and one-half months after the reference period.[67] For example, on April 12, advance estimates of retail sales are released for March, preliminary estimates are released for February, and final estimates are released for January.

Limitations: Inventories are difficult to measure because of the absence or inadequacy of company records of stocks, differences in valuation methods, determination of the ownership of inventories to avoid missing or double coverage of goods on consignment or returned or goods received but not invoiced or paid, inconsistent reporting between shipments and inventories in the manufacture of military hardware, and in-transit considerations.[68]

Two types of errors are possible in sales in an estimate based on a sample survey: sampling and nonsampling. Sampling errors occur because observations are made only on a sample, not on the entire population. Estimates of sampling variability for retail sales are published by the Bureau of the Census. Nonsampling errors can be attributed to many sources.

For retail sales, a major source of bias in the publishing estimates is attributable to imputing data for nonrespondents, for late reporters, and for data that fail edit. For all kinds of business combined, imputed sales amount to about 13 percent of the national sales estimates. Although no direct measurement of the biases due to nonsampling errors has been obtained, precautionary steps are taken in all phases of the collection, processing, and tabulation of the data in an effort to minimize their influence.

Publications: Current Data:

Council of Economic Advisers, *Economic Indicators,* Washington, D.C.: U.S. Government Printing Office. Monthly.

U.S. Department of Commerce, Bureau of the Census, Business Division, *Monthly Retail Trade: Sales and Inventories.* Monthly.

U.S. Department of Commerce, Bureau of Economic Analysis, *Survey of Current Business.* Monthly.

Publications: Historical Data:

Council of Economic Advisers, *Economic Report of the President,* Washington, D.C.: U.S. Government Printing Office. Annual. See statistical appendix.

U.S. Department of Commerce, Bureau of the Census, Business Division, *Annual Retail Trade.* Annual. Monthly since 1971.

U.S. Department of Commerce, Bureau of Economic Analysis, *Business Statistics,* Washington, D.C.: U.S. Government Printing Office, 1980, and earlier editions. Monthly since 1967.

References:

U.S. Department of Commerce, Bureau of the Census, Business Division, *Annual Retail Trade.*

Mail and Telephone Reference:

U.S. Bureau of the Census
Economic Census Staff
Suitland, MD   20233
(301) 763-4040

Wholesale Trade: Inventories and Sales

Issuing Agency: U.S. Department of Commerce, Bureau of the Census, Business Division.

Coverage: Wholesale trade includes establishments or places of business primarily engaged in selling merchandise to retailers; to industrial, commercial, institutional, farm or professional business users, or to other wholesalers; or acting as agents or brokers in buying merchandise for or selling merchandise to such persons or companies. The wholesale trade survey is limited to merchant wholesalers who take title to the goods they sell, such as wholesale merchants or jobbers, industrial distributors, voluntary group wholesalers, drop shippers, major distributors, retail cooperative warehouses, terminal elevators, and cooperative buying associations. Merchant wholesalers constitute the major portion of the broad field of wholesale trade. The survey excludes other categories of wholesale trade: sales branches and sales offices (but not retail stores) maintained by domestic manufacturing or mining enterprises apart from their plants or mines for the purpose of marketing their products; and agents, merchandise, or commodity brokers, and commission merchants.

Data Available: Wholesale sales and inventories are reported monthly by kind of business. More-recent data are available on a more-comprehensive industry basis than the historical data. Major categories of business-in-kind are shown in table 2-14.

Annual estimates are also available for nine geographic areas of the country, as shown in table 2-15.

Related Series: Inventory-sales ratios (or stock-sales ratios) are also available for trade. The stock-sales ratios are percentages derived by dividing the dollar value of inventories, at cost, by the dollar value of sales. No adjustment is made in these ratios for the markup in sales, which may vary from trade to trade.

Source of Data: Estimates of merchant wholesale sales and inventories are based on a monthly Census Bureau survey of merchant wholesalers. These establishments account for about 55 percent of all wholesale sales and about 80 percent of wholesale inventories. Probability sampling procedures are used, and the canvass is carried out by mail.

When Series Become Available: Estimates of wholesale trade are released between the fifth and tenth of each month. Preliminary estimates are released with a lag of about one month, and final figures are released with a

Table 2-14
Wholesale Trade Sales and Inventories: Major Categories

Merchant wholesalers' sales, total
  Durable goods
    Motor vehicles and auto parts and supplies
    Furniture and home furnishings
    Lumber and other construction materials
    Electrical goods
    Hardware, plumbing, heating, equipment, and supplies
    Machinery equipment and supplies
    Scrap and waste material

  Nondurable goods
    Paper and paper products
    Drugs, drug proprietaries and druggists' sundries
    Apparel, piece goods, and notions
    Groceries and related products
    Farm products raw materials
    Beer, wine and distilled alcoholic beverages
    Miscellaneous nondurable goods

Merchant wholesalers' inventories, total (book value end of period)
  Durable goods
    Motor vehicles and automotive parts and supplies
    Furniture and home furnishings
    Lumber and other construction materials
    Electrical goods
    Hardware, plumbing, heating equipment and supplies
    Machinery, equipment, and supplies

  Nondurable goods
    Paper and paper products
    Drugs, drug proprietaries, and druggists' sundries
    Groceries and related products
    Beer, wine, and distilled alcoholic beverages

Table 2-15
Wholesale Trade by Geographic Areas

New England
Middle Atlantic
East North Central
West North Central
South Atlantic
East South Central
West South Central
Mountain
Pacific

lag of about two months. For example, around April 5, preliminary estimates of wholesale inventories and sales are released for February, and final estimates are released for January.

Limitations: Although no direct measurement of the biases due to non-sampling errors has been obtained, precautionary steps are taken in all phases of the collection, processing, and tabulation of the data in an effort to minimize their influence.

A major source of possible bias in the published estimates is due to imputing data for nonrespondents, for late reporters, and for data that fail edit. For all kinds of business combined, imputed sales amount to about 15 percent of the sales estimates and 25 percent for inventories.[70]

Publications: Current Data:

Council of Economic Advisers, *Economic Indicators,* Washington, D.C.: U.S. Government Printing Office. Monthly.

U.S. Department of Commerce, Bureau of the Census, Business Division, *Current Business Reports: Monthly Wholesale Trade; Sales and Inventories.* Monthly.

U.S. Department of Commerce, Bureau of Economic Analysis, *Survey of Current Business.* Monthly.

Publications: Historical Data:

Council of Economic Advisers, *Economic Report of the President,* Washington, D.C.: U.S. Government Printing Office. Annual. See statistical appendix.

U.S. Department of Commerce, Bureau of the Census, Business Division, *Current Business Reports: Revised Monthly Wholesale Trade; Sales and Inventories January 1973-December 1980,* BW-13-805, April 1981.

U.S. Department of Commerce, Bureau of the Census, Business Division, *Current Business Reports: Monthly Wholesale Trade; Sales and Inventories January 1967-August 1977* (Revised), BW-13-775.

References:

U.S. Department of Commerce, Bureau of the Census, Business Division, *Current Business Reports: Monthly Wholesale Trade; Sales and Inventories January 1967-August 1977* (Revised), BW-13-775, 1977.

U.S. Department of Commerce, Bureau of the Census, Business Division, *Current Business Reports: Monthly Wholesale Trade; Sales and Inventories.* Monthly.

Mail and Telephone Reference:

U.S. Bureau of the Census
Economic Census Staff
Suitland, MD   20233
(301) 763-4040

Notes

1. An explanation of why the different measures exist and the reasons for these differences are presented in Frank de Leeuw, "Why Capacity Utilization Estimates Differ," *Survey of Current Business,* May 1976, U.S. Department of Commerce, Bureau of Economic Analysis, pp. 45-55. Also reprinted in *Measures of Capacity Utilization: Problems and Tasks,* Board of Governors of the Federal Reserve System, 1979.

2. Differences among the estimates of capacity-utilization rates reflect the problems involved in measuring capacity. These differences are largely attributable to the different methods that can be used to quantify capacity and utilization. Another problem is that there is not a uniform universally accepted definition of capacity utilization, and the data available to arrive at such estimates for production facilities are limited. For an explanation of how the estimates differ, see Richard D. Raddock, "How Capacity Utilization Estimates Differ: Comparisons of Census, BEA, McGraw-Hill, Federal Reserve, and Wharton Series," *Measures of Capacity Utilization: Problems and Tasks,* Board of Governors of the Federal Reserve System, 1979.

3. A description of the Bureau of Economic Analysis's measure of capacity utilization and a synopsis of the other measures can be found in Marie P. Hertzberg, Alfred I. Jacobs, and Jon E. Trevathan, "The Utilization of Manufacturing Capacity, 1965-73," *Survey of Current Business,* July 1974, U.S. Department of Commerce, Bureau of Economic Analysis, pp. 47-57.

4. Advanced processing includes the following industries: food, tobacco, apparel, furniture, printing, chemical products such as drugs and toiletries, leather, machinery, transportation equipment, instruments, miscellaneous manufacturing, and ordnance.

Primary processing, which incorporates many of the same manufacturing industries that are represented in materials, includes textiles, lumber, paper, industrial chemicals, petroleum refining, rubber and plastics, stone, clay and glass, and primary and fabricated metals.

5. The U.S. Department of Commerce, Bureau of Economic Analysis estimate of manufacturers' capacity utilization (which is a quarterly series) can be found in the back page of the December issue of the U.S. Department of Commerce, Bureau of Economic Analysis, *Survey of Current Business.* The estimate becomes available with about a two and one-half month lag. Thus the estimate for the first quarter becomes available about mid-June.

6. A second approach is to define capacity from a cost perspective. Some define capacity as the output at which average cost is a minimum, while others define it as the rate at which costs start to rise sharply. There

are a number of practical problems with this concept, however: few firms maintain the type of cost information necessary to arrive at such an output rate, some show that there is not a simple relationship between cost and output rate and that cost can be somewhat constant over a wide range of outputs, and for some products, costs apparently do not show signs of rising even at very high output rates.

7. This source provides estimates of the Commerce Department, Federal Reserve, and Wharton series for capacity utilization.

8. This source provides estimates of the Commerce Department, Federal Reserve, and Wharton series for capacity utilization.

9. U.S. Department of Commerce, Office of Federal Statistical Policy Standards, *A Framework for Planning U.S. Federal Statistics for the 1980s,* 1978, p. 46.

10. U.S. Department of Commerce, Bureau of Economic Analysis, "Revised Deflators for New Construction," 1947-73, *Survey of Current Business,* August 1974, pp. 18-27.

11. See selected issues of U.S. Department of Commerce, Bureau of the Census, *Construction Reports: Value of Construction Put in Place,* series C30; for example, for 1973-1978, see the issues for July 1979, August 1978, July 1977.

12. A description of the procedures used to develop current estimates of value of new construction put in place appears in the following: U.S. Department of Commerce, Bureau of the Census publications: *Construction Reports: Value of New Construction Put in Place, May 1980,* C30-80-5, July 1980; *Construction Report: Value of New Construction Put in Place,* C30-78-5, July 1978; *Construction Report: Value of New Construction Put in Place: 1947-1974,* C30-74S, December 1975.

The methods and indexes used to convert construction costs from current to constant dollars are explained in the following publications: U.S. Department of Commerce, Bureau of the Census, *Construction Report: Value of New Construction Put in Place,* May 1980, pp. 35-59; U.S. Department of Commerce, Domestic and International Business Administration, Bureau of Domestic Commerce, Elliot Levy, "Construction Cost Indexes, 1915-76," *Construction Review,* June-July 1977, pp. 4-16; U.S. Department of Commerce, Bureau of Economic Analysis, "Revised Deflators of New Construction, 1947-73," *Survey of Current Business,* August 1974, Part I, pp. 18-27.

13. Department of Commerce, *Framework*, p. 46. For a list of the cost indexes used for deriving the value of new construction put in place in constant 1972 dollars, see U.S. Department of Commerce, Bureau of the Census, *Value of New Construction Put in Place May 1980,* appendix B, p. 39.

14. Department of Commerce, "Revised Deflators," pp. 18-27.

15. Capital expenditures have two major components: plant and structures, and machinery and equipment. The distinction is not always clear-cut between the two categories; however, a useful guideline is that plant and structures are not movable (as are automobiles, trucks, computers, furniture, and fixtures).

16. More precisely, at the two-digit Standard Industrial Classification level. See appendix C.

17. See Frank de Leeuw and Michael J. McKelvey, "The Realization of Plans Reported in the BEA Plant and Equipment Survey," *Survey of Current Business,* October 1981, U.S. Department of Commerce, Bureau of Economic Analysis, pp. 28-37.

18. Our description of the available data is by no means comprehensive. Instead we have concentrated on a few of the widely used, easily available sources of such information.

19. William F. Sharpe, *Investments,* 2nd ed., © 1981, pp. 561-567. Reprinted by permission of Prentice-Hall, Inc., Englewood Cliffs, N.J.

20. Supplementing the annual bound *Manuals* are twice-weekly looseleaf *News Reports* (Transportation-weekly and International biweekly).

21. Standard & Poor's, *Outlook,* published weekly, supplements these publications.

22. Securities & Exchange Commission, 500 N. Capital Street, Washington, D.C.   20549.

23. Many of these organizations advertise their services in publications such as the *Wall Street Journal.* They photocopy the information from the SEC and forward it to the requester. The Washington Service Bureau is one such organization. The day a request is made, the organization copies the information requested and sends it out overnight through a delivery service, for a fee. Material ordered through the SEC involves a longer waiting time.

24. For a more-precise or technical description of the two methods of measuring GNP and the components of the national product and national income, see Carol S. Carson and George Jaszi, "The National Income and Products Accounts of the United States: An Overview," *Survey of Current Business,* February 1981, U.S. Department of Commerce, Bureau of Economic Analysis, pp. 22-34.

For an explanation and example of problems involved with intermediate products in calculating GNP, see appendix D.

25. There are three key features to the concept. GNP measures final output, output produced during the year per year, and output produced from productive transactions.

Final output: In the U.S. economy, it is rare for one firm to perform every stage of the production process. Usually the product passes through several intermediate firms before it is completed and goes to market for final sale. GNP ignores intermediate goods or inputs used up entirely in the production of final products; including them would result in double count-ing and thus overstate GNP. A numerical example is provided in appendix D.

Annual output refers to a flow of production. A nation produces at a certain rate, and individuals receive income at a certain rate. Your income flow might be at a rate of $5,000 per year, or $50,000 per year. Suppose you are told that someone earns $500. Would you consider this a good salary? There is no way you can answer that question unless you know whether the person is earning $500 per month, per week, or per day. Thus, you have to specify a time period for all flows; income received is a flow. You must con-trast this with, for example, your total accumulated savings, which are a stock measured at a point in time, not across time. Implicit in just about everything the GNP measures is a time period—usually a year. All of the measures of national product and income are specified as rates measured in billions of dollars per year.

Exclude nonproductive transactions: GNP measures only produc-tive transactions, or transactions that involve some final purchase of newly produced goods or services. Numerous nonproductive exchanges occur as well. They are not included in GNP.

One category of nonproductive transactions, so-called financial transactions, include the buying and selling of securities (the security dealer's commission, however, is part of GNP; the dealer performs the ser-vice of bringing the buyer and seller together and helps execute the transac-tion), government transfer payments, and private transfer payments. These transactions involve either a transfer of ownership rights in which no pro-ductive activity was consummated (buying and selling securities) or a pay-ment for which no goods were produced or services were performed (transfer payments). Hence, these transactions are not included in GNP.

A second category of nonproductive transactions involves the transfer of ownership of used goods. The purchase prices of used products were included in GNP when they were produced. To include them again would be double counting; hence such transactions are excluded from GNP.

26. Most of the following definitions and the section data available are from Carson and Jaszi, "National Income," pp. 31, 32.

27. Capital consumption allows for the consumption of capital during the period. More precisely, it consists of two elements: depreciation charges and accidental damages to fixed business capital.

28. Personal income is sometimes used as a proxy measure of produc-tion because it is available for regions of the nation and because the national measure is available monthly. It differs from production because it excludes some incomes that represent production but are not distributed to per-sons—for example, social security taxes and undistributed corporate prof-its—and includes some incomes that do not represent current produc-tion—for example, transfer payments. Because some of these incomes do not

follow the course of total production, especially in the short run, the proxy is imperfect.

29. For a concise description of the many sources, see Edward F. Denison and Robert P. Parker, "The National Income and Product Accounts of the United States: An Introduction to the Revised Estimates for 1929-80," *Survey of Current Business,* December 1980, U.S. Department of Commerce, Bureau of Economic Analysis, pp. 1-26; U.S. Department of Commerce, Bureau of Economic Analysis, "Key Source Data and Projections for National Income and Product Estimates: Fourth Quarter 1978," *Survey of Current Business,* January 1979, pp. 19-21.

30. This section is adapted from Roger LeRoy Miller, *Economics Today,* 4th ed., New York, Harper & Row, 1982, pp. 199, 200.

31. Nordhaus and Tobin are certainly aware of these problems. The intent and the conclusions of their study are best summarized in their own words: "We recognize that our proposal is controversial on conceptual and theoretical grounds and that many of the numerical expedients in its execution are dubious. Nevertheless, the challenge to economists to produce relevant welfare-oriented measures seems compelling enough to justify some risk-taking. We hope that others will be challenged, or provoked, to tackle the problem with different assumptions, more refined procedures, and better data. We hope also that further investigations will be concerned with the distribution, as well as the mean value, of a measure of economic welfare, an aspect we have not been able to consider." William Nordhaus and James Tobin, "Is Growth Obsolete?" in *Economic Growth, Fiftieth Anniversary Colloquuim, vol. 5,* New York: National Bureau of Economic Research, 1972, p. 26.

32. On a monthly basis, the data are available for 137 large metropolitan areas and 8,000 permit-issuing areas. On an annual basis, data are available for 318 metropolitan areas and all 16,000 permit-issuing entities in the United States. Annual data become available around June each year.

33. Frequently, housing permits and housing starts are used jointly as indicators of housing activity. Over time, series of starts and permits tend to move together; and moreover, these series tend to peak and trough at about the same time. Sometimes, however, the two series move in opposite directions. When that occurs, the analysts should investigate the underlying data more carefully.

Both starts and permits can fluctuate widely from month to month, thus some analysts focus on moving averages of the two series.

Finally, *Existing Home Sales,* available monthly from the National Association of Realtors, is useful in assessing housing activity.

34. See note 33.

35. Housing starts are seasonally adjusted. Data for the winter months—December, January, and February—are especially sensitive to seasonal adjustments. During the winter, building activity slows in many

parts of the country. To compensate for this, the seasonal adjustments can be quite large during those months. During a mild winter, building activity can be somewhat higher than normal. After the large seasonal adjustment is applied to the data, however, the seasonally adjusted figures can exaggerate the extent of an increase in building activity in those months.

36. See U.S. Department of Commerce, Bureau of the Census, *Construction Reports: Price Index of New One-Family Houses Sold,* Series C27. The standard is refined periodically.

37. The official designator of the reference dates for the beginning and end of recessions takes into account a lot of different information relating to the total economy. The National Bureau of Economic Research (NBER) designates the dates of recessions that are used for most official purposes. The U.S. Department of Commerce uses the loose definition of two consecutive quarters of negative real economic growth as an indicator of possible recession. That indicator is used only until the NBER sets the official date. Since World War II through 1980, the NBER has defined six official recessions. Only three of the six (1953-1954, 1960-1961, and 1973-1975) have had two consecutive quarters of declining real GNP.

The expansion phase of a business fluctuation occurs after business activity turns upward. The official turning point is decided on after the fact by the NBER.

The dating of recessions and expansions is arbitrary. The NBER has decided on a set or criteria, but the decision as to what to include in that set has no basis in positive economic theory. Nevertheless it is convenient to be able to agree on the dating of recessions and expansions.

38. The justification for a composite series made up of several leading indicators has been stated by the Commerce Department. First, if the relative importance of different causal factors varies in different business cycles, then it is helpful to consider a variety of indicators. Second, measurement errors of individual series can be large. If such errors are independent, then looking at a number of series lessens the possibility of being misdirected by erratic movements of a particular component. Finally, the volatility of individual series, which arises from short-term random disturbances, may be ironed out in a smoother composite index. This rationale for generating a composite of leading indicators reflects some of the reasoning behind recent studies of the predictive value of combining separate forecasts. A primary conclusion of these analyses is that in most circumstances a combination of forecasts from different models is more accurate than any single model taken by itself.

39. For a detailed explanation of how the indexes are compiled, see Victor Zarrowitz and Charlotte Boschan, "Cyclical Indicator: An Evaluation and New Leading Indexes," *Handbook of Cyclical Indicators,* U.S. Department of Commerce, Bureau of Economic Analysis, Washington, D.C.:

U.S. Government Printing Office, 1977, pp. 170-184; Victor Zarrowitz and Charlotte Boschan, "New Composite Indexes of Coincident and Lagging Indicators," *Handbook of Cyclical Indicators*, U.S. Department of Commerce, Bureau of Economic Analysis, Washington, D.C.: U.S. Government Printing Office, 1977, pp. 185-199.

40. For a detailed description of each of these series included in the indexes of leading, coincident, and lagging indicators, see U.S. Department of Commerce, Bureau of Economic Analysis, *Handbook of Cyclical Indicators*, Washington, D.C.: U.S. Government Printing Office, 1977; and, U.S. Department of Commerce, Bureau of Economic Analysis, *Business Conditions Digest*, March 1983, pp. 107-109. The handbook also provides descriptions and sources of over 300 time series useful to business analysts and forecasters. These series are regularly presented in charts and tables in U.S. Department of Commerce, Bureau of Economic Analysis, *Business Conditions Digest*, published monthly.

41. Historical values are published in Department of Commerce, *Handbook of Cyclical Indicators*. Recent data and some historical data are published monthly in U.S. Department of Commerce, Bureau of Economic Analysis, *Business Conditions Digest*.

42. See Geoffrey Moore, "Generating Leading Indicators from Lagging Indicators," *Western Economic Journal*, vol. 7, no. 2, June 1969, pp. 135-144.

43. Zarnowitz and Boschan, "New Composite Indexes," p. 198.

44. For an easily understandable nontechnical article, see Gary Girton, "Forecasting with the Index of Leading Indicators," *Business Review*, November-December 1982, Federal Reserve Bank of Philadelphia, pp. 15-27. For more-technical articles, see H.O. Steckler and Martin Schepsman, "Forecasting with an Index of Leading Series," *Journal of the American Statistical Association*, June 1973, pp. 291-296; Alan J. Auerbach, "The Index of Leading Indicators: 'Measurement without Theory,' Twenty-five Years Later," National Bureau of Economic Research, Working Paper No. 761; Sahil N. Neftci, "Lead-lag Relations, Exogeneity and Prediction of Economic Time Series," *Econometrica*, January 1979, pp. 101-113.

45. Zarnowitz and Boschan, "New Composite Indexes."

46. The proportions or weights are shown in table 2-8. For example, by major market group, 60.71 percent of the output is accounted for by products such as automotive products, home appliances, and clothing, and the remainder, or 39.29 percent, is accounted for by materials, such as equipment parts, textiles, paper, and chemical materials. Similarly by industry group, utilities and mining accounted for 12.05 percent of total output and manufacturing 87.95 percent. The weights are based on the value added by manufacturers—the difference between the value of production and the cost of materials or supplies consumed.

47. Like many other statistics, the Index of Industrial Production is compiled from data collected through other government agencies, private organizations, and trade associations. Consequently the Federal Reserve has less direct control over the quality of those data than of the data it collects directly, such as the data from power companies.

48. Shipments are comparable to sales at the wholesale-retail levels.

49. Inventories are difficult to measure because of the absence or inadequacy of company records of stocks, differences in valuation methods, determination of the ownership of inventories to avoid missing or double coverage of goods on consignment or returned goods received but not invoiced or paid, inconsistent reporting between shipments and inventories in the manufacture of military hardware, and in-transit considerations.

The methodology used to estimate the constant value of manufacturing inventories (which make up more than 40 percent of the total) is described in John C. Hinrichs and Anthony D. Eckman, "Constant-Dollar Manufacturing Inventories," *Survey of Current Business,* November 1981, U.S. Department of Commerce, Bureau of Economic Analysis, pp. 16-23. Also see Edward F. Denison and Robert P. Parker, "National Income and Product Accounts of the United States: An Introduction to the Revised Estimates for 1929-1980," *Survey of Current Business,* December 1980, U.S. Department of Commerce, Bureau of Economic Analysis, p. 9. The procedure uses industry detail available by stage of fabrication—materials and supplies, work in progress, and finished goods.

Because the information about inventories comes from the accounting records of business (which does not include records of physical stocks), an indirect estimating procedure must be used to obtain constant-dollar stocks. The procedure converts the value of inventories reported by business (book value) to base-year prices (currently at 1972 prices).

50. The monthly shipments and inventory data are comparable to the totals published in the Annual Survey of Manufacturers (ASM). The ASM is a sample survey of approximately 70,000 manufacturing establishments drawn from a five-year census of a manufacturers' universe of about 350,000 manufacturing establishments. In the ASM, each manufacturing location reports data on value of shipments, beginning and end-of-year inventories, as well as various other economic variables.

51. See appendix C.

52. The definitions are taken directly from James C. Byrnes, Gerald F. Donahoe, Mary W. Hook, and Robert P. Parker, "Monthly Estimates of Personal Income, Taxes and Outlays," *Survey of Current Business,* November 1979, U.S. Department of Commerce, Bureau of Economic Analysis, pp. 19-23, 31.

Personal income as measured in the national income and product accounts differs from the Internal Revenue Service measure of adjusted gross income. For a reconciliation between the two income measures, see

Thae S. Park, "Relationship between Personal Income and Adjusted Gross Income, 1947-78," *Survey of Current Business,* November 1981, U.S. Department of Commerce, Bureau of Economic Analysis, pp. 24-28, 46.

53. Because the bulk of personal income is derived from production, personal income is used widely as an indicator of economic activity; however, it is not a measure of the value of national output. Not only does it include certain incomes that do not accrue in production (transfer payments and government interest), but it also excludes certain incomes that do accrue in production that are not distributed to persons (such as undistributed corporate profits and contributions for social insurance).

54. Employer contributions to publicly administered funds such as old-age, survivors', disability, and hospital insurance, unemployment insurance, and civilian government employees' retirement are excluded from other labor income and personal income.

55. For an explanation of the sources and methods used to prepare the constant-dollar estimates, see Byrnes et al., "Monthly Estimates," pp. 18-38.

56. Per-capita personal income is computed by dividing the total personal income by midyear population estimates. Population data for July for each year are provided by the Bureau of the Census; the college student population, however, is measured as of April 1.

"The per capita personal income estimates should be used with caution for several reasons. In many instances, an unusually high (or low) per-capita personal income is the temporary result of unusual conditions, such as a bumper crop, a major construction project (for example, a defense facility, nuclear plant, or dam), or a catastrophe (for example, a tornado or drought). In some cases, a high per capita personal income is not representative of the standard of living in an area. For example, a construction project may attract a large number of high-paid workers who are included in the population, but who send a substantial portion of their wages to dependents living in other areas. Conversely, a county with a large institutional population (for example, residents of a college, correctional institution, or domiciliary medical facility) may show an unusually low per capita personal income, which is not necessarily indicative of the economic well-being of the noninstitutional population. Moreover, population is measured at midyear, whereas income is measured as a flow over the year. Therefore, a significant change in population during the year can cause a distortion in the per capita personal income estimates, particularly if the change occurs around midyear." U.S. Department of Commerce, Bureau of Economic Analysis, Regional Economic Measurement Division, "County and Metropolitan Area Personal Income," *Survey of Current Business,* April 1981, p. 42.

57. Copies of the computer tapes may be purchased from the Data and Systems Branch, Regional Economic Analysis Division, Bureau of Eco-

nomic Analysis, U.S. Department of Commerce, Washington, D.C.   20230. A set of eleven volumes, containing all of the projected data and a detailed discussion of methodology, was published by BEA in July 1981.

State population projections to the year 2000 are also available from the Bureau of the Census. They are based on demographic trends and, unlike the BEA projections, do not reflect economic trends.

For a summary of the regional and state projections of income, employment and population, see U.S. Department of Commerce, Bureau of Economic Analysis, Regional Economic Analysis Division, ''Regional and State Projections of Income, Employment, and Population to the Year 2000,'' *Survey of Current Business,* November 1980, pp. 44-70.

58. The definitions underlying the local area estimates are, for the most part, the same as those underlying the personal income estimates in the national income and product accounts. The major difference is in the treatment of U.S. citizens temporarily working on assignment abroad. The national estimates include not only federal personnel—civilian and military—stationed abroad but also—since the 1976 benchmark revision—U.S. residents employed by private U.S. firms on temporary foreign assignment. The local area estimates include only persons residing in the fifty states and the District of Columbia.

59. In each volume, part 1 of the methodology section discusses the characteristics and applications of the personal income estimates. Part 2 describes the types of income payments and how they were estimated.

A detailed description of the sources and methods used in making estimates, including an explanation of revisions that affect the state and local area estimates, is presented in volume 1 of the set.

60. The REIS includes an active information-retrieval service, which provides a variety of standard and specialized analytic tabulations for counties and specified combinations of counties. A sample set of standard tabulations available through this system is included in volume 1 as appendix C. All of the tabulations are available in magnetic tape, microfiche, and computer printout form. The REIS data base currently includes the following data sets:

Quarterly state personal income. These estimates, available approximately four months after the close of the subject quarter, are published regularly in the January, April, July, and October issues of the *Survey.* As of April 1981, quarterly estimates are available from the first quarter of 1958 through the fourth quarter of 1980. Quarterly estimates for years prior to 1958 have not yet been adjusted to the revised national income series.

Annual state personal income. Annual estimates for states are published twice each year. Preliminary estimates of total and per-capita personal income, derived from the quarterly estimates, are published in the April issue of *Survey* (four months after the close of the subject year). A revised set of estimates, based on more-complete data and therefore more reliable, is presented in greater detail in the August issue of the *Survey*. Tabulations at the two-digit Standard Industrial Classification (SIC) code level are available as of August 1981 through REIS. Estimates for years prior to 1958 have not yet been adjusted to the revised national income series.

Annual state disposable personal income. Annual estimates of total and per-capita disposable personal income for states are released as a companion series to the revised annual state estimates of personal income and are published in the August issue of the *Survey*. The state disposable personal income series is consistent with the state personal income series for 1967 and subsequent years.

Annual county personal income. These estimates, published in this volume, become available approximately sixteen months after the close of the subject year. Summary statistics are published in the April issue of the *Survey*. Estimates are available for 1959, 1962, and 1965-79. County estimates for selected years back to 1929 have not yet been adjusted to the revised national income series.

Transfer payments. The component estimates of transfer payments by county are unpublished. However, tabulations of transfer payments by type of program are available from REIS for the years corresponding to the county personal income series.

Farm income and expenditures. These estimates of gross receipts and expenditures of farms, which underlie the net farm income estimates in the state and county personal income series, are unpublished. However, tabulations for the years 1969-1979 are available on request from REIS.

Average annual employment for states and counties. These unpublished estimates are a companion series to the personal income estimates. They are constructed from similar sources using the same concepts and definitions. Tabulations are available from REIS for 1967-1979. Source: *Area Personal Income 1974-79: Southwest Region,* vol. 7, U.S. Department of Commerce, 1981, p. v.

61. Data published by BLS are described in *BLS Handbook of Methods, vol. 1.* Tax-return tabulations prepared by the IRS are described in the *Statistics of Income* reports series. Estimates of retail sales, prepared by the Bureau of the Census, are described in the *Current Business Reports* series. A comprehensive description of the sources and methods used to prepare the estimates of personal income is provided in Byrnes et al., pp. 18-38.

62. Productivity is also available by output per employee.

63. When productivity declines, it does not necessarily mean that the population is worse off overall, as is sometimes inferred, particularly if the number of people employed has been rising relative to the population (a development important to the U.S. experience). This means that the characteristics of the work force may have changed. It also means that although the percentage employed may reduce the average level of output per worker (productivity), total output and output per capita may nonetheless increase. For example, suppose there are 200 people in the work force and 100 are employed and each produces 10 widgets for a total of 1,000 widgets or 5 per capita. If 120 persons (instead of 100 persons) become employed in total and the 20 newcomers produce only 7 widgets each, productivity has per person employed dropped to 9.5 (from 10) widgets, but the total output is 1,140 (compared to a total of 1000) and output per capita is 5.7 (instead of 5 per capita). The population as a whole has more widgets per person despite the fall in productivity.

64. A category called "GAF" is reported for many geographic areas. The GAF figure represents the sales of stores that specialize in department-store types of merchandise. It is not added directly into retail sales; to do so would result in some double counting.

65. The inventories-sales ratios indicate the relationship of end-of-month inventories to sales during the month. The ratios shown are derived by dividing the seasonally adjusted inventories estimates by the corresponding seasonally adjusted sales estimates. No adjustment is made in these ratios for markup in sales, which may vary from one kind of business to another.

66. Inventories estimates are developed from a fixed sample of respondents; the same respondents are canvassed each month. Therefore the differences between the preliminary and final inventories estimates for the same month are due to nonsampling errors.

67. The advance-sales estimates are based on early reporting of sales by a small subsample of the bureau's retail survey panels. Because of the early reporting and the sampling variability between the subsample and the full sample, the advance estimates will differ from the subsequent estimates for the same month. There are also differences between the preliminary and final sales estimates because some additional information that becomes available is incorporated into the final estimates (the differences involve both sampling and nonsampling errors).

68. The method used to estimate constant dollar inventories is summarized in Edward F. Denison and Robert P. Parker, "The National Income and Product Accounts of the United States; An Introduction to the Revised Estimates for 1929-80," *Survey of Current Business,* December 1980, U.S. Department of Commerce, Bureau of Economic Analysis, pp. 9, 10.

69. In 1967, data were available at the four-digit level for forty-eight industries under the Standard Industrial Classification (SIC). See appendix C. In 1972, the industries were expanded to sixty-one four-digit industries. In addition, the definitions of some industries were changed. Monthly data for the broad categories are available from 1947.

70. Inventories are difficult to measure because of the absence or inadequacy of company records of stocks, differences in valuation methods, determination of the ownership of inventories to avoid missing or double coverage of goods on consignment or returned or goods received but not invoiced or paid, inconsistent reporting between shipments and inventories in the manufacture of military hardware, and in-transit considerations. The method used to estimate constant dollar inventories is described in Denison and Parker, "National Income and Product Accounts," pp. 9-10.

3 Interest Rates and Other Financial Indicators

Bankers Acceptances and Interest Rates

Issuing Agency: Board of Governors of the Federal Reserve System.

Coverage and Source: A bankers acceptance is a draft or an order to pay a specified amount at a specified time and is drawn on individuals and businesses. When the party on whom the draft is drawn, usually a bank, acknowledges an obligation to pay at maturity, usually by writing "accepted" across the draft, it becomes an acceptance. Typically acceptances are liabilities of well-known, financially sound banks. Usually banks accept drafts in behalf of their customers when they present the bank with a letter of credit; then the customer is obligated to pay the bank on or before the maturity date of the draft. Typically bankers acceptances are created through letters of credit in financing foreign trade.[1]

Bankers acceptances are negotiable and can be sold to or discounted by third parties. Bankers acceptances are short-term instruments that carry a high degree of safety; they represent an obligation to both the accepting bank and the person who sells it.

Maturities and bankers acceptances range from 30 to 180 days; most have an original maturity of around 90 days. Typically, banks charge for issuing acceptances; consequently, the cost to the borrower is the fee plus the discount on the acceptance.

The market for bankers acceptances is an over-the-counter market made by about ten to fifteen dealers; some have nationwide branches. Most of the firms deal in a variety of obligations, and bankers acceptances are one part of their overall activities. The most-active institutions are foreign banks, and financial institutions, a small group of private domestic investors, and some U.S. government security dealers.

The interest rate published for bankers acceptances is the most-representative dealer closing offered rate for top-rated banks. The rate may be (but not necessarily need be) the average of the rates quoted by dealers.

When Series Become Available: Estimates are available on Monday for the week ending the previous Saturday. For the approximate release dates see also, each year, the June issue of Board of Governors of the Federal Reserve System, *Federal Reserve Bulletin*.

Publications: Current Data:

Board of Governors of the Federal Reserve System, *Federal Reserve Bulletin*. Monthly.
Board of Governors of the Federal Reserve System, *Selected Interest Rates*, H.15 (519) statistical release. Weekly.

Board of Governors of the Federal Reserve System, *Selected Interest Rates*, G.13 (415) statistical release. Monthly.

Publications: Historical Data:

Board of Governors of the Federal Reserve System, *Banking and Monetary Statistics, 1941-70*, 1976.
Board of Governors of the Federal Reserve System, *Annual Statistical Digest, 1970-79*, 1981.
Board of Governors of the Federal Reserve System, *Annual Statistical Digest, 1980*, 1981.
Board of Governors of the Federal Reserve System, *Annual Statistical Digest, 1981*, 1982.

References:

Duffield, Jeremy and Bruce Summers, "Bankers Acceptances," *Instruments of the Money Market*, Federal Reserve Bank of Richmond, 1981, pp. 114-122. No charge for this book.
Helfrich, Ralph T., "Trading in Bankers Acceptances: A View from the Acceptance Desk of the Federal Reserve Bank of New York," *Monthly Review*, Federal Reserve Bank of New York, February 1976, p. 51.
Melton, William and Jean M. Mahr, "Bankers Acceptances," *Quarterly Review*, Federal Reserve Bank of New York, Summer 1981, pp. 39-55.

Mail and Telephone Reference:

Board of Governors of the Federal Reserve System
Division of Research and Statistics
20th and Constitution Ave., N.W.
Washington, D.C.   20551
(202) 452-3000

Certificates of Deposit (Negotiable) and Interest Rates

Issuing Agency: Board of Governors of the Federal Reserve System.

Coverage and Source: A large negotiable certificate of deposit (CD) is a receipt for funds deposited in a bank for a specified period of time at a stated rate of interest. The receipt or certificate indicates the amount of money deposited, the rate of interest to be paid, and the principal amount due on the maturity date. The receipt is salable or negotiable so that title to the deposit can be transferred to another investor before the maturity date. Typically, the minimum size or denomination in which the CDs are sold is $100,000.

Because CDs are time deposits, they are subject to Federal Reserve regulations, which require time deposits to have a minimum maturity of thirty days. Since deposits cannot be accepted by a bank on a discount basis, CDs are issued at par and are traded on an interest-bearing basis.

Generally negotiable CDs are actively issued only by large commercial banks; the hundred largest banks account for about 90 percent of all large CDs issued. Negotiable CDs are among the most-important sources of purchased funds of U.S. money-market banks.

The new-issue market is called the primary CD market, and interest rates paid on newly issued CDs are primary rates.

Outstanding large negotiable CDs may be traded in a secondary market. The existence of such a market improves their liquidity and makes them attractive relative to both nonnegotiable instruments and negotiable instruments having poorly developed secondary markets. However, the secondary market rate generally exceeds the interest rate at which CDs are originally issued. The reason is that the CDs available in the secondary market may not match the maturities or be issued by the banks desired by investors, and investors have the option of buying CDs of any desired maturity of at least thirty days from preferred issuing banks. As a result, yields in the secondary market must often be increased relative to primary yields to induce investors to purchase them.

Interest on CDs is computed on the basis of a 360-day year instead of the 365-day year used to calculate the investment yield (or bond equivalent yield). The published rate is the unweighted average of offered rates quoted by at least five dealers early in the day.[2]

When Series Become Available: Estimates are available on Monday for the week ending the previous Saturday. For the approximate release dates see also, each year, the June issue of Board of Governors of the Federal Reserve System, *Federal Reserve Bulletin*.

Publications: Current Data:

Board of Governors of the Federal Reserve System, *Federal Reserve Bulletin*. Monthly.

Board of Governors of the Federal Reserve System, *Selected Interest Rates*, H.15 (419) statistical release. Weekly.

Board of Governors of the Federal Reserve System, *Selected Interest Rates*, G.13 (415) statistical release. Monthly.

Publications: Historical Data:

Council of Economic Advisers, *Economic Report of the President*, Washington, D.C.: U.S. Government Printing Office. Annual. See statistical appendix.

Board of Governors of the Federal Reserve System, *Banking and Monetary Statistics, 1941-70*, 1976.

Board of Governors of the Federal Reserve System, *Annual Statistical Digest, 1970-79*, 1981.

Board of Governors of the Federal Reserve System, *Annual Statistical Digest, 1980*, 1981.

Board of Governors of the Federal Reserve System, *Annual Statistical Digest, 1981*, 1982.

References:

Melton, William, "The Market for Large Negotiable CDs," *Quarterly Review*, Federal Reserve Bank of New York, Winter 1977-1978.

Summers, Bruce J., "Negotiable Certificates of Deposit," *Instruments of the Money Market*, Federal Reserve Bank of Richmond, 1981, pp. 73-93. No charge for this book.

Mail and Telephone Reference:

Board of Governors of the Federal Reserve System
Division of Research and Statistics
20th and Constitution Ave., N.W.
Washington, D.C.   20551
(202) 452-3000

Commercial Paper and Interest Rates

Issuing Agency: Board of Governors of the Federal Reserve System.

Coverage and Source: Commercial paper is an unsecured short-term promissory note sold by financially strong, highly rated firms on a discount basis to investors. Issuers usually arrange forms of indirect assurance, such as backing by bank lines and letters of credit, that the debt will be repaid at maturity. Commerical paper typically is issued in maturities of fewer than 270 days because longer maturities are subject to a costly registration process with the Securities and Exchange Commission. Most commercial paper, however, carries an initial maturity of less than 60 days.

Commercial paper is sold to investors directly (directly issued commercial paper) and through dealers (dealer-issued commercial paper). Directly issued commercial paper is sold directly to investors by large companies using their own sales force and distribution channels. Dealer-issued commercial paper is sold through dealers who initially purchase the paper from issuers.[3] Typically, the dealers charge somewhat less than one-eighth of a percentage point (0.00125) as their fee. The method used to raise funds depends primarily on the relative costs of these alternatives.

Most direct placers of commercial paper are large finance companies and medium to large-sized bank holding companies that are highly rated and need large amounts of short-term funds on a continuous basis. Borrowing costs must be sizable to justify the substantial fixed costs of distributing paper without dealer assistance.

In the dealer market, most issuers are nonfinancial firms—principally industrial companies, public utilities, and foreign nonfinancial entities. Major financial issuers in the dealer market are finance companies (often subsidiaries of manufacturers and retailers), medium-sized bank holding companies, and foreign banks; mortgage companies and insurance companies issue smaller amounts.

There is no active resale market or secondary market in commerical paper, as there is in Treasury bills or negotiable certificates of deposits that can be resold after issuance. Moreover, dealers and direct issuers discourage early redemption of commercial paper, although it may occur occasionally.

Of the one thousand or so firms that issue commercial paper, most obtain, for a fee, at least two ratings from one of the five companies that rates commercial paper. The five companies that rate paper for underlying financial quality or soundness are Moody's Investors Service; Standard & Poor's Corporation; Fitch Investors Service; Duff and Phelps, Inc.; and McCarthy, Crisanti, Maffei, Inc.[4]

The published interest rates of commercial paper are the unweighted average of offering rates quoted by at least five dealers (in the case of commercial paper) or finance companies (in the case of finance paper). The yields are quoted on a bank-discount basis (360-day year) instead of on an investment or bond-equivalent yield basis (365-day year) which would give a higher figure.

When Series Become Available: Estimates are available on Monday for the week ending the previous Saturday. For the approximate release dates see also, each year, the June issue of Board of Governors of the Federal Reserve System, *Federal Reserve Bulletin.*

Publications: Current Data:

Council of Economic Advisers, *Economic Indicators*, Washington, D.C.: U.S. Government Printing Office. Monthly.

Board of Governors of the Federal Reserve System, *Federal Reserve Bulletin.* Monthly.

Board of Governors of the Federal Reserve System, *Selected Interest Rates*, H.15 (519) statistical release. Weekly.

Board of Governors of the Federal Reserve System, *Selected Interest Rates*, G.13 (415) statistical release. Monthly.

Publications: Historical Data:

Council of Economic Advisers, *Economic Report of the President*, Washington, D.C.: U.S. Government Printing Office. Annual. See statistical appendix.

Board of Governors of the Federal Reserve System, *Banking and Monetary Statistics, 1941-1970*, 1976.[5]

Board of Governors of the Federal Reserve System, *Annual Statistical Digest, 1970-79*, 1981.

Board of Governors of the Federal Reserve System, *Annual Statistical Digest, 1980*, 1981.

Board of Governors of the Federal Reserve System, *Annual Statistical Digest, 1981*, 1982.

References:

Abken, Peter A., "Commercial Paper," *Instruments of the Money Market*, Federal Reserve Bank of Richmond, 1981. No charge for this book.

Hurley, Evelyn, "The Commercial Paper Market," *Federal Reserve Bulletin*, June 1977, Board of Governors of the Federal Reserve System, pp. 525-536.

Hurley, Evelyn, "The Commercial Paper Market Since the Mid-Seventies," *Federal Reserve Bulletin*, June 1982, Board of Governors of the Federal Reserve System, pp. 327-334.

Mail and Telephone Reference:

Board of Governors of the Federal Reserve System
Division of Research and Statistics
20th and Constitution Ave., N.W.
Washington, D.C.   20551
(202) 452-3000

Consumer Credit

Issuing Agency: Board of Governors of the Federal Reserve System, Mortgage and Consumer Finance Section.

Coverage and Source: Consumer credit has influenced many aspects of economic activity since its development shortly before World War I.[6] The practice has played an important role in the development of the market for consumer durable goods. In recent years, the practice has extended to the purchase of nondurable goods and services.

By using consumer credit, many persons are able to spread their purchases of goods and services more evenly over time. They can acquire the use of the products they want sooner (such as automobiles, appliances, furniture) while meeting monthly payments convenient for their budgets. The alternative is waiting until they have saved enough money to purchase the products outright, thereby concentrating their purchases in the future.

Consumer credit consists mainly of short- and intermediate-term credit. It excludes real-estate and mortgage credit, which is almost entirely long term. To provide consumer credit, an elaborate structure of financial and service organizations has been developed.

Consumer credit includes all short- and intermediate-term credit extended through regular business channels to finance the purchase of commodities and services for personal consumption or to refinance debts incurred for these purposes.[7] Consumer credit can be divided into two major types: installment and noninstallment.[8]

Installment credit represents all consumer credit that is to be repaid in two or more payments.[9] The four major categories of installment credit are automobile credit, revolving credit, mobile-home credit, and other.

Each of these types of installment credit is subdivided according to the type of institution holding the credit: commercial banks, finance companies, credit unions, retailers, savings and loan associations, gasoline companies, and mutual savings banks. This method of classification does not necessarily indicate the originator of the credit. Thus, credit held by financial institutions is classified according to its current holder, whether the institutions made the loans directly to consumers or purchased the paper from the retail outlet that originated the credit.[10]

Estimates of installment credit extended, liquidated, and outstanding are summaries of accounting statements. Credit extensions represent all debit entries to the installment receivable accounts of financial institutions and retail outlets. Credit liquidations covers all of the credit entries.[11] Credit extensions are much more volatile than liquidations and more directly reflect the effects of changing market conditions.

Data Available: Consumer installment credit is published monthly by the amount outstanding, net change,[12] extensions, and liquidations. Each of these categories is subdivided into the major type of credit (automobile, revolving, mobile home, and other) and the major holder (commercial banks, finance companies, credit unions, retailers, savings and loan associations, gasoline companies, mutual savings banks). Table 3-1 provides an example of the type of information available for each of the categories.

Related Series: The Federal Reserve also publishes quarterly estimates of finance rates on selected consumer installment loans.[13]

Table 3-1
Total Outstanding Consumer Installment Credit, 1980
(millions of dollars)

	1980
Total	313,472
By major holder	
Commercial banks	147,013
Finance companies	76,756
Credit unions	44,041
Retailers	28,448
Savings and loans	9,911
Gasoline companies	4,468
Mutual savings banks	2,835
By major type of credit	
Automobile	116,838
Commercial banks	61,536
Indirect paper	35,233
Direct loans	26,303
Credit unions	21,060
Finance companies	34,242
Revolving	58,352
Commercial banks	29,765
Retailers	24,119
Gasoline companies	4,468
Mobile home	17,322
Commercial banks	10,371
Finance companies	3,745
Savings and loans	2,737
Credit unions	469
Other	120,960
Commercial banks	45,341
Finance companies	38,769
Credit unions	22,512
Retailers	4,329
Savings and loans	7,174
Mutual savings banks	2,835

When Series Become Available: Data on consumer credit become available with a lag of about five weeks. For example, in early May, estimates become available for March. For the estimated release dates see also, each year, the June issue of the Board of Governors of the Federal Reserve System, *Federal Reserve Bulletin*.

Publications: Current Data:

Council of Economic Advisers, *Economic Indicators*, Washington, D.C.: U.S. Government Printing Office. Monthly.

Board of Governors of the Federal Reserve System, *Consumer Installment Credit*, G.19 (421) statistical release. Monthly.

Board of Governors of the Federal Reserve System, *Federal Reserve Bulletin*. Monthly.

Publications: Historical Data:

Council of Economic Advisers, *Economic Report of the President*, Washington, D.C.: U.S. Government Printing Office. Annual. See statistical appendix.

Board of Governors of the Federal Reserve System, *Consumer Installment Credit: Historical Series*, G.19 statistical release.[14]

Mail and Telephone Reference:

Board of Governors of the Federal Reserve System
Division of Research and Statistics
20th and Constitution Ave., N.W.
Washington, D.C.   20551
(202) 452-3000

Corporate Bonds and Corporate Bond Indexes

Issuing Agency: Various private organizations.

Coverage and Source: Corporations sell both bonds and stocks. Corporate bonds are available with a wide range of expected returns, risks, and other characteristics.[15] That is because corporations differ greatly in their abilities to generate the earnings and cash flow necessary to make interest payments and to repay the principal amount of the bonds at maturity. Furthermore, corporate bonds are only part of the total debt and overall financial structure of corporate business.

Because debt financing (issuing bonds) represents a legal obligation on the part of the corporation, the terms of a particular bond issue are specified in a lending agreement, called a bond indenture. A corporate trustee, often a commercial-bank trust department, ensures that the terms of the bond issue are met by the corporation. Most corporate bonds pay semiannually a coupon rate of interest on the $1,000 face amount of the bond. Thus if you owned a 6 percent corporate bond, you would receive $30 interest every six months. The indenture also indicates if any portion of the bond is to be retired each year in a series of so-called sinking-fund payments. Any collateral for the bond issue, such as buildings or equipment, also is indicated. Additionally, the indenture indicates how you as a bondholder would fare—along with other creditors of the business firm—should the firm get into serious financial difficulty and not be able to meet all of its legal obligations.

There are several different types of corporate bonds. No specific assets of the corporation are pledged as backing for debentures. Rather, the general credit rating of the corporation is at stake, plus any assets that can be seized if the corporation allows the bonds to fall into default. Mortgage bonds are secured by a mortgage on all or part of the corporate-owned real property. The backing for equipment trust bonds is a specific piece of equipment. The title to the equipment is vested in a trustee, who holds it for the benefit of the owners of the bonds. Collateral trust bonds are secured by anything that is not real estate, such as shares of stock in another corporation or accounts receivable. Convertible bonds can be exchanged for a specified number of shares of common stock, when and if the bondholder so desires. The rate of conversion is determined when the convertible bond is issued. Debentures or any other kind of bond may be callable, which means that the corporation can take the bond back and repay the principal whenever it wants to. The callable provision is put into the bond when it is issued.

New corporate bonds are sold in one of two ways: in the public market (public placements) or to particular lenders (private placements). Investment banking firms are the major underwriters of corporate bond issues.

A large issue requires the participation of many investment banking firms, which combine under the leadership of a particular underwriter or group of underwriters to form a syndicate. The underwriter and/or syndicate then sells the bonds to the public.

Many organizations compile representative yields for different categories of corporate bonds. Average yields compiled by three of these organizations are particularly widely used: The Board of Governors of the Federal Reserve System, Moody's Investors Service, and Standard & Poor's Corp. Typically the yield is an average of the yield on selected bonds in a specific category. They tend to be reasonably representative of the rates for the underlying group.[16]

The Board of Governors of the Federal Reserve System compiles two corporate bond yields for high-grade (Aaa) utility bonds: one for bonds that are newly issued and the other for bonds that are recently offered (included only for the first four weeks after termination of underwriter restrictions). The new-issue series attempts to adjust for any undesirable features that may be included in a series for seasoned issues.[17]

> Both the new-issue and the recently offered series represent estimates for a standard bond, which is defined as a new, straight-debt, long-term (20 years or longer) utility issue, rated Aaa by Moody's Investors Service, Inc., and AAA by Standard and Poor's, Inc., that carries 5-year call protection and is underwritten by a process of competitive bidding. New corporate debt issues with characteristics other than those of the standard bond are included in determining the newly issued yield series by using a nonlinear regression model to calculate the basis-point values of the heterogeneous characteristics.[18]
>
> There are several differences between the two yield series. First, bonds that meet the criteria for inclusion in the new-issue series are employed in the calculation of that series only in the week in which they are initially offered to investors; bonds in the recently offered series are the same as those in the newly issued series, but they are employed in calculating the series for each of the first 4 weeks after termination of underwriter price restrictions.[19] Second, yields on bonds in the series for new issues are based on prices asked by underwriting syndicates; yields on recently offered bonds, on the other hand, are based on prices determined in the free market and hence approximate market clearing prices. Third, yields on recently offered bonds are derived from quotes at the close of trading on Friday, while new issues, may be offered on any day of the week. Fourth, no adjustment is made for type of underwriting in the recently offered series because such differences as may exist due to the underwriting process are assumed not to exist in market-determined yields.[20]

Moody's Investors Service compiles the average yields for a wide variety of selected long-term taxable, nonconvertible, corporate bonds. Table 3-2 shows frequently used yield averages, how often the average is available, and where to obtain current and historical data. Categories are shown for

Table 3-2
Frequently Used Moody's Bond Averages

Type of Bond	Rating Class	Frequency	Source
Newly issued corporate bonds	Aaa Aa A Baa Composite of newly issued corporates	Monthly from 1952	Moody's *Industrial Manual*
Seasoned corporate bonds	Aaa Aa A Baa Composite of seasoned corporates	Monthly from 1929	Moody's *Industrial Manual*
Newly issued industrial bonds	Aaa Aa A Baa Composite of newly issued industrials	Monthly from 1952	Moody's *Industrial Manual*
Seasoned industrial bonds	Aaa Aa A Baa Composite of seasoned industrials	Monthly from 1929	Moody's *Industrial Manual*
Newly issued public utility bonds	Aaa Aa A Baa Composite of newly issued utilities	Monthly from 1957	Moody's *Public Utility Manual*
Seasoned public utility bonds	Aaa Aa A Baa Composite of seasoned utilities	Monthly from 1919	Moody's *Public Utility Manual*
Railroad bonds[a]	Aa A Baa Composite of seasoned corporates	Monthly from 1919	Moody's *Transportation Manual*

[a]Moody's monthly average yields on railroad bonds are based on approximately thirty long-term railroad bonds (ten Aa, ten A, and ten Baa). The yields extend back to 1919. Prior to 1928, twenty bonds were used. All yields are calculated to maturity dates, and the list of bonds is adjusted when required to reflect rating changes or other reasons so that each of the series is comparable throughout the entire period.

seasoned bonds: four by quality ratings (Aaa, Aa, A, and Baa), three by industry (industrials, railroads, public utility, and a total or corporate category), and two by time outstanding (newly issued or seasoned).

Moody's uses approximately ten representative bonds in each of the quality rating groups, including ten industrial, ten railroad, and ten public utility bonds. However, there are not always ten bonds in each classification that adequately meet all of the suitability criteria.[21] The average maturity of the long-term bonds included has also varied over time somewhat. Moody's aims at an average maturity of around twenty years for long-term corporates; sometimes it is somewhat longer than twenty years and sometimes shorter than twenty years.

The daily yield for each bond is calculated on the basis of its closing price (based on dealer-ask quotes). The closing price is adjusted when necessary for abnormally wide spreads between bid and asked quotes or for other distorting factors. The figures for each industry grouping of each rating group are unweighted arithmetic averages of the issues in the ratings group. The industry groups are the averages of all ratings for the industry. The total (corporates) is an unweighted average of the three industry groups.

Issues used in these averages are chosen to represent typical long-term bonds for the categories. Substitutions are made when a rating is changed and when a bond is called or sells too high above its call price, or when it approaches maturity. When necessary, adjustments are made to prevent substitutions from adversely affecting the comparability of the series.[22]

Table 3-3
Frequently Used Standard & Poor's Bond Averages

Type of Index	Rating Class	Frequency	Source
Composite (by quality rating)[a]	AAA AA A	Monthly from 1937[c] Weekly from 1970	Security Price Index Record, 1980 ed.
	BBB	Weekly over previous year	Current Statistics
Industrial bonds	AAA[b] AA A	Monthly from 1937[c] Weekly from 1970	Security Price Index Record, 1980 ed.
	BBB	Weekly over previous year	Current Statistics
Public-utility bonds	AAA[b] AA AAA	Monthly from 1937[c] Weekly from 1970	Security Price Index Record, 1980 ed.
	BBB	Weekly over previous year	Current Statistics

[a]Based on an average of the industrial and utility issues of the same credit quality. For example, the AA composite is an average of the AA industrial and AA utility bonds. Prior to September 1973, railroad bonds (of the same quality) were included in the composites.

[b]High-grade (AAA) corporates, public utilities, and the composite are also published in Security Price Index Record on a monthly basis from about 1900.

[c]Weekly averages are available from 1937 and can be obtained by writing to Standard & Poor's Corp., 25 Broadway, New York, NY 10004.

Standard & Poor's calculates average yields for groups of different long-term, taxable, nonconvertible corporate bonds. Table 3-3 shows the frequently used averages, how often the average is available, and when and where to obtain current and historical data. All of the averages apply to seasoned bonds. Four are by quality rating—AAA, AA, A, BBB—and two are by industry—industrials and public utility (and a total or composite).

S&P's uses about seven or eight representative issues in each of the four quality-ratings categories. The issues have about twenty years to maturity, and the yields are based on Wednesday price quotes. Each index is calculated as an arithmetic average of the yield to maturity of the issues making up the index.

The Discount Rate

Issuing Agency: Board of Governors of the Federal Reserve System.

Coverage and Source: When a depository institution wants to increase its reserves, it can borrow from the Federal Reserve. The depository institution requests from its district Federal Reserve bank a loan for a certain amount of reserves. The interest rate the Federal Reserve bank charges these institutions for the reserves it lends is called the *discount rate*.[23] In most other English-speaking countries, it is called the *bank rate*.

The Federal Reserve also has authority to impose a surcharge on certain types of discount lending. For example, in March 1980, the Board of Governors imposed a 3 percent surcharge on adjustment credit of member banks, with over $500 million in deposits, when the borrowing occurred in two or more successive statement weeks or when the borrowing occurred in more than four weeks in a calendar year. The purpose of the surcharge was to discourage frequent use of the discount window. In May 1980 the surcharge was eliminated. Thus, both the discount rate and any additional surcharge should be taken into account to estimate the effective interest rate on borrowing from the Federal Reserve.

In addition to the discount rate and surcharge, a wide variety of nonprice methods are used to affect the amount of borrowing through the discount window. These techniques range from moral suasion to rationing and even outright denial of the loans.

Publications: Current Data:

Council of Economic Advisers, *Economic Indicators*, Washington, D.C.: U.S. Government Printing Office. Monthly.

Board of Governors of the Federal Reserve System, *Federal Reserve Bulletin*. Monthly.

Board of Governors of the Federal Reserve System, *Selected Interest Rates*, H.15 (519) statistical release. Weekly.

Board of Governors of the Federal Reserve System, *Selected Interest Rates*, G.13 (415) statistical release. Monthly.

Publications: Historical Data:

Council of Economic Advisers, *Economic Report of the President*, Washington, D.C.: U.S. Government Printing Office. Annual. See statistical appendix.

Board of Governors of the Federal Reserve System, *Banking and Monetary Statistics, 1941-1970*, 1976.[24]

Board of Governors of the Federal Reserve System, *Annual Statistical Digest, 1970-79*, 1981.

Board of Governors of the Federal Reserve System, *Annual Statistical Digest, 1970-79*, 1981.
Board of Governors of the Federal Reserve System, *Annual Statistical Digest, 1980*, 1981.
Board of Governors of the Federal Reserve System, *Annual Statistical Digest, 1981*, 1982.

References:

Parthemos, James, and Walter Varvel, "The Discount Window," *Instruments of the Money Market*, Federal Reserve Bank of Richmond, 1981, pp. 59-72. No charge for this book.
Taylor, Herb, "The Discount Window and Monetary Control," *Business Review*, May/June 1983, Federal Reserve Bank of Philadelphia, pp. 3-12.

Mail and Telephone Reference:

Board of Governors of the Federal Reserve System
Division of Research and Statistics
20th and Constitution Ave., N.W.
Washington, D.C.   20551
(202) 452-3000

Eurodollar Deposits and Interest Rates

Issuing Agency: Board of Governors of the Federal Reserve System.

Coverage: Eurodollars are deposit liabilities, denominated in dollars, in banks located outside the United States.[25] Eurodollar deposits are created when the owner of a demand deposit at a U.S. bank transfers ownership of that deposit to a foreign bank in exchange for a dollar-denominated claim against the foreign bank, including the foreign branch of an American bank. Eurodollar deposits can be made by individuals, corporations, or other institutions depositing dollars obtained through transactions or the foreign-exchange markets.

The Eurodollars are usually fixed-rate deposits; maturities range from overnight to several years. Most Eurodollar money is held in the one-week to six-month range. The bulk of the Eurodollar time deposits are interbank liabilities.

Participants in the Eurodollar market are located throughout the world and transactions are carried out by telex, cable, and telephone. Funds are transferred either directly through correspondent banks or according to the brokers instructions.

A secondary market for Eurodollars enables investors to sell Eurodollars before the time deposits mature.

Interest rates on Eurodollar borrowings are averages of daily quotations of the London bid rate.

When Series Become Available: Estimates are available on Monday for the week ending the previous Saturday. For the approximate release dates see also, each year, the June issue of Board of Governors of the Federal Reserve System, *Federal Reserve Bulletin*.

Publications: Current Data:

Board of Governors of the Federal Reserve System, *Federal Reserve Bulletin*. Monthly.

Board of Governors of the Federal Reserve System, *Selected Interest Rates*, H.15 (519) statistical release. Weekly.

Board of Governors of the Federal Reserve System, *Selected Interest Rates*, G.13 (415) statistical release. Monthly.

Publications: Historical Data:

Board of Governors of the Federal Reserve System, *Banking and Monetary Statistics, 1941-70*, 1976.

Board of Governors of the Federal Reserve System, *Annual Statistical Digest, 1970-79*, 1981.
Board of Governors of the Federal Reserve System, *Annual Statistical Digest, 1980*, 1981.
Board of Governors of the Federal Reserve System, *Annual Statistical Digest, 1981*, 1982.

References:

Goodfriend, Marvin, "Eurodollars," *Instruments of the Money Market*, Federal Reserve Bank of Richmond, 1981, pp. 134-145. No charge for this book.

Mail and Telephone Reference:

Board of Governors of the Federal Reserve System
Division of Research and Statistics
20th and Constitution Ave., N.W.
Washington, D.C.   20551
(202) 452-3000

Federal Funds, Repurchase Agreements, and Interest Rates

Issuing Agency: Board of Governors of the Federal Reserve System.

Coverage and Source: Among the most-important financial developments in the postwar period has been the growth in trading of federal funds and repurchase agreements. Both markets involve the borrowing and lending of funds for periods as short as one day. The crucial feature of these transactions is that they are settled in immediately available funds; that is, the funds are available the same day the transaction takes place.

Banks, financial institutions, and firms in the course of daily business transfer enormous amounts of money among each other. The cost and inconvenience of transporting large amounts of cash among businesses would be prohibitive (when they want to make payment on the same day). Instead, they can transfer immediately available funds in the form of deposits the recipient can use that same day. (Since these transfers are made in immediately available funds, there is no time period, such as several days, involved in waiting for the funds to be collected.)[26]

Normally federal funds transactions are not secured by anything other than the promise of the borrower to repay. Accordingly, federal funds transactions take place only among credit-worthy institutions.

Most federal funds transactions are overnight loans ("overnight money")—funds lent out on one day and repaid the following morning. By convention, federal funds borrowing has come to mean an overnight loan between any two institutions exempt from reserve requirements.[27] Loans of longer maturity, however, known as *term federal funds*, also occur.

The market for repurchase agreements is closely related to the federal funds market. Immediately available funds are acquired through repurchase agreements by selling securities and at the same time agreeing to buy them back, or repurchase them, at a later date.[28]

Usually repurchase agreements are made for one day; however, they can also be made for longer periods of time. As long as the funds the banks acquire through repurchase agreements involve U.S. government or federal agency securities, the funds borrowed are not subject to reserved requirements.

The federal funds interest rate is the average of the rates on a given day weighted by the volume of transactions at those rates. The weekly and monthly figures are averages of all calendar days. By convention, weekly figures represent bank-statement week averages—averages for the week ending Wednesday.[29]

When Series Become Available: Estimates are available on Monday for the week ending the previous Saturday. For the approximate release dates see also, each year, the June issue of Board of Governors of the Federal Reserve System, *Federal Reserve Bulletin.*

Publications: Current Data:

Board of Governors of the Federal Reserve System, *Federal Reserve Bulletin.* Monthly.

Board of Governors of the Federal Reserve System, *Selected Interest Rates*, H.15 (519) statistical release. Weekly.

Board of Governors of the Federal Reserve System, *Selected Interest Rates*, G.13 (415) statistical release. Monthly.

Publications: Historical Data:

Board of Governors of the Federal Reserve System, *Banking and Monetary Statistics, 1941-70,* 1976.

Board of Governors of the Federal Reserve System, *Annual Statistical Digest, 1970-79,* 1981.

Board of Governors of the Federal Reserve System, *Annual Statistical Digest, 1980,* 1981.

Board of Governors of the Federal Reserve System, *Annual Statistical Digest, 1981,* 1982.

References:

Bowsher, Norman, "Repurchase Agreements," *Review*, September 1979, Federal Reserve Bank of St. Louis.

Lucas, Charles, Marcos T. Jones, and Thom B. Thurston, "Federal Funds and Repurchase Agreements," *Quarterly Review*, Summer 1977, Federal Reserve Bank of New York. Also available in *Instruments of the Money Market*, Federal Reserve Bank of Richmond, 1981. No charge for this book.

Pence, Barbara K., "Repurchase Agreements: Their Dramatic Growth," *Review*, Winter 1979, Federal Reserve Bank of Cleveland.

Purchase and Sale of Fed Funds, Fedpoints 15, Federal Reserve Bank of NY, 1978.

Repurchase and Matched Sale-Purchase Transactions, Fedpoints 4, Federal Reserve Bank of New York, 1979.

Mail and Telephone Reference:

Board of Governors of the Federal Reserve System
Division of Research and Statistics
20th and Constitution Ave., N.W.
Washington, D.C.   20551
(202) 452-3000

Flow of Funds Accounts

Issuing Agency: Board of Governors of the Federal Reserve System, Flow of Funds and Savings Section.

Coverage: The flow of funds accounts provide a comprehensive source of financial and nonfinancial statistical information. An explanation of the ways in which the flow of funds can be used and are generated, the types of information available, and the many sources from which the data are drawn is available elsewhere.[30] In this section some of the statistical information generated is highlighted briefly.

The flow of funds accounts focus on the relation between financial activities in the United States and nonfinancial activities that generate income and production. The purpose of the accounts is to provide, systematically, aggregate measures of transactions needed to identify both influences of the nonfinancial economy on the financial market and reciprocal influences of financial-market developments on the demand for goods and services, sources and amounts of savings and investment, and structure of income.

At the most-detailed level, statistical information is divided into about twenty sectors, as shown in table 3-4. The accounts for each of these detailed sectors are available, as well as for the broader groupings into which these sectors are aggregated. For example, accounts of savings institutions are generated by combining the accounts of savings and loan associations, mutual savings banks, and credit unions. For each sector, the accounts are organized into categories of transactions. Transactions are divided into three major groups: current nonfinancial transactions, capital nonfinancial transactions (savings and investment), and financial transactions. In addition to the sector accounts, separate tables of accounts are shown for different types of financial claims (table 3-5). The items listed are normally shown in the tables. Some sums of subcategories of accounts are also maintained (the subcategories are indented).

Data Available: Flow of funds data reported between 1946 and 1951 are in annual form. Beginning in 1952, the data are in quarterly form.

The data presented consist of two types: stocks or amount outstanding and flows or changes (increases or decreases) in outstanding accounts. Both seasonally adjusted and not seasonally adjusted is available.

When Series Become Available: Quarterly flow of funds data become available about one and one-half months after the end of each quarter. For example, estimates for the first quarter become available around May 15. For the estimated release dates see also, each year, the June issue of the Board of Governors of the Federal Reserve System, *Federal Reserve Bulletin.*

126

Table 3-4
Flow of Funds Sector Structure

Households			Private domestic nonfinancial	Non-financial
Farm business	Noncorporate business	Nonfinancial business		
Nonfarm noncorporate business				
Corporate nonfinancial business				
State and local governments—general funds				
Rest of the world				
U.S. government				
Federally sponsored credit agencies				Finance
Mortgage pools				
Monetary authorities				
Domestic commercial banks	Commercial banking			
Domestic affiliates of commercial banks				
Foreign banking offices in the United States				
Banks in U.S. territories and possessions				
Savings and loan associations	Savings institutions		Private nonbank finance	
Mutual savings banks				
Credit unions				
Life insurance companies	Insurance			
Other insurance companies				
Private pension funds				
State and local government employee retirement funds				
Finance companies	Finance not elsewhere classified			
Real-estate investment trusts				
Open-end investment companies				
Money market funds				
Security brokers and dealers				

Source: Board of Governors of the Federal Reserve System, *Introduction to Flow of Funds*, 1980, p. 32.

Table 3-5
Flow of Funds Financial Transactions Categories

Gold and special drawing rights	
Official foreign exchange position	
IMF gold tranche position	Monetary reserves
Convertible foreign exchange	
Treasury currency	
Demand deposits and currency	
Private domestic	
U.S. government	
Foreign	Deposit claims on
Time deposits at commercial banks	financial institutions
Savings accounts at savings institutions	
Money market fund shares	
Federal funds and security repurchase agreements	
Interbank claims	Interbank claims
Life insurance reserves	Insurance and pension
Pension fund reserves	reserves
Corporate equities	Corporate equities
U.S. government securities	
Treasury issues	
Short-term	
Other marketable	
Savings bonds	
Federal agency issues	
Loan participation certificates	
Sponsored agency issues	
Mortgage pool securities	
State and local government obligations	
Corporate and foreign bonds	
Mortages	
Home (one- to four-family) mortgages	Credit market
Multifamily residential	instruments
Commercial	
Farm	
Consumer credit	
Installment	
Noninstallment	
Bank loans not elsewhere classified	
Other loans	
Open market paper	
Finance company loans to business	
U.S. government loans	
Sponsored credit agency loans	
Loans on insurance policies	
Security credit	
Owed by brokers and dealers	
Owed by others	
Taxes payable	
Trade credit	
Equity in noncorporate business	Other claims
Miscellaneous	
Foreign claims	
U.S. government claims	
Insurance claims	
Unallocated claims	
Sector discrepancies	

Source: Board of Governors of the Federal Reserve System, *Introduction to Flow of Funds,*
1980, p. 39.

Publications: Current Data:

Council of Economic Advisers, *Economic Indicators*, Washington, D.C.: U.S. Government Printing Office. Monthly.
Board of Governors of the Federal Reserve System, *Federal Reserve Bulletin*. Monthly. Contains summary tables.
Board of Governors of the Federal Reserve System, *Flow of Funds*, Z.1 (780) statistical release. Quarterly.

Publications: Historical Data:

Board of Governors of the Federal Reserve System, *Flow of Funds Accounts, Assets and Liabilities Outstanding 1957-80*, 1981.

References:

Board of Governors of the Federal Reserve System, *Introduction to Flow of Funds*, 1980.

Mail and Telephone Reference:

Flow of Funds Section
Room B-5100   Stop 95
Board of Governors of the Federal Reserve System
20th and Constitution Ave., N.W.
Washington, D.C.   20551
(202) 452-3482

Monetary Aggregates: M1, M2, M3, L

Issuing Agency: Board of Governors of the Federal Reserve System, Banking Section.

Coverage and Limitations: The money supply has become one of the most closely watched economic statistics in recent years.[31] Unexpected large drops or bulges in the money supply can lead to sizable gains or declines in the stock market. Such movements stem in part from the expressed policy of the Federal Reserve of controlling the money-supply growth and the anticipated effects of the policy on economic activity.

During the late 1970s and early 1980s, sweeping changes, both technological and regulatory in nature, occurred throughout in the U.S. financial system. These changes have expanded the traditional means of payment, thereby directly affecting the money supply. Throughout this period, the items included in the money supply, as defined by the Federal Reserve, have changed several times and undoubtedly will change again in the future.

As the term suggests, monetary aggregates are aggregations or summations of the public's financial assets that appear to function as money. This raises the more-fundamental questions of what money is—the functional characteristics and the assets that possess those characteristics.

Economists do not completely agree on the answers to these questions so there is no one universally accepted definition of the money stock. As a result, the Federal Reserve has taken a more eclectic approach and defines several monetary aggregates it believes relevant to monetary analysis. Each aggregate is designated by the letter M and carries a number: M1, M2, M3. Higher numbers are more-inclusive or broader measures of the aggregates.[32] The organizing principle underlying each measure is that similar kinds of monetary assets are combined at each level of aggregation.

At present, there are two leading concepts of what money is.[33] The more restrictive of the concepts, M1, focuses on money as a medium of exchange. According to this definition, money consists of assets that are widely used in payment for goods and services.

The second and broader concept, applicable to M2 and M3, suggests money has another role as well; it is a temporary store of value. Between the time of sale and purchase of an item, the proceeds need not be kept in the form of the medium of exchange. They can be kept in other financial assets, which themselves are not a means of payment but are a store of value. If this occurs and these assets are considered by the public to be close substitutes for the medium of exchange, then the relevant concept of money includes both the medium of exchange and store of values.

The Federal Reserve tries to identify the assets that correspond to each of these concepts. At present, there is no clear-cut way to identify which

130

assets act as a medium of exchange and which serve as a temporary store of value. Both direct and indirect evidence are used to determine whether a financial asset serves as a medium of exchange or store of value.

Direct evidence is both qualitative and quantitative. The qualitative information is based on the character and use of financial assets. The quantitative information includes amounts of the financial assets outstanding, the distribution of the assets among different holders, and the frequency with which the assets are used to make transactions.

The indirect evidence that the Federal Reserve uses to help determine whether a financial asset is money is statistical. A variety of statistical tests are conducted between the assets that are prospects to be included in money and the nonmonetary variables that ought to be correlated with money, according to the different monetary theories. For example, under one set of statistical tests, a search is conducted for the financial assets that are most highly correlated with a group of variables (such as national income and interest rates) used to explain the public's demand for money.

Even with both the direct and indirect evidence, however, the Federal Reserve's assessment of the roles of any specific asset usually requires a substantial use of judgment.

The Federal Reserve must also contend with the problem of data availability in its attempts to match financial assets and the concepts of money. If observation suggests the importance of a specific financial asset in the definition of money, its inclusion will depend in part on the availability of accurate and comprehensive data on the amount outstanding. If the data are not available, the Federal Reserve will weigh the cost of collecting them against the potential significance of the item. The goal is to identify the financial assets with the characteristics that correspond to the related concepts of money.

During the 1970s and early 1980s major financial innovations changed the meaning and significance of existing measures of the money stock. For example, the introduction of negotiable order withdrawal accounts (NOW accounts), credit-union share drafts, demand deposits at thrift institutions, and automatic transfer systems (ATS accounts) increased the number of ways in which payments could be made. Also, the number of liquid investment alternatives increased through the development of money-market mutual funds, security-repurchase agreements, and Eurodollar deposits. Moreover, legal and regulatory changes have given depository institutions more flexibility in competing for customers. Because of these and other developments, it was increasingly argued that the existing measures of the monetary aggregates no longer measured the true financial position of the public and therefore were inadequate tools for monetary policy.

In a response to these developments, the Board of Governors of the Federal Reserve System, after extensive study, announced on February 7,

1980, the redefinitions of the monetary aggregates.[34] The problems involved in defining the monetary aggregates have continued to become more complex in the 1980s in the face of rapid financial innovation.[35] They have been reflected by the subsequent changes (and changes that may occur in the future) in the items that constitute the monetary aggregates.[36]

Table 3-6 provides the precise definition of the monetary aggregates. A less-technical description of M1, M2, M3, and L follows.

Medium of Exchange—M1. All sorts of checking-type accounts are available. Traditionally money included currency in the hands of the public and demand deposits held only in commercial banks (excluding those held by foreign banks and official institutions). Many depository institutions,[37] other than commercial banks, offer NOW accounts, ATS accounts (whereby funds from savings accounts can be automatically transferred to checkable deposits), share-draft accounts, and travelers' checks (of nonbank issuers). In order to take account of all of these additional checkable deposits in all depository institutions, the definition of the money supply was expanded to include NOW accounts, ATS accounts, credit-union share drafts, demand deposits at mutual savings banks, and travelers' checks of nonbank issuers.[38]

Near Monies—M2 and M3. Near monies are other assets that are almost, but not exactly, like money. Their values are known in terms of money, and they have relatively high liquidity; that is, they can be converted into money relatively quickly and without risk of loss of value.

Table 3-6
Composition of the Money Stock Measures

M1: Averages of daily figures for (1) currency outside the treasury, Federal Reserve Banks, and the vaults of commercial banks; (2) traveler's checks of nonbank issuers; (3) demand deposits at all commercial banks other than those due to domestic banks, the U.S. government, and foreign banks and official institutions less cash items in the process of collection and Federal Reserve float; and (4) negotiable order of withdrawal (NOW) and automatic transfer service (ATS) accounts at banks and thrift institutions, credit union share-draft (CUSD) accounts, and demand deposits at mutual savings banks.

M2: M1 plus savings and small-denomination time deposits at all depository institutions, overnight repurchase agreements at commercial banks, overnight Eurodollars held by U.S. residents other than banks at Caribbean branches of member banks, and balances of money-market mutual funds (general purpose and broker/dealer).

M3: M2 plus large-denomination time deposits at all depository institutions, term RPs at commercial banks and savings and loan associations, and balances of institution-only money-market mutual funds.

L: M3 plus other liquid assets such as term Eurodollars held by U.S. residents other than banks, bankers acceptances, commercial paper. Treasury bills and other liquid Treasury securities, and U.S. savings bonds.

Source: Board of Governors of the Federal Reserve System, *Federal Reserve Bulletin,* March 1983.

M2. The major components of M2 added to M1 to form M2 are:

1. Small-denomination time deposits. These are deposits that, in principle, have a specified time period that they must be held before being liquidated.[39] An example of a time deposit might be a six-month certificate of deposit offered by a savings and loan association. If that time deposit is cashed before the end of six months, the holder suffers a substantial penalty for early withdrawal in the form of a lower interest rate than is stated on the certificate of deposit and possibly a complete loss of interest for a portion of the time that the deposit was held.

2. Savings deposits. Savings-account balances are a special type of time deposit which, in principle, require thirty days notice of intent to withdraw, although in practice this notice is rarely required at this time.

3. Money-market mutual-fund shares. Many people keep part of their assets in the form of shares in money-market mutual funds; these are mutual funds that invest only in government and corporate bonds. Many of these money-market mutuals allow check-writing privileges.[40]

4. Retail repurchase agreements. Repurchase agreements involve two transactions: the sale of a financial asset (usually U.S. Treasury or federal agency securities) and the repurchase of that asset by the original seller. The terms of both transactions are agreed on in advance with the original seller agreeing to repurchase the securities for a higher price than the original sale price. Retail repurchase agreements are issued in denominations of less than $100,000 with maturity of eighty-nine days or less.[41]

5. Certain specialized overnight assets.[42]

M3. The components of M3 consist of M2 plus financial assets that are very liquid but are more restrictive in use because of size or conversion. These financial assets are primarily used by institutions, not individuals. The major items in M3 are large-denomination time deposits ($100,000 and over); repurchase agreements $100,000 and over and more than one-day maturity (also called *term RPs*), and institutional money-market fund shares, which cater to institutional investors and require substantial minimum initial investments, ranging as high as $250,000.

Bank Credit—L. Bank credit, L, consists of M3 plus other liquid assets such as Eurodollars held by U.S. residents other than banks, bankers acceptances, commerical paper, Treasury bills and other liquid Treasury securities, and U.S. savings bonds.

Data Available: Monetary aggregates and the components of the aggregates are available on both a seasonally and not seasonally adjusted basis.

Source of Data: To provide quantitative measures of the monetary aggregates, the Federal Reserve undertakes a multistage process of collecting and processing data.[43] The basic data come from the institutions that issue money—the Federal Reserve itself, the U.S. Treasury, bank and thrift depositories, money-market mutual funds, and nonbank issuers of travelers' checks.

Depositories—about 40,400—are the largest number of reporters of data. Of these, 17,800 are not members of the Federal Reserve system. They submit quarterly or semiannual balance-sheet figures to their chartering agencies, and this information is obtained by the Fed (sometimes with considerable lag). The remaining 22,600 depositories supply data directly to the Fed. The reporting burden is heaviest for the largest organizations—some 14,900 weekly reporters that provide seven days of selected balance-sheet data with each report. The 7,700 smaller depositories report quarterly.

Around the end of 1982, there were about ten nonbank issuers of travelers' checks; they furnish end-of-the-month data to the Fed on their outstanding checks. Money-market mutual funds, of which there are about 220, report their end-of-the-week outstanding shares to the Investment Company Institute, the industry trade organization that provides data to the Fed.

The balance-sheet information these organizations provide goes through several processing steps. First, it is carefully reviewed for errors. Since the basic data obtained from some institutions are not complete, statistical procedures are used to fill the gaps. Adjustments are made to eliminate double counting. The results of these procedures are the Fed's estimates of the money supply. Finally, the figures are seasonally adjusted. Both seasonally adjusted and not seasonally adjusted money-supply figures are provided by the Federal Reserve.[44]

When Series Become Available: Estimates for M1 become available on Friday for the week ended Wednesday of the previous week. The broader aggregates (M2, M3, L) have a lag of a few weeks.[45] For the estimated release dates see also, each year, the June issue of the Board of Governors of the Federal Reserve System, *Federal Reserve Bulletin*.

Publications: Current Data:

Council of Economic Advisers, *Economic Indicators*, Washington, D.C.: U.S. Government Printing Office. Monthly.

Board of Governors of the Federal Reserve System, *Federal Reserve Bulletin*. Monthly.

Board of Governors of the Federal Reserve System, *Money Stock Measures and Liquid Assets*, H.6 (508) statistical release. Weekly.

Publications: Historical Data:

Council of Economic Advisers, *Economic Report of the President*, Washington, D.C.: U.S. Government Printing Office. Annual. See statistical appendix.

The most-up-to-date back data are available from the Banking Section, Division of Research and Statistics, Board of Governors of the Federal Reserve System, Washington, D.C.   20551.

References:

Axilrod, Stephen H., "Monetary Policy, Money Supply, and the Federal Reserve's Operating Procedures," *Federal Reserve Bulletin*, January 1982, Board of Governors of the Federal Reserve System, pp. 13-24.

Duprey, James H., "How the Fed Defines and Measures Money," *Quarterly Review*, Spring-Summer 1982, Federal Reserve Bank of Minneapolis, pp. 10-19.

Pierce, David A., and William P. Cleveland, "Seasonal Adjustment Methods for the Monetary Aggregates," *Federal Reserve Bulletin*, December 1981, Board of Governors of the Federal Reserve System, pp. 875-887.

Simpson, Thomas, "A Proposal for Redefining the Monetary Aggregates," *Federal Reserve Bulletin*, January 1979, Board of Governors of the Federal Reserve System, pp. 13-42.

Simpson, Thomas, "The Redefined Monetary Aggregates," *Federal Reserve Bulletin*, February 1980, Board of Governors of the Federal Reserve System, pp. 97-114.

Mail and Telephone Reference:

Board of Governors of the Federal Reserve System
Division of Research and Statistics
20th and Constitution Ave., N.W.
Washington, D.C.   20551
(202) 452-3000

Monetary Base, or High-Powered Money

Issuing Agency: Board of Governors of the Federal Reserve System, Banking Section.

Coverage: Given that most money-supply watchers are merely interested in knowing what the Fed has done to affect monetary policy, some suggest that the monetary aggregates not be looked at at all. Rather, these economists look at only the monetary base, the raw material from which money is produced. The Fed at times calls the monetary base *high-powered money*. These terms come from the fact that the liabilities of the Federal Reserve system—currency and depository institutions deposits—constitute the base of the money supply. Reserves and currency are the base on which the money supply is built. The monetary base is distributed among the following uses:[46]

monetary base =   vault cash held by depository institutions
                + depository institutions deposits in Federal Reserve banks + currency in the hands of the public.

Prior to the advent of the Federal Reserve system in 1914, the monetary base consisted solely of currency in the hands of the public and in the vaults of banks. With the advent of the Federal Reserve, high-powered money had to include the banks' reserve accounts with the Federal Reserve system. More recently, the Monetary Control Act of 1980 enabled other financial institutions along with commercial banks to offer checklike deposits. Depository institutions that offer such checklike deposits also become subject to legal reserve requirements; consequently, the monetary base was broadened to include the legal reserves of all depository institutions as well.

Data Available: The monetary base is available in two forms: adjusted for changes in reserve requirements (and seasonally adjusted) and not adjusted for changes in reserve requirements (and not seasonally adjusted).

Source of Data: Data for the monetary base are obtained primarily from the balance sheet of the Federal Reserve banks and the U.S. Treasury, as well as from vault cash data received from member banks. Estimates of the monetary base are available the day after the end of each banking statement week and are subject to minor revisions. These revisions include estimates of depository institutions' vault cash (other than member banks) and revisions of the seasonal factors. Consequently, the estimates of the monetary base become available more quickly and are subject to less revision and estimation problems than, for example, the monetary aggregates.[47]

When Series Become Available: Estimates of the monetary base are available on Monday for the week ended the previous Wednesday. For the estimated release dates see also, each year, the June issue of the Board of Governors of the Federal Reserve System, *Federal Reserve Bulletin.*

Publications: Current Data:

Board of Governors of the Federal Reserve System, *Aggregate Reserves of Depository Institutions and the Monetary Base*, H.3 (502) statistical release. Monthly.
Board of Governors of the Federal Reserve System, *Federal Reserve Bulletin.* Monthly.

Publications: Historical Data:

Council of Economic Advisers, *Economic Report of the President*, Washington, D.C.: U.S. Government Printing Office. Annual. See statistical appendix.

The most up-to-date back data are available from the Banking Section, Division of Research and Statistics, Board of Governors of the Federal Reserve System, Washington, D.C.   20551.

References:

Burger, Albert E., "Alternative Measures of the Monetary Base," *Review*, June 1979, Federal Reserve Bank of St. Louis, pp. 2-8.
Davis, Richard G., "The Monetary Base as an Intermediate Target for Monetary Policy," *Quarterly Review*, Winter 1979-80, Federal Reserve Bank of New York, pp. 1-10.
Tatom, John A., "Issues in Measuring an Adjusted Monetary Base," *Review*, December 1980, Federal Reserve Bank of St. Louis, pp. 11-29.

Mail and Telephone Reference:

Board of Governors of the Federal Reserve System
Division of Research and Statistics
20th and Constitution Ave., N.W.
Washington, D.C.   20551
(202) 452-3000

Mortgages and Mortgage Interest Rates

Issuing Agency: Federal Home Loan Bank Board and Department of Housing and Urban Development.

Coverage:

Major Types of Mortgages: Most homes are financed through a mortgage, which is a loan on a house.[48] In some states, the purchaser holds title to the house, and in others the mortgagee does. In nine states and the District of Columbia, a special arrangement is made whereby the borrower (mortgagor) deeds the property to a trustee, a third party, on behalf of the lender (mortgagee). The trustee then deeds the property back to the borrower when the loan is repaid.

There are four basic sources of mortgage money. The most common are savings and loan associations; the second most common are mortgage companies. Commercial banks are third, and mutual savings banks make some mortgage loans, particularly in the Northeast. There is a category of "other," which includes pension funds, mortgage pools, insurance companies, mortgage investment trusts, and state and local credit agencies. (Only under special circumstances, can a buyer get a mortgage loan from one of these institutions.)[49]

There are three kinds of mortgages: conventional mortgages, Veterans Administration mortgages (VA loans), and Federal Housing Administration mortgages (FHA loans). Although an individual may not be eligible for all of them, each is available from the same sources: commercial banks, savings banks, mortgage companies, savings and loan associations, and insurance companies.

Conventional mortgages run for about twenty to thirty years. The rate of interest is also subject to state and usury laws. With a conventional mortgage loan, the money the lender risks is secured by the value of the mortgaged property and the financial integrity of the borrower. To protect the investment from the start, the conventional lender, such as a savings and loan association, usually requires a down payment of 5 to 35 percent of the value of the property. Some private insurers will protect lenders against the loss on at least part of the loan (the borrower pays the insurance cost). In practice, most borrowers pay off their mortgages well before maturity (after nine or ten years).

VA loans can be obtained only by qualified veterans or their spouses or widows. The interest charged is administered, rather than determined strictly, by supply and demand in the money market. The VA loan is guaranteed (or underwritten by the government) rather than insured. That is, the government promises, on an approved loan, that it will repay up to a certain amount—say $20,000—or a certain percentage—say 69 percent. The borrower has no insurance premium to pay.

On FHA loans, the FHA insurance covers the entire amount of the loan. The security enables qualified borrowers to obtain a more-generous loan, in relation to the value of the property, than they could obtain with an uninsured loan. The maximum interest rate that can be charged usually has been below current market interest rates. But a .5 percent premium for the insurance and a 1 percent origination fee (for the work of drawing up the papers) are also permitted. The loan can be for as long as thirty-five years, not to exceed three-fourths of what the FHA estimates is the remaining economic life of the dwelling. There are no penalties for prepayment. A home buyer applies for an FHA-insured mortgage loan just as he or she would for any other loan. The lender, be it a savings and loan association, commercial bank, or mortgage company, supplies the necessary forms.[50]

The major difference between FHA loans and conventional loans is that the FHA interest is not determined strictly by market conditions but is set at an arbitrary rate by the secretary of housing and urban development. Usually the secretary tries to fix the rate below the lowest prevailing market rate. This practice has resulted in the point system on both FHA and VA loans.[51]

In the late 1970s and early 1980s, a number of more-flexible payment arrangements were established for home buyers. Five kinds of mortgages are shown in table 3-7: graduated payment, variable rate, rollover, price-level adjusted, and reverse annuity.

Mortgage Interest Rates: For conventional mortgages, the Federal Home Loan Bank Board in cooperation with the Federal Deposit Insurance Corporation, compiles and publishes the terms and yields on home mortgages closed.[52] The terms are weighted averages based on a probability sample survey of characteristics of mortgages originated by major institutional lending groups: savings and loan associations, mortgage bankers, commercial banks, and mutual savings banks.[53] The loans are for fully amortized first mortgage loans that are both secured by and for the purchase of single-family nonfarm residential property (homes). Table 3-8 shows some of the information available. The contract rate is the stated rate of interest charged on a mortgage loan.[54]

Initial fees and charges include any general or specific charges paid by the borrower, or seller, to obtain the loan (such as loan commissions, fees, or discounts) but exclude charges for mortgage credit, life, or property insurance, property transfer, and title search and insurance.

The effective rate (also called the Federal Home Loan Bank Board— FHLBB—series) is the contract rate and the initial fees and charges amortized over ten years, which is the assumed actual average life of a conventional mortgage; (prepayment is assumed at the end of ten years).[55] Other

Table 3-7
Five Kinds of Mortgages

Type of Mortgage and How It Works	Pros and Cons	Who Benefits
Graduated payment mortgage (GPM). Monthly payments are arranged to start out low but get bigger later, perhaps in a series of steps at specified intervals. The term of the loan and the interest rate remain unchanged.	The main object is to make buying easier in the beginning. Initial payments have to be balanced by larger payments later. One disadvantage: Possible "negative amortization" in the early years, which means that for a time your debt grows instead of diminishing.	Mainly first-time home buyers, who have a hard time becoming homeowners but can reasonably look forward to higher earnings that will enable them to afford the bigger payments coming later.
Variable rate mortgage (VRM). Instead of a fixed interest rate, this loan carries an interest rate that may change within limits—up or down—from time to time during the life of the loan, reflecting changes in market rates for money.	Because the size of the payments you'll have to make in the future is uncertain, this loan is a bit of a gamble. If money rates go down in the future, your payments will go down. But if rates go up, so will your payments.	Helps lenders keep their flow of funds in step with changing conditions, and this in turn could make home loans easier to come by when money is tight. You may get fractionally lower interest at first or other inducements to make future uncertainties more palatable.
Rollover mortgage. The rate of interest is fixed and the size of the monthly payment is fixed, but the whole loan—including principal, rate of interest and term—is renegotiated, or rolled over, at stated intervals, usually every five years.	If interest rates go up, you can expect to be charged more when you renegotiate. But you'll also have opportunity to adjust other aspects of the loan, such as term and principal. Or you can pay off the outstanding balance without penalty. Renegotiation is guaranteed.	Lenders, for the same reason variable rate loans are good for them. Benefits to borrowers are as shown for variable rate loans, with this plus: Periodic renegotiation gives you a chance to rejigger the loan to suit your changing needs without all the expense of refinancing.
Price-level adjusted mortgage (PLAM). The interest rate remains fixed, but the outstanding balance and monthly payments change according to fluctuations in a specified price index.	If interest cost is your big worry, this plan at least ties down the percentage rate. All else remains uncertain, including how much you'll have to pay in toto and each month.	If this plan gets you a loan when you can get one no other way, then it helps you. Otherwise it mainly helps lenders. Not likely to become popular with borrowers.
Reverse annuity mortgage. You take out a loan secured by the accumulated equity in your house. The money is used to purchase an annuity that provides monthly income to you. You continue to live in the house. Its sale pays off the loan.	This is not a plan for putting money *into* a house. It's a plan for taking money *out*. It converts an existing frozen asset into current income that you can use without giving up your house.	Homeowners, principally older and retired people who have paid for or substantially paid for their homes but need additional current income to live on.

Source: Roger LeRoy Miller, *Personal Finance Today,* New York: West Publishing Co., 1979, p. 167.

Table 3-8
Terms on Conventional Home Mortgage Loans Made: National Averages for All Major Types of Lenders

Period	Contract Interest Rate (percent)	Initial Fees and Charges (percent)	Effective Rate (percent)	Term to Maturity (years)	Loan Amount (thousands)	Purchase Price (thousands)	Loan-to-Price Ratio (percent)	Percentage Distribution of Estimated Number of Loans by Loan-to-Price Ratio Class			
								70.0 Percent or Less	70.1-80.0 Percent	80.1-90.0 Percent	Over 90.0 Percent
1977	8.82	1.22	9.02	26.2	36.2	49.5	75.0	NA	NA	NA	NA
1978	9.34	1.30	9.56	26.7	41.2	56.8	74.7	NA	NA	NA	NA
1979	10.60	1.51	10.87	27.4	48.3	68.0	73.5	33	43	18	7
1980	12.48	1.96	12.86	27.2	51.6	73.4	72.7	35	41	16	9

Source: Federal Home Loan Bank Board, *Journal*, July 1981, p. 92.

major features of the conventional loans are also shown in table 3-8: term to the term to maturity in years (or the length of the mortgage loan), the loan amount (the amount of the mortgage loan), the purchase price of the home, and ratio of the loan to purchase price of the home.

The rate on FHA-insured loans[56] is based on opinion reports of the seventy-five FHA field offices on prevailing conditions in their localities as of the first of the month.[57] Yields are derived from secondary market prices for thirty-year-minimum-down payment FHA-insured first mortgages with minimum down payment and an assumed prepayment at the end of fifteen years. The mortgages are for immediate delivery in the secondary market. Gaps in monthly data are caused by periods of adjustment to changes in maximum permissible contract interest rate. The data represent the gross yield to the investor—that is, yield to the purchaser before deduction of servicing costs.[58]

Data Available: Data for terms on conventional home mortgage loans, compiled by the Federal Home Loan Bank Board, are available for all home loans made, for the purchases of newly built homes, and for the purchase of previously occupied homes.[59] The data are available on a national basis, for states, and for thirty-two standard metropolitan statistical areas.[60]

The yields on FHA-insured loans in the secondary market are available on a national and regional basis. Each of the seventy-five field offices is classified into one of six geographic regions, and a yield is derived for each of the six regions.

When Series Become Available: Yields on conventional mortgages compiled by the Federal Home Loan Bank Board are published on a monthly basis and become available with a lag of about one month.

Yields on FHA mortgages in the secondary market are published monthly by the Department of Housing and Urban Development and become available with a lag of about two weeks.

Publications: Current Data:

Council of Economic Advisers, *Economic Indicators*, Washington, D.C.: U.S. Government Printing Office. Monthly. [For conventional mortgages]

Department of Housing and Urban Development, *Secondary Market Prices and Yields*, statistical release. Monthly. [For FHA-insured mortgages]

Federal Home Loan Bank Board, *Journal*. Monthly. [For conventional mortgages]

Publications: Historical Data:

Council of Economic Advisers, *Economic Report of the President*, Washington, D.C.: U.S. Government Printing Office. Annual. See statistical appendix.

Data for conventional mortgages are available from 1963. They can be obtained by writing to the Federal Home Loan Bank Board, Office of Policy and Economic Research, Statistical Analysis Division, 1700 G Street, N.W., Washington, D.C.   20552. Data for FHA-insured mortgages can be obtained from: Department of Housing and Urban Development, Office of Financial Management, Financial Analysis Division, Washington, D.C. 20410.

References:

Larkins, Daniel J., "Recent Developments in Mortgage Markets," *Survey of Current Business*, February 1982, U.S. Department of Commerce, Bureau of Economic Analysis, pp. 19-36.

Mail and Telephone Reference:

Conventional Mortgages:

Federal Home Loan Bank Board
Office of Policy and Economic Research
Statistical Analysis Division
1700 G Street, N.W.
Washington, D.C.   20552
(202) 377-6769

FHA-Insured Mortgages

Department of Housing and Urban Development
Public Affairs
451 7th Street, S.W.
Washington, D.C.   20410
(202) 755-5284

Municipal Bonds and Municipal Bond Indexes

Issuing Agency: Various private organizations.

Coverage and Source: State bonds are issued by the fifty state governments; municipal bonds are issued by cities, townships, and school districts and for special purposes and by special authorities.[61] These bonds differ in their issue purpose and their maturity schedule. Municipal bonds are usually issued in serial form; for example, one group matures a year after issue, another two years after issue, and so on.

Municipal bonds can generally be divided into two categories: general-obligation bonds and revenue bonds. General-obligation bonds are backed by the full faith and credit (meaning the taxing power) of their issuing agency. Revenue bonds are backed by the proceeds from a specific tax and/or revenues from the project. Revenue bonds, for example, are issued to finance capital expenditures of public utilities, public transportation, new sewer systems, the purchase and/or construction of industrial facilities, and various housing projects..

Interest on municipal bonds is exempt from federal income taxes and in some cases from state taxes as well. As a result, such issues can be sold to yield a considerably lower rate of interest than that required from taxable securities. It also lowers the cost of financing to the issuer, in effect providing a federal subsidy to agencies permitted to issue tax-exempt bonds.

Differences in yields among the bonds and notes of state and local governments reflect risk differences, as well as varying maturities. Several private organizations rate securities for credit quality.

Municipal bonds are usually offered by the issuer on a negotiated or competitively bid basis. The underwriting group then reoffers the securities to the public, either publicly through the public market or privately to a particular lender.

Several organizations compile representative yields for different categories of tax-exempt bonds. Yield indexes compiled by three organizations are particularly widely used: the Bond Buyer, Moody's Investor Service, and Standard & Poor's Corp. Typically the index is an average of the yield of selected bonds in a specific category. The indexes tend to be reasonably representative of the rates for the underlying group.[62]

The Bond Buyer compiles a weekly index for general-obligation bonds, issued by twenty state and local governments of mixed credit quality. The computations do not necessarily refer to specific issues. The yields are applicable to bonds selling near par with about twenty years to maturity. Ratings of the issues in the index are in the top four classifications, according to Moody's Investors Service (Aaa, Aa, A, and Baa), and are concentrated in the second and third categories. The index is based on figures for Thursday.[63]

144

Moody's Investors Service prepares municipal-bond yield averages for long-term bonds (about twenty years to maturity) for tax-exempt long-term bonds in each of the four highest rating groups: AAA, AA, A, and Baa. The yields to maturity have been compiled weekly since December 1936.[64] An average or composite municipal yield is reported as well.[65]

The averages have been constructed from a small sample of selected general market issues.[66] About twenty general-obligation issues are included in the composite (five in each of the four quality rating groups). The yield for each group is an unweighted arithmetic average for the five bonds included and are computed from Thursday closing asked quotations and adjusted as necessary for abnormally wide spreads between bid and asked quotations and for other distorting factors.

Standard & Poor's Corporation publishes an index of high-quality municipal bonds. The index is based on an arithmetic average of approximately fifteen high-grade bonds. For the most part, the bonds are serial issues with about a twenty-year period to maturity and are selected to maintain representative regional distribution.[67]

The Prime Rate

Issuing Agency: Board of Governors of the Federal Reserve System.

Coverage and Source: The prime rate is the interest rate charged by banks for money lent to businesses with high credit ratings.[68] The posted prime rate is usually lower than most other commercial interest rates because there is very little risk of nonpayment and relatively few expenses are incurred by the lending bank in investigating the credit worthiness of the borrowing company.

The prime rate has come to serve several primary functions since it was originated in 1933. It is the interest rate applicable to the most credit-worthy customers of a bank, the base to which higher interest rates on many non-prime bank loans are tied, and an index for floating-rate bank loans (contracts that allow interest charges to fluctuate with market rates over the period of the loan). Over the years, banks tried to adopt lending practices that would permit the prime rate to serve its multiple tasks. Difficulties developed, however, which can make the prime rate a misleading indicator of the actual or effective rate paid on a loan by a bank's most credit-worthy customer.[69]

Borrowers in the prime lending category have become more heterogenous, broadening the idea of the most credit-worthy customer. At the same time, the floating-rate function of the prime rate has become increasingly important as the levels of interest rates have risen and fluctuations have become more pronounced. Under these conditions, banks started lending to some customers at special rates below the prime (for example, in 1977 when loan demand was slack). Much of the below-prime lending appeared to be the result of pricing policies introduced by large banks to meet competition from the commercial paper market, finance companies, and branches and agencies of foreign banks.

Banks sometimes require that borrowers maintain compensating balances, which are deposits that must be held with the bank, as a condition for obtaining a loan. Suppose that the General Motors Acceptance Corporation (GMAC) wants a $10 million loan from Citibank. Assume that Citibank agrees to issue the loan at the published 12 percent prime rate. Suppose that it requires GMAC to leave $1 million in a noninterest-bearing checking account. The true interest payment is therefore $1.2 million for borrowing, effectively, only $9 million that is, GMAC would end up paying 13 1/3 percent, and not the published 12 percent. Unless one knows what compensating balances are required for any type of bank loan, one cannot be sure that the reported interest rate is the actual interest charge paid.

Banks in other countries quote prime rates; however, lending practices differ among countries so the rates may not be directly comparable.

146

The prime rate can differ among banks. The prime rate quoted by a bank is determined under the discretion of the officers of the bank in accord with market conditions and competition from other sources of loans. "The" prime rate, which is widely quoted as the prevailing level of the prime, is the level quoted by most large major banks. The weekly figures represent bank-statement week averages, averages for the week ending Wednesday.

When Series Become Available: Estimates are available on Monday for the week ending the previous Saturday. For the approximate release dates see also, each year, the June issue of Board of Governors of the Federal Reserve System, *Federal Reserve Bulletin*.

Publications: Current Data:

Council of Economic Advisers, *Economic Indicators*, Washington, D.C.: U.S. Government Printing Office. Monthly.
Board of Governors of the Federal Reserve System, *Federal Reserve Bulletin*. Monthly.
Board of Governors of the Federal Reserve System, *Selected Interest Rates*, H.15 (519) statistical release. Weekly.
Board of Governors of the Federal Reserve System, *Selected Interest Rates*, G.13 (415) statistical release. Monthly.

Publications: Historical Data:

Council of Economic Advisers, *Economic Report of the President*, Washington, D.C.: U.S. Government Printing Office. Annual. See statistical appendix.
Board of Governors of the Federal Reserve System, *Banking and Monetary Statistics, 1941-1970*, 1976.[70]
Board of Governors of the Federal Reserve System, *Annual Statistical Digest, 1970-79*, 1981.
Board of Governors of the Federal Reserve System, *Annual Statistical Digest, 1980*, 1981.
Board of Governors of the Federal Reserve System, *Annual Statistical Digest, 1981*, 1982.

References:

"Bank Loan Charges," *Business Conditions*, Federal Reserve Bank of Chicago, June 1974, pp. 14-15.
Gendreau, Brian C., "When Is the Prime Rate Second Choice?", *Business Review*, May/June 1983, Federal Reserve Bank of Philadelphia, pp. 13-23.

Merris, Randall C., "Prime Rate," *Business Conditions*, Federal Reserve Bank of Chicago, April 1975, pp. 3-12.

Merris, Randall C., "Prime Rate Revisited," *Economic Perspectives*, Federal Reserve Bank of Chicago, July 1977, p. 17.

Merris, Randall C., "Prime Rate Update," *Economic Perspectives*, Federal Reserve Bank of Chicago, May 1978, pp. 14-16.

Mail and Telephone Reference:

Board of Governors of the Federal Reserve System
Division of Research and Statistics
20th and Constitution Ave., N.W.
Washington, D.C.   20551
(202) 452-3000

Bond Ratings and Commercial Paper Ratings

Issuing Agency: Moody's Investors Service, Standard & Poor's Corp., Fitch Investors Service.

Coverage and Source: Several firms rate corporate bonds, municipal bonds, and commercial paper for credit quality. They also rate securities offered by foreign or international issuers. Hundreds of corporations and municipalities issue debt; moreover, debt issued by individual firms may offer different security pledges or different creditor standings, in case of bankruptcy, and different provisions such as convertibility or call features. The task facing an individual investor in assessing the credit risk of different firms or municipalities, or one firm that may offer a variety of different debt instruments, is formidable, if not impossible. Several firms perform this function; Standard & Poor's Corp., Moody's Investors Service, and Fitch Investors Service rate securities. After analyzing the information about an issue offered by a company, the rating service assigns a letter symbol to the issue denoting the relative credit risk.

Moody's ratings consist of nine different classes and grades ranging from Aaa (best quality) to Baa (lower medium quality) to Caa (poor standing) to C (extremely poor prospects).[71] The rating scales of the individual companies are well known among investors. Knowledge of the symbol transmits to investors information about the credit risk associated with the issue. Ratings services continue to monitor the performance of companies whose issues they rate and when appropriate upgrade or downgrade the ratings assigned to those issues.

The rating services are independent firms. The rating companies charge a fee for the service they perform. Companies sometimes have more than one service rate their securities. Ratings are not an indication of whether to buy a security; they look at only one aspect of the security: credit quality. Many other features enter the decision-making process; most important is the trade-off between risk and return an issuer is willing to undertake in the overall portfolio.

Publications:

Moody's Investors Service, *Moody's Bond Record*, New York: Moody's Investors Service. Monthly.
Standard & Poor's Corp., *CreditWeek*, Ephrata, PA: Standard & Poor's Corp. Weekly.

References:

Standard & Poor's Ratings Guide: Corporate Bonds, Commercial Paper, Municipal Bonds, International Securities, McGraw-Hill Book Co., New York, 1979.

Moody's Investors Service publishes an annual bound *Manual* in each of six areas of specialization: bond and finance, industrial international, over-the-counter industrial, public utility, and transportation. Each *Manual* describes the ratings and lists ratings for securities issued by different companies.

Reserves: Required, Excess, and Borrowed, Nonborrowed

Issuing Agency: Board of Governors of the Federal Reserve System, Banking Section.

Coverage: Depository institutions are required to maintain a specified percentage of their customer deposits as reserves. For example, if the required level of reserves is 20 percent and a bank has $1 billion in customer deposits, it must have at least $200 million as reserves. These reserves can be either deposits with the district Federal Reserve bank or vault cash. Nonmember banks and other depository institutions may also treat as reserves their deposits with a correspondent depository institution holding required reserves at a Federal Reserve bank, deposits with a Federal Home Loan bank, or with the National Credit Union Administration central liquidity facility, if such reserves are passed through to a Federal Reserve bank.[72]

Legal reserves constitute anything that depository institutions are allowed by law to claim as reserves. Currently that consists of only deposits held at the district Federal Reserve bank plus vault cash. Government bonds, for example, are not legal reserves, even though the owners and managers of the member bank may consider them to be a type of reserve since they can easily be turned into cash should the need arise to meet unusually large net withdrawals by clients.

Total or legal reserves can be subdivided in a variety of ways. Two of the most frequently used classifications of total reserves are required and excess reserves, and nonborrowed and borrowed reserves.

Required reserves are the minimum amount of legal reserves—cash plus deposits at the Fed—that a member bank must have to back its deposits. Required reserves are reserves that depository institutions must hold, on average each week, either as vault cash or on deposit with the Federal Reserve bank. Required reserves are expressed as a ratio (in percentage terms) of required reserves to total deposits.[73]

Depository institutions often hold reserves in excess of what is required by law. This difference between actual (legal) reserves and required reserves is called *excess reserves*. Since reserves produce no income, profit-seeking financial institutions have an incentive to minimize any excess reserves. For example, they can use them to purchase income-producing securities or to make loans with which they earn income through interest payments. In equation form, total reserves can be defined as: total or legal reserves = required reserves + excess reserves.

If a depository institution wants to increase its reserves, it can borrow reserves from the Federal Reserve itself. The depository institution asks the district Federal Reserve bank for a loan of a certain amount of reserves. The Fed charges these institutions for any reserves that it lends the institution.[74] These reserves are known as *borrowed reserves*. The interest rate that the Fed charges used to be called the *rediscount rate*, but now it is typically called the *discount rate*. In most other English-speaking countries, it is called the *bank rate*.

Until passage of the Monetary Control Act of 1980, the discounting privilege was available only to commercial banks that were members of the Federal Reserve system. The new legislation required depository institutions to maintain reserves against transaction and nonpersonal time deposits. In addition, these institutions were granted access to the discount window.

Federal Reserve banks make credit available to depository institutions for different reasons and for different lengths of time. To ensure that credit is extended for the appropriate purposes, guidelines have been developed as a basis for granting loans. The purposes of the loan can be classified into four categories:

1. Adjustment credit is available to meet unexpected temporary credit demands caused by sudden deposit withdrawals or unanticipated increase in loan demand.
2. Seasonal credit is available to depository institutions with deposit levels below specified totals that have seasonal patterns in their deposits in loans.
3. Emergency credit is available to depository institutions with severe financial difficulties.
4. Extended credit is available for depository institutions with financial difficulties caused by exceptional circumstances such as sudden deposit withdrawals, impaired access to money-market funds, or sudden deterioration in loan repayments.

For purposes of monetary policy, the key feature of depository institutions' borrowing from Federal Reserve banks is that borrowing from the Fed increases reserves and thereby aids depository institutions' abilities to engage in deposit creation, thus increasing the money supply.

Depository institutions do not often borrow reserves from the Federal Reserve because the Fed will not lend them all they want. In addition, the Fed can refuse to lend reserves even when the depository institutions need the reserves to make their reserve account meet legal requirements.

Nonborrowed reserves are reserves held by depository institutions that have not been borrowed from the Federal Reserve banks.

In equation form, we can classify total or legal reserves as follows: total or legal reserves = borrowed reserves + nonborrowed reserves.

Data Available: The values of the reserve measures and components are available on a monthly and weekly basis. They are reported in two forms: adjusted for changes in reserve requirements (and seasonally adjusted) and not adjusted for changes in reserve requirements (and not seasonally adjusted).

Required and excess reserves are reported for all commercial banks, U.S. agencies and branches, and all other institutions.

Alternatively, total reserves can be calculated by combining specified components from the consolidated balance sheet of the Federal Reserve banks and the Treasury.[75]

Source of Data: All depository institutions are subject to reserve requirements. The procedure through which reserve requirements are calculated, thereby also determining excess reserves, and transmitted to the Federal Reserve System and affected institutions can be illustrated by describing the procedure followed by member banks.[76]

At the end of the settlement week (each seven-day period ending in Wednesday), member banks send written reports to Federal Reserve banks indicating the amount of their liabilities, subject to reserve requirements. They also indicate the amount of vault cash for each day. The Federal Reserve banks then send reports to member banks indicating the average reserve balances they must hold for the coming settlement week (Thursday through Wednesday).

When Series Become Available: Estimates of reserves become available on Monday for the week ended the previous Wednesday. For the estimated release dates see also, each year, the June issue of the Board of Governors of the Federal Reserve System, *Federal Reserve Bulletin.*

Publications: Current Data:

Council of Economic Advisers, *Economic Indicators*, Washington, D.C.: U.S. Government Printing Office. Monthly.

Board of Governors of the Federal Reserve System, *Aggregate Reserves of Depository Institutions and Monetary Base*, H.3 (502) statistical release. Weekly.

Board of Governors of the Federal Reserve System, *Federal Reserve Bulletin*. Monthly.

Publications: Historical Data: The most up-to-date back data and estimates of the impact on required reserves and changes in reserve requirements are available from the Banking Section, Division of Research and Statistics, Board of Governors of the Federal Reserve System, Washington, D.C. 20551.

Mail and Telephone Reference:

Board of Governors of the Federal Reserve System
Division of Research and Statistics
20th and Constitution Ave., N.W.
Washington, D.C.   20551
(202) 452-3000

Stock Price Indexes

Issuing Agency: Various private organizations.

Coverage, Data Available, and Source: The prices of individual stocks fluctuate from day to day, yet it is difficult, if not impossible, to describe how the market or some group of stocks performed without looking at some representative measure of changes in stock prices.[77] How did the market do today? How does it compare with what it did yesterday? What would an unmanaged portfolio have returned last year? These are some of the questions answered by stock-market indexes.

There are a wide variety of stock-market indexes. They differ in the stocks included, the weighting given to the individual stocks, and the procedures used to compute the indexes. The 1981 averages of seven composite stock price indexes are shown in table 3-9. Clearly the values all differ; moreover, the number of points equivalent to a 1 percent change differs among the indexes. But the function of all these averages is the same: to give a general rather than a precise idea of fluctuations in the securities markets and to reflect the historical continuity of security price movements.

Perhaps the most-common misconception about the averages is that they reflect the true dollar value of stocks or the actual degree of increase in a given day of trading. In fact, the averages are a generalization, an overview of market performance, values as a measure of trading conditions rather than a specific reference to actual stock prices.[78]

Dow Jones Averages: Dow Jones publishes an index of stock prices for thirty industrial stocks, twenty transportation stocks, fifteen utility stocks, and for a composite of the sixty-five stocks that make up the other three averages. Although all use the same general methodology, the Dow Jones

Table 3-9
Selected Composite Stock-Price Indexes, 1981 Averages

Dow Jones Composite	364.61
Standard & Poor's 500	128.05
New York Stock Exchange Composite	74.02
American Stock Exchange Market Value Index	361.05
NASDAQ Over-the-Counter Composite	214.98
Value Line Index	155.60
Wilshire 5000 Equity	1,395.75

Industrial Average is probably the best-known indicator of market performance. It has been used since the end of the nineteenth century, when it was constructed by Charles Dow.

The stocks in the industrial average were selected on the basis of their total market value, broad public ownership, and high quality. In short, the index is aimed at reflecting representative price movements of mature, blue-chip stocks.[79]

The first index was constructed by taking a simple mathematical average of closing prices. For example, if there are three stocks (A, B, and C) selling at $5, $15, and $10, respectively, the average price of all three is $10—their total value divided by 3:

$$\frac{5 + 15 + 10}{3} = 10.$$

With increased pace and volatility in stock transactions, new formulas were necessary to reflect market conditions more accurately. The rise in stock prices that accompanied business growth prompted the practice of stock splitting, distorting the picture of market performance presented by figuring a simple average of stock prices.[80]

In addition, infrequent changes are made in the stocks that make up the index in order to make it more representative of market performance. For example, the first major revision to the industrial index in twenty years occurred on June 29, 1979, when International Business Machines and Merk displaced Chrysler and Esmark.

The Dow Jones averages are computed by summing the closing prices of the stocks in the index and then dividing by a constant. This means that the index is price weighted and emphasizes high-priced stocks relative to low-priced stocks. Thus if a company's share price falls, the weight of that company in the index falls and vice versa. The constant or divisor reflects the effect of adjustments necessary to correct the index for distortions that occur when stocks in the index are split or have significant stock dividends. The divisor was originally equal to the number of stocks in the index or one share for each of the thirty stocks. At that time the index represented the average price of the thirty stocks. Over the years, however, many of the thirty stocks have split and have been replaced, requiring adustments to the index to eliminate distortions. The effect of the adjustment on the index is to assume that the extra shares are sold and the proceeds invested in an equal share amount of each of the thirty stocks. As a result, instead of corresponding to one share of each of thirty stocks, the hypothetical portfolio by 1983 consisted of around twenty-three shares of each stock (the divisor has declined from 30 to about 1.3 as a result of adjustments). The effect of the adjustment procedure prevents a precise, easy interpretation of the average. In general, the indexes reflect the price movements of mature blue-chip stocks.

Standard & Poor's Indexes: Standard & Poor's Corporation (S&P's) has been calculating stock-price indexes since 1923. One of the most widely used, which S&P's began publishing in 1957, is Standard & Poor's 500 stock index, a value-weighted index of 500 stocks. Most of the stocks are listed on the New York Stock Exchange. Each of these stocks is weighted by the market value of its outstanding shares, and since about 75 percent of the value of all stocks listed on the New York Stock Exchange are included, the index is representative of activity in this sphere of the capital markets. The index includes 400 industrial (formerly 425), 20 transportation (formerly 15 rail), 40 public utility (formerly 60), and 40 financial companies.[81] Standard & Poor's also publishes an Industrial Index, Transportation Index, Public Utility Index, and a Financial Index.

The Standard & Poor's indexes, such as the S&P 500, are not expressed in dollars per share but as an index number. The average market value of the stocks over the 1941-1943 period was arbitrarily assigned an index number of 10. Thus, if the average aggregate market value in the 1941-1943 period was around $44 billion and the aggregate market value doubled by 1950 to about $88 billion, the index would double from 10 to 20. In effect, the ratio of the aggregate current market value of the 500 stocks to the value of the stocks in the base period 1941-1943 is multiplied by 10 to come up with the current value of the index—for example, [($88 billion/$44 billion) × 10 = 20].

So that the indexes will reflect only fluctuations in current market values, adjustments in the base-period value are made when necessary to offset the effect of issuance of rights, consolidations, and acquisitions. The base is also adjusted when there are additions to or deletions from the list of stocks in the index.

New York Stock Exchange Indexes: On July 14, 1966, the New York Stock Exchange (NYSE) began to publish indexes of the prices of all common stocks listed on the exchange. These include a composite index covering all of the more than 1,250 common stocks listed and four separate indexes representing broad industry components of the whole list: the Transportation Index (rail, airline, shipping, motor transport, and other transportation companies); the Utility Index (operating, holding, and transmission companies in gas, electric power, and communications); the Financial Index (financial, banking, insurance, closed and investment, and similar companies); and the Industrial Index (the remaining companies on the New York Stock Exchange).[82]

The NYSE indexes are designed to measure changes in the aggregate value of the listed stocks and are adjusted to eliminate the effect of capitalization changes, new listings, and old listings. The method for calculating the NYSE indexes is similar to that used in the S&P's indexes. The relative importance of each stock is obtained by multiplying the stock price by the number of shares in the company. The values of individual issues are then totaled to obtain the aggregate market value of all stocks. This is then related to base-market value and expressed as an index.

The base selected was the close of the market on December 31, 1965. The indexes were deliberately set at 50 for that date so that the index level for all issues would start reasonably close to their actual average price. (On the base date, the actual average price of all common stocks listed on the exchange was $53.33.) For example, if the average price of all stocks listed on the exchange doubled between 1965 and 1980, the index value would rise from 50 to 100.

In order to keep the current index numbers comparable to the base period, the base-market values are adjusted daily to correct for the effect of stock splits, rights offerings, and so on.[83]

Value Line Indexes: Value Line publishes a popular set of stock price indexes: a composite and one for each of three groups—industrials, rails, and utilities.[84] The composite covers about 1,700 stocks. The indexes are all based on the same method of calculation. Value Line indexes are based on a geometric mean rather than an arithmetic mean and is recalculated daily.[85] In effect, the index implicitly assumes that all of the stocks in the index (implicit portfolio) are sold off at the end of each day—those that do well, as well as those that perform less well—and equal dollar amounts are maintained in each stock.[86]

The Value Line Composite Index is based to June 30, 1961 equals 100. The daily closing price of each stock is expressed as a ratio of the previous day's closing price. The ratios are averaged geometrically; the resulting geometric mean daily price ratio is compounded on an index basis, starting with the base period June 30, 1961, equal to 100.

Other Stock Price Indexes: Other market-value-weighted indexes for U.S. stocks are also computed. The American Stock Exchange (AMEX) computes an index based on the average market values of all of its stocks. The AMEX index is based to August 31, 1973, equals 100.[87] The National Association of Securities Dealers, using its Automated Quotation Service (NASDAQ), computes indexes based on the market value of more than 2,000 over-the-counter stocks (industrial, bank, insurance, other finance, transportation, utilities, and a composite index).[88] The NASDAQ Index is based to February 5, 1971, equals 100. Wilshire Associates computes the

Wilshire 5000 Equity Index, which indicates the total market value of all stocks listed on the New York and American Stock exchanges plus those actively traded over the counter.[89] It is indexed in billions of dollars.

Capital International Perspective publishes market-value-weighted indexes using various combinations of 1,100 stocks from eighteen different countries.[90] An overall World Index is provided, along with eighteen national and thirty-eight international industry indexes. The 1,100 stocks account for approximately 60 percent of the aggregate market value of all stocks listed on the national exchanges of the countries represented. Month-end values, adjusted for changes in foreign-exchange rates, are used to compute returns in U.S. dollars and in other currencies.

Related Series: Daily stock prices are available in book form for individual companies traded on the New York Stock Exchange, the American Stock Exchange, and over the counter. Daily prices of companies traded on the New York Stock Exchange and the American Stock Exchange are available from the first quarter of 1962 and for companies traded over the counter from the first quarter of 1968.[91]

Publications: Specific references are cited in the discussion of each stock-price index.

References:

American Stock Exchange, "Amex Introduces New Market Value Index System: Includes Trends by Industry and Region," 1973. (Address: 86 Trinity Place, New York, NY   10006.)

Butler, Hartman L. and J. Devon Allen, "The Dow Jones Indusrial Average Reexamined," *Financial Analysts Journal*, November-December 1979, pp. 23-30.

Dow Jones & Company, Education Service Bureau, *The Dow Jones Averages: A Non-professional's Guide.* (Address: P.O. Box 300, Princeton, NJ   09540).

Latané, Henry A. and Donald L. Tuttle, *Security Analysis and Portfolio Management*, New York: The Ronald Press, Co., 1970.

Rudd, Andrew T., "The Revised Dow Jones Industrial Average: New Wine in Old Bottles?," *Financial Analysts Journal*, November-December 1979, pp. 57-63.

Standard & Poor's Corp., *Statistical Service: Security Price Index Record*, New York: Standard & Poor's Corp., 1980.

U.S. Treasury Securities: Bills, Notes, and Bonds

Issuing Agency: Board of Governors of the Federal Reserve System.

Coverage and Source: To meet its financing requirements, the federal government can issue three types of securities: Treasury bills, Treasury notes, and Treasury bonds. All of these securities are obligations of the U.S. government.[92]

Two attractive features of Treasury securities (also called U.S. government securities) are their safety and liquidity. Since they are backed by the taxing power of the U.S. government, the risk of default is negligible. There is also an active secondary or resale market in U.S. government securities, so they can be sold fairly easily. Although interest on Treasury securities is subject to federal income taxes, it is exempt from state and local income taxes.

The Treasury sells securities to the public through the twelve Federal Reserve banks and their branches. The securities can also be purchased through commercial banks or financial institutions; however, a fee is usually charged for this service.

New Treasury securities are sold through an auction procedure; individuals wishing to obtain securities can make either a competitive or noncompetitive bid. Competitive bids are ordinarily submitted by professionals skilled in the buying of securities. Noncompetitive bids are usually submitted by small bidders or inexperienced investors. With the noncompetitive bid, prospective purchasers are not required to state a price or yield. Instead, they indicate the amount of securities they wish to purchase and agree to accept the average price or yield established in the auction.

There is also an active resale or secondary market in Treasury securities that centers around three dozen dealers that report daily activity to the Federal Reserve Bank of New York (about one-third of these dealers are commercial banks and the other two-thirds are nonbank dealers). Reporting dealers conduct a sigificant amount of business in Treasury securities with customers and with other dealers, operate in significant volume in most maturity areas of the market, and are adequately capitalized and managed by responsible personnel.

In the dealer market, most trading is transacted over the telephone. There is no centralized marketplace, such as an exchange. The market is made up of a decentralized group of firms, each willing to quote prices for the purchase and sale of treasury securities.

Treasury bills are issued with maturities of three, six, and twelve months and are available in minimum denomination of $10,000 and multiples of $5,000 above the minimum. Treasury bills are issued only in book-entry form. Purchasers receive a receipt rather than an engraved security as evidence of their purchase. Ownership is electronically recorded in a book-entry account established for purchasers at the Treasury.

Treasury notes have an original maturity of more than one year and less than ten years, and bonds can be any maturity but are usually more than ten years. Notes and bonds are generally issued in minimum denominations of $1,000 and $5,000 (notes with original maturities of less than four years are not issued in denominations of less than $5,000).

Notes and bonds are issued in two forms: registered and bearer. Bearer instruments are payable to anyone in possession of the securities. Registered securities are registered with respect to interest and principal and bear the owner's name on the face of the security.

Yields on Treasury bills are quoted on a bank-discount basis (360-day year) rather than on an investment yield or bond equivalent-yield basis (365-day year), which would give a higher figure. Secondary market rates are based on an unweighted average of closing bid rates, quoted by at least five dealers.

Yields on Treasury notes and bonds, following the usual convention, are calculated on an investment yield. The yields are based on the unweighted average of closing bid prices, quoted by at least five dealers. The Federal Reserve publishes several interest rates on Treasury notes and bonds assuming constant maturity. For example, it publishes an interest rate for Treasury securities with a time to maturity of four years and an interest rate for Treasury securities with a time to maturity of five years. In effect, the yields are adjusted to constant maturities by the U.S. Treasury. To do this, the yields are read from a yield curve at fixed maturities and are based only on recently issued, actively traded securities.[93]

When Series Become Available: Estimates are available on Monday for the week ending the previous Saturday. For the approximate release dates see also, each year, the June issue of Board of Governors of the Federal Reserve System, *Federal Reserve Bulletin.*

Publications: Current Data:

Council of Economic Advisers, *Economic Indicators*, Washington, D.C.: U.S. Government Printing Office. Monthly.

Board of Governors of the Federal Reserve System, *Federal Reserve Bulletin.* Monthly.

Board of Governors of the Federal Reserve System, *Selected Interest Rates*, H.15 (419) statistical release. Weekly.

Board of Governors of the Federal Reserve System, *Selected Interest Rates*, G.13 (415) statistical release. Monthly.

Publications: Historical Data:

Council of Economic Advisers, *Economic Report of the President*, Washington, D.C.: U.S. Government Printing Office. Annual. See statistical appendix.

Board of Governors of the Federal Reserve System, *Annual Statistical Digest, 1972-76*, 1977.

Board of Governors of the Federal Reserve System, *Annual Statistical Digest, 1974-78*, 1980.

Board of Governors of the Federal Reserve System, *Annual Statistical Digest, 1970-79*, 1981.

Board of Governors of the Federal Reserve System, *Annual Statistical Digest, 1980*, 1981.

Board of Governors of the Federal Reserve System, *Annual Statistical Digest, 1981*, 1982.

References:

Cook, Timothy Q., and Jimmie R. Monhollon, "Treasury Bills," *Instruments of the Money Market*, Federal Reserve Bank of Richmond, 1981. (No charge for this book.)

Garbade, Kenneth, "Electronic Quotation Systems and the Market for Government Securities," Federal Reserve Bank of New York, *Quarterly Review*, Summer 1978, p. 13.

McCurdy, Christopher, "The Dealer Market for U.S. Government Securities," *Quarterly Review*, Federal Reserve Bank of New York, Winter 1977-1978; also in *Instruments of the Money Market,* Federal Reserve Bank of Richmond, 1981. (No charge for this book.)

Tucker, James, *Buying Treasury Securities at Federal Reserve Banks*, Federal Reserve Bank of Richmond, 1980.

Mail and Telephone Reference:

Board of Governors of the Federal Reserve System
Division of Research and Statistics
20th and Constitution Ave., N.W.
Washington, D.C.   20551
(202) 452-3000

Notes

1. For example, consider an importer purchasing merchandise from abroad. Typically, the exporter or seller wants payment immediately, while the importer or buyer wants to pay later (when the merchandise arrives). The exporter (seller) sends the merchandise to a shipping firm, and the

goods are forwarded. The importer (buyer) asks its bank to issue a letter of credit in favor of (extending credit to) the exporter (seller). The bank issues the letter (if the importer's credit standing is satisfactory), authorizing the foreign seller to draw a draft on it for payment of the merchandise. The exporter (seller) can present the letter of credit to its bank, along with shipping documents. The exporter (seller) can then receive payment immediately by discounting the draft with his or her bank. The exporter's bank usually ships the documents to its U.S. correspondent who presents them to the importer-buyer's bank for acceptance.

2. The Board of Governors of the Federal Reserve System also publishes, in addition to interest rates, *Maturity Distribution of Outstanding Negotiable Time Certificates of Deposit*, G.9 statistical release. The data are released around the twentieth of each month for the previous month.

3. As of the early 1980s, there were about nine major commerical paper dealers.

4. From highest to lowest quality, paper ratings run: P-1, P-2, P-3 for Moody's; A-1+, A-1, A-2, A-3 for Standard & Poor's; and F-1, F-2, F-3 for Fitch.

5. Another volume of historical statistics is also available: Board of Governors of the Federal Reserve System, *Banking and Monetary Statistics, 1914-1941*, 1976; however, only part I is available.

6. This section is taken largely from Board of Governors of the Federal Reserve System, *Banking and Monetary Statistics, 1941-1970*, 1976, pp. 1051-1079.

7. In this sense, consumer credit can be either an advance of funds for the purchase of goods or services or an advance of goods and services in exchange for a promise to pay later.

8. In late 1975, the board stopped publishing figures on total consumer credit and noninstallment credit (credit scheduled to be repaid in a lump sum, including single-payment loans, charge accounts, and service credit). In a note to the tables published on consumer installment credit, however, the board does publish annual noininstallment credit outstanding for the past several years.

9. More precisely, it covers most short- and intermediate-term credit extended to individuals through regular business channels, usually to finance the purchases of consumer goods and services or to refinance debts incurred for such purposes, and scheduled to be repaid (or with the option of repayment) in two or more installments. Published estimates of installment credit outstanding generally include the financing charges on such credit and the cost of insurance or other fees included in the credit contract.

10. For a detailed description of the source of consumer credit and the methods used to compile estimates, see *Banking and Monetary Statistics, 1941-1970*, pp. 1051-1079. Some of the information in this article is out of date, or the technique may have changed. At the time of this writing, how-

ever, this is the most-current description of the series that has been published. For a more-timely article on finance companies only, see Evelyn M. Hurley, "Survey of Finance Companies, 1980," *Federal Reserve Bulletin*, May 1981, Board of Governors of the Federal Reserve System, pp. 398-407.

11. The amount of outstanding credit represents the sum of the balances in the accounts. The difference between credit extended and liquidated (repaid) during any period is equal to the change in the outstanding balance during the period, after allowances for losses and charge-offs.

12. Net change equals extensions minus liquidations (repayments, charge-offs, and other credit). Yearly, noninstallment credit is published as a note to the tables on installment credit.

13. See Board of Governors of the Federal Reserve System, *Finance Rates on Selected Consumer Installment Loans at Reporting Commercial Banks*, E.12 (122) statistical release. The data are released quarterly with a lag of about two weeks. Thus, estimates released around the fifteenth of March, June, September, and December are for the months of February, May, August, and November, respectively.

14. A copy of the historical data can be obtained from Nellie Middleton or Jim Pflueger, MAC Finance Section, Division of Research and Statistics, Board of Governors of the Federal Reserve System, Washington, D.C. 20551.

15. Several private organizations rate corporate bonds by credit quality.

16. Market yields indicate the percentage rate of return to investors on securities purchased at current market prices and held to maturity (taking into account the effect of differences in the length of time to maturity and in coupon rates). Those yields, however, do not necessarily reflect the return realized by purchasers on other dates or by investors who dispose of their obligations before maturity, because of the capital gains or losses arising out of subsequent price changes.

Yields do not necessarily reflect the cost of funds to the borrower. When a new security is marketed, its yield is related to the market yield on outstanding issues of comparable quality and terms. The yield on a new issue, however, is generally greater than the yield on outstanding issues by the flotation costs—including underwriters' compensation—and any discount from market price that is necessary to place the issue initially.

In addition to the general level of interest rates, yields on long-term securities also reflect relative supplies of various types of securities, preferences, relative amounts of funds available to investors, and characteristics of the various types of securities, such as the market's evaluation of differences in the underlying risk, marketability, the tax status of the income return to investors, and term to maturity.

17. For example, a lag in yield adjustments between new issues and seasoned issues, noncurrent coupons, and the lack of reliable bid and asked

quotations on seasoned issues. The rates are published monthly in Board of Governors of the Federal Reserve System, *Federal Reserve Bulletin.*

18. Details of the model, the estimation procedures, and a discussion of the results are presented in a Federal Reserve Staff Economic Study, "Obtaining the Yield on a Standard Bond from a Sample of Bonds with Heterogeneous Characteristics," by James L. Kichline, P. Michael Laub, and Guy V.G. Stevens.

19. During the four-week interval, trading is generally active, and reliable quotes are usually available. In addition, coupons on the bonds in the series do not differ appreciably from coupons on bonds in the new-issue market. In contrast, bonds outstanding for significantly longer periods of time often have thin markets and may carry noncurrent coupons. Both of these factors influence the yield and often make seasoned yield indexes less sensitive to current market developments and, at times, less representative of the underlying market situation.

20. *Banking and Monetary Statistics, 1941-1970,* p. 649.

21. For newly issued bond averages, there are a limited number of suitable bonds in some periods. In more extreme cases, no corporates are issued under a particular rating during some months. This tends to happen especially during periods of high interest rates for newly issued low-quality bonds. Moody's leaves those months blank for such bonds (the series is not continuous). Thus, annual averages are not necessarily twelve-month averages. As a result, when yearly yields are calculated by averaging the available monthly figures, it is possible for the yearly yield on high-quality bonds to be above the yield on low-quality bonds. For example, the 1974 yield on Moody's newly issued long-term corporate bonds of high quality (Aa) was 9.23, which was above the 9.14 yield on lower quality (Baa) issues.

22. Current data can also be found in U.S. Department of Commerce, Bureau of Economic Analysis, *Survey of Current Business,* published monthly. Historical data can also be found in U.S. Department of Commerce, Bureau of Economic Analysis, *Business Statistics 1979,* 22nd ed., 1980.

23. Changes in the discount rate are recommended by the board of directors of district Federal Reserve Banks in accord with current economic conditions; final approval is extended by the Board of Governors of the Federal Reserve System.

24. Another volume of historical statistics is also available: Board of Governors of the Federal Reserve System, *Banking and Monetary Statistics, 1914-1941,* 1976; however, only part I is available.

25. The market is also called the Eurocurrency market because it refers to deposits whenever a bank in one country accepts a deposit denominated in the currency of another. This term is also imprecise because non-European countries such as Canada, Japan, and Caribbean countries are active in this market; nevertheless, the term is market convention.

26. Ultimately payment in immediately available funds involves transfers of deposits at Federal Reserve banks (federal reserve deposits). Not everyone, however, can make deposits at a Federal Reserve bank. A Federal Reserve bank is a bankers' bank. These banks maintain Federal Reserve deposits which, in effect, are checking accounts for banks and some other depository institutions. Federal Reserve deposits can be transferred on request, almost instantaneously over an electronic network among Federal Reserve banks located throughout the country. By this means enormous amounts of funds can be transferred the same day transactions occur.

27. By regulation, depository institutions are required to hold reserves against certain liabilities, such as checking accounts (demand deposits). For example, if a bank has demand deposits of liabilities of $100,000 and reserve requirements are 6 percent, the bank must maintain minimum reserves of $6,000 (6 percent of $100,000). These reserves can be held either as vault cash or as Federal Reserve deposits. Under Federal Reserve regulations, depository institutions are not subject to these reserve requirements if they borrow immediately available funds overnight (for one day) from certain institutions such as other commercial banks, federal agencies, savings and loan associations, mutual savings banks, domestic agencies and branches of foreign banks, and to some extent U.S. government security dealers.

28. For example, a bank with funds available to lend might agree through a dealer to buy a specified amount of securities at a stated price and rate. At the same time, the lender simultaneously agrees to resell the same securities to the borrower, with payment and redelivery made on the maturity date of the repurchase agreement. The borrower delivers the securities to the bank or its depository. Sales and purchases are made in federal funds or immediately available funds, and the investing or lending bank receives the interest income for the agreed-on period of time it holds the funds. Repurchase agreements are called several names: *repos*, *buy backs*, and *RPs*.

A reverse repurchase agreement is the opposite or reverse of a repurchase agreement. The distinction refers to the two different sides of viewing the same exchange or transaction. In a repurchase agreement, the recipient sells securities to obtain funds and repurchases the securities at maturity by redelivering the funds. In a reverse repurchase agreement, the opposite occurs: the supplier of funds buys securities by delivering funds and at maturity resells the security for the funds. Reserve repos are sometimes called *reverse RPs* or *matched-sale-purchase agreements*.

29. Interest rates on repurchase agreements are not published by the Federal Reserve.

30. The flow of funds accounts are described in detail in Board of Governors of the Federal Reserve System, *Introduction to Flow of Funds*, 1980.

31. For more detail, see James H. Duprey, "How the Fed Defines and Measures Money," *Quarterly Review*, Spring-Summer 1982, Federal Reserve Bank of Minneapolis, pp. 10-19.

Why are consistent measures of the monetary aggregates important? The actions of the Federal Reserve have a major impact on economic activity and the price level. The effects of the actions cannot be observed apart from other influences such as government spending and taxing policies. The Federal Reserve, thus, must rely on other intermediate variables, such as the money supply and interest rates, to gauge the effects of its policies on the economy. To be reliable, the measure should be stable and predictably related to economic activity and subject to Federal Reserve control.

Recent technological and regulatory changes in the U.S. financial markets have been changing the relationships temporarily. As a result, the impact of monetary policy on economic activity has become more difficult to assess than in the past. For example, because of the increases in the variety of higher-yielding substitutes for conventional M1-type means of payment, slower observed growth in the money stock may not be accompanied by a slowdown in economic activity. The key point is that the Federal Reserve has to adjust for the major distortions that occur in this environment, or monetary policy may not have the intended effect on economic activity.

The Federal Reserve has used several methods to minimize the effects of financial innovations and regulatory changes on the monetary aggregates and their relationship to economic activity. One of these ways involves redefining the monetary aggregates. In 1980, for example, major changes were made in the definitions of the monetary aggregates. Since then, financial assets that constitute the different aggregates have been changed when necessary. Other methods used by the Federal Reserve involve adjusting the monetary aggregates observed growth rates to reflect shifts of funds accounted for by financial innovations or shifting the target ranges of the aggregates to incorporate the effects of shifts of funds among the aggregates. The Federal Reserve has also tended to put greater emphasis than in the past on the more broadly defined monetary aggregates that are less affected by financial innovations involving shifts of funds.

32. The most-inclusive measure, bank credit, is denoted by L.

33. A third concept, the base or high-powered money, is that money is nonmarket-interest-bearing government debt. This definition represents nonmarket-interest bearing claims of the private sector against the federal government, as well as part of the net wealth of the private sector. In the United States, these liabilities are the currency listed by the Federal Reserve and the U.S. Treasury and deposits held by depository institutions at the Fed.

34. See "Announcement," Board of Governors of the Federal Reserve System, February 7, 1980.

35. For example, see Stephen H. Axilrod, "Monetary Policy, Money Supply, and the Federal Reserve's Operating Procedures," *Federal Reserve Bulletin*, January 1982, Board of Governors of the Federal Reserve System,

pp. 12-24, and Lyle E. Gramley, "Financial Innovation and Monetary Policy," *Federal Reserve Bulletin*, July 1982, Board of Governors of the Federal Reserve System, pp. 393-400.

36. For example, sweep accounts, which have features similar to savings accounts and checking accounts, are becoming widespread. There are usually five basic features of the sweep account: a high-yielding money-market fund into which the idle funds are automatically swept by computer; check-writing privileges; access to brokerage services; a credit or debit card for each withdrawal; and a line of credit (typically a standard margin account).

A second example concerns the Depository Institution Deregulation Committee's (DIDC) authorization of two accounts: the money-market deposit account and the Super NOW account. These accounts allow depository institutions to compete more effectively for funds, especially during periods of high or rising interest rates.

The money-market deposit account (MMDA), effective December 14, 1982, has no interest-rate ceiling as long as a minimum balance of $2,500 is maintained. Whenever the balance falls below $2,500, the allowable interest rate declines to the ceiling rate on NOW accounts. The MMDA has a limit of six transfers per month: preauthorized transfers, third-party checks, or telephone transfers. No more than three of these may be third-party checks. There are no limitations on the size or frequency of additions, however made, or on the number of withdrawals effected by mail, messenger, automated teller machine, or in person. The account is available to all depositors: individuals, partnerships, corporations, and governmental units. (Nonpersonal accounts are subject to a reserve requirement.)

The Super NOW account, available beginning January 5, 1983, has the same features as the MMDA, with two exceptions: an unlimited number of transfers are permitted, and the account is available only to individuals, certain nonprofit corporations, and governmental units.

37. Under the Monetary Control Act, depository institutions include commercial banks, savings and loan associations, mutual savings banks, credit unions, agencies and branches of foreign banks, and Edge Act corporations.

38. Initially two M1 measures were adopted, M1A and M1B, primarily because of uncertainties that would arise during a transition period when NOW accounts were permitted nationwide. M1A included currency in the hands of the public plus demand deposits held only in commerical banks, excluding those held by foreign banks and official institutions. (Both old M1 and M1A included currency in the hands of the nonbank public and demand deposits at commercial banks. Old M1 included deposits of foreign official institutions as well. M1A excluded demand deposits held in commercial banks by foreign banks and official institutions. M1B included M1A plus other checkable deposits at all financial institutions, including

ATS and NOW accounts.) NOW accounts have properties of both a transaction account and a savings account, and thus newly opened NOW accounts attracted funds from both household demand deposits and savings accounts and other liquid assets.

During a conversion period, growth in M1B could significantly overstate underlying growth in the public's transaction balances. M1A, in contrast, could understate such growth as households converted demand-deposit balances into NOW accounts. In practice, because the extent of the shift from demand deposits and other accounts to NOW accounts would be uncertain, the availability of both M1 measures helped in the interpretation of growth in the narrow money stock during the transition period.

A shift-adjusted M1B was introduced in February 1981. See Paul A. Volcker, "Monetary Report to Congress," *Federal Reserve Bulletin*, March 1981, pp. 195-208. Shift-adjusted M1B is M1B minus an estimate of the other checkable deposit account balances that originate from shifts of non-demand deposit funds. The rational was to adjust the observed growth rates of the aggregates to account for distortions caused by shifts of funds among financial assets.

39. Small-denomination time deposits are those issued in amounts for less than $100,000.

40. Money-market mutual funds in M2 refer to the general-purposes (household) funds. Institutional money-market fund shares, which cater to institutional investors, require substantial minimum investments, ranging as high as $250,000, and are included in M3.

41. The maximum maturities have been limited to eighty-nine days to comply with rulings imposing interest-rate ceilings on longer maturities.

42. These include overnight repurchase agreements at commercial banks and overnight Eurodollars held by U.S. residents other than banks at Caribbean branches of member banks.

43. For more detail, see Duprey, "How the Fed," pp. 14, 15.

44. See David A. Pierce and William Cleveland, "Seasonal Adjustment Methods for the Monetary Aggregates," *Federal Reserve Bulletin*, December 1981, Board of Governors of the Federal Reserve System, pp. 875-887.

45. Specifically, the broader aggregates usually appear on the last weekly H.6 statistical form of the month.

46. More precisely, the monetary base includes: reserve balances at Federal Reserve banks in the current week plus vault cash held two weeks earlier used to satisfy reserve requirements at all depository institutions; plus currency outside the U.S. Treasury, Federal Reserve banks, and the vaults of depository institutions; and surplus vault cash at depository institutions.

47. Some economists argue that the monetary base is useful as a single measure of the effect of all Federal Reserve actions on the money supply.

The base can be readily computed and reported almost immediately. It is not subject to periodic revisions or significant measurement errors. Any change in reserve requirements, however, affects the amount of money and bank credit that a given volume of bank reserves can support. The monetary base needs to be adjusted for the impact of changes in reserve requirements ratios. Thus, a related technical problem is how to adjust the monetary base for the effects of changes in reserve requirements. The adjusted monetary base can be viewed as a single measure of all Federal Reserve actions that affect the monetary policy, including reserve requirements.

A more-complex question is how to adjust the monetary base for changes in reserve requirements since there is more than one way and the choice of the appropriate method is not clear-cut. In part, the choice depends on the uses of the data. The Federal Reserve Board adjusts the base for changes in legal reserve requirements. The St. Louis Federal Reserve Bank, however, adjusts the base to take into account changes in legal reserve requirements and shifts among deposit categories with different reserve requirements.

For a brief description of the complexities in using the base or any of the reserve measures as a target for controlling money stock growth, see Axilrod, "Monetary Policy," pp. 13-24, and Lyle E. Gramley, "Financial Innovations and Monetary Policy," *Federal Reserve Bulletin*, July 1982, Board of Governors of the Federal Reserve System, pp. 393-400.

48. The following section is adapted from Roger LeRoy Miller, *Personal Finance Today*, New York: West Publishing Company, 1979, pp. 163-166.

49. In the past several years, owner financing of homes has also become a source of mortgage loans.

50. The FHA also sponsors a subsidy program for low- and moderate-income families.

51. Sometimes borrowers may be asked to pay discount points. The point system is a device to raise the effective rate of interest on a mortgage. It is employed whenever there are restrictions on the legal interest rate that can be charged on a mortgage loan.

A point is a charge of 1 percent of the loan. The charge may be assessed against the buyer or the seller or both. Suppose that you have to pay four discount points on a $25,000 loan; that means you get a loan of $25,000 minus 4 percent of $25,000, or only $24,000. You pay interest, however, on the full $25,000. The interest paid on the $25,000 loan understates the actual interest paid because the borrower gets only $24,000. Some states have laws against discount points, and the FHA and VA have restrictions on buyers' paying points. They are charged to the seller but are in reality passed on to the borrower in the form of a higher price on the housing unit.

52. These series cover all purchase loans closed (entered on the books) by participants during the first five full working days of a month. During months when lending terms are in the process of change, the averages may not be representative of the month as a whole. Most mortgage lending, moreover, is based on prior commitments made by lenders. The averages, therefore, should not be interpreted as measures of market rates and terms during the reporting period. The commitment rate-lending policy series should be used for this purpose. Moreover, the closed-loan series will reflect changes in relative lending volumes among lender types, among geographic areas, and among sizes of lenders.

53. These lenders have accounted for about 90 percent of all conventional home-mortgage-loan originations since 1972. The weights represent the relative total lending volumes of participants during a fixed-base period as estimated from the loan volumes reported in the closed-loan survey.

54. It excludes the estimated cost of private (nongovernmental) mortgage insurance from the contract rate for the relatively small number of loans, including such costs in the rate.

55. The effective rate shown in table 3-8 is on all conventional mortgage loans closed. The FHLBB also compiles the information for conventional mortgages on new homes and existing homes; for example, the effective rate on new homes was 10.77 in 1979 and 12.65 in 1980; in previously occupied homes it was 10.92 in 1979 and 12.95 in 1980. The effective interest rates, prior to 1973, are not completely comparable with later periods due to revisions in the series effective January 1973.

56. The data are compiled by the Department of Housing and Urban Development (HUD). HUD does not maintain a separate series for the yields on VA-guaranteed loans.

57. Representatives in each of the seventy-five field offices call lenders on the first of the month (usually the same lenders) and obtain prices on actual transactions; the yields are derived from these reports. The mortgage rates refer to rates on or about that date, not an average or opinion of the average level over the month. HUD, the Federal Reserve, and the Federal Home Loan Bank Board treat the month to which the rate on FHA-insured mortgages in the secondary market refers differently. HUD reports the yield as of the month in which the survey is taken, whereas the Federal Reserve and the Federal Home Loan Bank Board report the yield as of the preceding month. For example, the survey conducted on November 1, 1981, resulted in a secondary yield of 17.43 percent. The Federal Reserve and Federal Home Loan Bank Board, however, report that figure (17.43 percent) as the yield for the preceding month, October 1981.

58. Yields are weighted by the activity in each of the seventy-five field offices during the preceding year.

59. Terms as described above are: contact interest rates; initial fees and charges; effective rates; loan amount; purchase price; loan-to-price ratio.

60. State and metropolitan area data are available from the Federal Home Loan Bank Board, Office of Policy and Economic Research, Statistical Analysis Division, 1700 G Street, N.W., Washington, D.C. 20552. (202) 377-6923.

61. The term *municipal bonds* can be used to refer to all of these issuers.

62. Market yields indicate the percentage rate of return to investors on securities purchased at current market prices and held to maturity (taking into account the effect of differences in the length of time to maturity and in coupon rates). Those yields, however, do not necessarily reflect the return realized by purchasers on other dates or by investors who dispose of their obligations before maturity because of the capital gains or losses arising out of subsequent price changes.

Yields do not necessarily reflect the costs of funds to the borrower. When a new security is marketed, its yield is related to the market yield on outstanding issues of comparable quality and terms. The yield on a new issue, however, is generally greater than the yield on outstanding issues by the flotation costs—including underwriters' compensation—and any discount from market price that is necessary to place the issue initially.

In addition to the general level of interest rates, yields on long-term securities also reflect relative supplies of various types of securities, preferences, relative amounts of funds available to investors, and characteristics of the various types of securities, such as the market's evaluation of differences in the underlying risk, marketability, the tax status of the income return to investors, and term to maturity.

63. Current data can be found in U.S. Department of Commerce, Bureau of Economic Analysis, *Survey of Current Business*, published monthly. Historical data can be found in U.S. Department of Commerce, *Business Statistics 1979*.

64. Weekly data, however, are not available before 1948.

65. Monthly averages of the weekly data are reported in the Moody's *Municipal and Government Manual*.

66. Under relatively stable market conditions, that system performed satisfactorily. However, when interest rates rise sharply, an average based on specific issues becomes an average based on discount bonds. Consequently Moody's averages have been in a transitory stage as consideration has been given not only to quality and maturity but also to the level of interest rates to determine what the present yields would be if bonds of the same quality bore current coupons. Thus, by degrees, Moody's averages have become influenced by the new-issue market.

67. For example, a representative list as of 1980 could have included Atlanta, Baltimore, California, Chicago Board of Education, Cleveland,

Houston, Illinois, Los Angeles, Memphis, New Orleans, Ohio, Oregon, Pittsburgh, Rhode Island, and St. Louis. Standard & Poor's Corp. also compiles an index of short-term (approximately six months to maturity) municipal issues.

Historical data are available monthly from 1900 and weekly from 1970 in the *Security Price Index Record.* (Weekly data are available from 1921 and can be obtained by writing to Standard & Poor's Corp., 25 Broadway, New York, NY   10004.) Current data are available weekly in *Current Statistics* for the previous year.

Current data can also be found in U.S. Department of Commerce, Bureau of Economic Analysis, *Survey of Current Business*, published monthly. Historical data can also be found in U.S. Department of Commerce, *Business Statistics 1979.*

68. This section is adapted from Roger LeRoy Miller and Arline Alchian Hoel, *Media Economics Source Book*, New York: West Publishing Co., 1982, pp. 61-62.

69. Randall C. Merris, "Prime Rate Update," *Economic Perspectives*, May 1978, Federal Reserve Bank of Chicago, pp. 14-16; and Brian C. Gendreau, "When Is the Prime Rate Second Choice," *Business Review*, May/June 1983, Federal Reserve Bank of Philadelphia, pp. 13-23.

70. Another volume of historical statistics is also available: Board of Governors of the Federal Reserve System, *Banking and Monetary Statistics, 1914-1941.*

71. Standard & Poor's Corp. ratings consist of ten categories ranging from AAA (best quality) to BBB (lower medium quality) to CCC (poor prospects) to D (default).

72. Under the Monetary Control Act, depository institutions include commercial banks, savings and loan associations, mutual savings banks, credit unions, agencies and branches of foreign banks, and Edge Act corporations.

73. Legislation enacted in March 1980 imposed Federal Reserve requirements on all depository institutions. Until then, only member banks were subject to reserve requirements of the Federal Reserve System.

Until September 1968, member banks based their calculations of reserve requirements on deposit liabilities at the start of each day, for the seven days ending on Wednesdays. Reserves held to meet reserve requirements were made up of vault cash at the start of each day, plus reserve balances at Federal Reserve banks at the end of each day for the seven days ending on Wednesdays. In effect, there was a one-day lag between the period over which deposit liabilities and vault cash were calculated and the period over which member banks held required reserve balances.

In September 1968, the Federal Reserve changed the timing of reserve accounting by extending the one-day lag to a two-week lag. Under this system, known as lagged reserve requirements (LRR), required reserves for each week (the seven days ending Wednesdays) are based on deposit liabilities held two weeks earlier. Average vault cash held two weeks earlier is counted as part of reserves in the current week, and vault cash in the current week is counted as reserve for two weeks in the future.

In February 1984 depository institutions will switch to a system of contemporaneous reserve requirements (CRR). Under CRR there will be considerable overlap between the reserve computation and maintenance periods. Required reserves in the current fourteen-day maintenance period will be held against the average level of transaction deposit liabilities over fourteen days ending two days before the end of the current maintenance period. For more detail see R. Alton Gilbert and Michael E. Trebing, "The New System of Contemporaneous Reserve Requirements," *Review*, December 1982, Federal Reserve Bank of St. Louis, pp. 3-7.

74. The term *discounting function* evolved from the means by which Federal Reserve banks extended credit to member banks in the early years of the Federal Reserve System. Member banks would sell short-term loans that had been made to their commercial customers. They endorsed the notes to their Federal Reserve banks and received a fraction of the face amounts of the notes. The fraction reflected the discount rate. This process was known as discounting a note. Now most Federal Reserve loans to member banks are called *advances*. Federal Reserve banks lend the amounts requested by depository institutions and various types of assets, such as government securities, are submitted to the Federal Reserve as collateral.

75. Specifically, reserves can be calculated by combining factors that supply and absorb reserve funds. See Board of Governors of the Federal Reserve System, *Factors Affecting Reserves of Depository Institutions and Condition Statement of Federal Reserve Banks*, H.4.1 (503) statistical release, published weekly. Also see Board of Governors of the Federal Reserve System, *Federal Reserve Bulletin*, published monthly.

76. The procedures are not quite the same for all other depository institutions. The procedure will change in February 1984 when CRR become effective, as explained in note 73.

77. Issuing stocks is one of the two major ways corporations obtain long-term financing. Stocks differ from bonds because they represent ownership in a business firm, whereas bonds represent borrowing by the firm. Stocks represent the equity capital in a company. The concept of equity might best be understood in terms of the equity that home owners have in their homes. If you own a house that has a market value (the price at which you could sell your house) of $100,000 and you owed $60,000 on your home mortgage, then you would have equity of $40,000 in your home.

COMPARING STOCKS AND BONDS

Common Stocks	Bonds
1. Stocks represent ownership.	1. Bonds represent owed debt.
2. Stocks do not have a fixed dividend rate.	2. Interest on bonds must always be paid, whether or not any profit is earned.
3. Stockholders can elect a board of directors, which controls the corporation.	3. Bondholders usually have no voice in or control over management of the corporation.
4. Stocks do not have a maturity date; the corporation does not usually repay the stockholder.	4. Bonds have a maturity date when the bondholder is to be repaid the face value of the bond.
5. All corporations issue or offer to sell stocks. This is the usual definition of a corporation.	5. Corporations are not required to issue bonds.
6. Stockholders have a claim against the property and income of a corporation after all creditors' claims have been met.	6. Bondholders have a claim against the property and income of a corporation that must be met before the claims of stockholders.

Steven L. Mandell, Scott S. Cowen, and Roger LeRoy Miller, *Introduction to Business: Concepts and Applications*, New York: West Publishing Co., 1981, p. 396.

Most stock is common stock, usually called equity. Common-stock shareholders are last in line in receiving payment for their investment. Suppliers, employees, managers, bankers, governments, bondholders, and preferred-stock shareholders must first be paid what is due them. Once those groups have been paid, however, common-stock shareholders are entitled to all of the remaining earnings. This is the central feature of ownership in any business. The common-stock owners occupy the riskiest position, but they can logically expect a greater return on their investment than that accruing to other groups.

78. The stock-price indexes we describe can be placed into two categories.

Average-price-level indexes: The most well-known example is the

Dow Jones Industrial Average. Average-price-level indexes primarily stress the price per share of the stocks that make up the index. They do not take the outstanding number of shares of stock of each company into account to reflect the aggregate market value of the companies. These indexes emphasize that a stock sells at a price of $10 per share, not that its 1,000 outstanding shares reflect a market value of $10,000 ($10 price per share times 1,000 shares). Average-price-level indexes in effect measure the performance of a portfolio, in which the relative value of each holding is proportional to the price of the stock relative to the other stocks in the index.

Aggregate-value indexes: Examples are Standard & Poor's (S&P's) averages and New York Stock Exchange (NYSE) indexes. Aggregate-value indexes stress the aggregate or total market value of the stocks in the index. They are constructed by weighting the price of each stock in the index by the corresponding number of outstanding shares, thereby reflecting the total market value of the common stock for each company. For example, the $10 price of a stock is weighted by the 1,000 outstanding shares to reflect a $10,000 aggregate market value for that stock in the index. These indexes in effect measure the performance of a portfolio in which the relative value of each holding is proportional to the value of each company's shares relative to the total value of all companies' shares. Aggregate-market-value indexes represent the average dollar invested in the stocks included in the index.

79. The Dow Jones Averages are published daily in the *Wall Street Journal*. Current data can also be found in the U.S. Department of Commerce, Bureau of Economic Analysis, *Survey of Current Business*, published monthly. Historical data are available in Phillis S. Pierce, *The Dow Jones Averages 1885-1980*, Homewood, Ill.: Dow Jones-Irwin, 1982; and U.S. Department of Commerce, *Business Statistics 1979*.

80. This note illustrates the effect of capitalization changes (splits, rights, warrants) on the Dow Jones averages. For example, if stock B split with three $5 shares for one $15 share, the market adjusts the price of stock B downward in exact proportion to the increased number of shares. Since the number of shares tripled, the price of stock B falls to $5, one-third of its original price.

A person who held one $15 share now had shares worth only $5 but holds three of those shares. If the average were computed with no adjustment adding $5, $5, and $10 for a total of $20 divided by 3, the new average would be $6.66, down from $10. But this would not be right since the dollar value of the outstanding shares of the companies has not decreased.

Thus, an adjustment must be made so that the average will remain at $10. There are different ways to make these adjustments. The method used by the Dow Jones is equivalent to a portfolio reallocation from the split stock to all other stocks in the index. In effect, the stocks that split most will play a smaller and smaller role relative to those that split least. For a more-detailed explanation, see Henry A. Latané and Donald L. Tuttle, *Security Analysis and Portfolio Management*, New York: Ronald Press Co., 1970, pp. 158-162.

81. Effective July 1976, S&P's added a new financial group, banks and insurance companies. The stocks used in the index were selected on the basis of the aggregate value of all outstanding shares of each stock, trading activity, and market representation.

The Transportation Index and Financial Index are based to 1970 = 10. The Public Utility Index, Indusrial Index and the S&P 500 Index (the composite or total index) are based to 1941-43 = 10.

For historical data and a detailed explanation of how to calculate the index, see Standard & Poor's, *Statistical Service: Security Price Index Record*, 1980 ed., New York: Standard & Poor's Corp., 1980. Current data are published weekly in the *Outlook*.

Current data are also available in U.S. Department of Commerce, Bureau of Economic Analysis, *Survey of Current Business*, published monthly. Historical data are available in U.S. Department of Commerce, *Business Statistics 1979*.

Standard & Poor's Corp. also publishes in the *Daily Stock Price Record* the daily high, low, and closing stock prices and volume for individual companies traded on exchanges. The *Daily Stock Price Records* are published four times a year; the New York Stock Exchange and American Stock Exchange books are available from the first quarter of 1962 forward. The over-the-counter books are available from the first quarter of 1968 forward.

82. Current data can be found in the U.S. Department of Commerce, Bureau of Economic Analysis, *Survey of Current Business*, published monthly. Historical data are available in U.S. Department of Commerce, *Business Statistics 1979*.

83. Although the method of calculating stock price averages is similar for the New York Stock Exchange and Standard & Poor's indexes, there are some differences. First, more-frequent adjustments must be made in the base aggregate values of the NYSE indexes than in the corresponding values of the S&P's indexes. Whereas the number of stocks in the S&P's indexes is fixed and the names of the S&P's stocks change infrequently, the number of stocks in NYSE indexes changes every time a common stock is newly listed on or deleted from the exchange. Second, the NYSE indexes each include more stocks than the corresponding S&P's indexes. Third, the NYSE indexes use a base of 50, which is more recent (December 31, 1965) than the S&P's indexes, which use a base of 10 (average weekly experience over the two years 1941-1943).

84. The stock-price indexes described implicitly assume a portfolio investment strategy of buy and hold. Average-price-level indexes, such as

the Dow Jones Industrial Average, emphasize the price per share: investing dollar amounts in each stock in the index (the implicit portfolio) in proportion to the price per share of the stocks in the index. (In the event of splits or stock dividends, the divisor is adjusted so that instead of investing the proceeds in one share of each of the original thirty stocks, the proceeds are spread among about twenty-three shares of each stock; the divisor has declined from 30 to about 1.3.) Aggregate-market-value indexes, such as the New York Stock Exchange Composite Price Index, emphasize investing in each stock in the index (the implicit portfolio) in proportion to the aggregate market value of each stock in the index.

Another type of stock-price index can be constructed that assumes an investment strategy of reallocation: the composition of the investment in each stock in the index changes over time. That is, some of these indexes are constructed so that all of the stocks are assumed to be sold off periodically (such as the end of each year) and immediately repurchased with equal dollar amounts going into each stock. Alternatively, the indexes can be constructed so that the composition of the investment in the stocks in the index is assumed to change continuously (daily)—for example, the Value Line Indexes.

85. The geometric mean is a somewhat more-technical concept than the arithmetic mean. An explanation of the geometric mean can be found in any finance book. Briefly, the geometric mean is obtained by raising the product of K price ratios to the $1/K$th power or by taking the Kth root of the product of the K price ratios.

86. Value Line Indexes are published in *Value Line Selection and Opinion*, New York: Arnold Bernhard and Co.

87. American Stock Exchange, "Amex Introduces New Market Value Index System: Includes Trends by Industry and Region," 1973. (Address: 86 Trinity Place, New York, NY   10006.)

88. National Association of Securities Dealers, Inc., 1735 K Street, N.W., Washington, D.C.   20006.

89. Wilshire Associates, 1299 Ocean Avenue, Suite 700, Santa Monica, CA   90401.

90. Capital International, S.A., 15, rue de Centrier, 1201 Geneva, Switzerland.

91. Specifically, the books published quarterly by Standard & Poor's Corp. are: *Daily Stock Price Record: New York Stock Exchange*, *Daily Stock Price Record: American Stock Exchange*, and *Daily Stock Price Record: Over-the-Counter*.

92. A related group of securities known as agency securities are issued by a group of institutions created under federal law to serve explicit public

purposes. Some are part of the federal government and are known as federal agencies; others are privately owned and have come to be known as federally sponsored agencies. In recent years, the agencies, which are part of the federal government, have not issued new debt but instead have been financed indirectly by the U.S. Treasury.

93. See note 16.

4 Measures of Employment, Unemployment, and Earnings

Earnings: Gross Average Hourly Earnings; Real Earnings; Hourly Earnings Indexes

Issuing Agency: U.S. Department of Labor, Bureau of Labor Statistics, Office of Wages and Industrial Relations (for the Hourly Earnings Index) and Office of Employment Structure and Trends (for gross average hourly earnings and real earnings).

Coverage and Limitations: The Bureau of Labor Statistics publishes several series that attempt to measure different concepts of earnings. None, however, measures the earnings of a representative household. A more-appropriate measure, based on demographic features, can be obtained from the weekly earnings data (released quarterly) described in the section "Earnings of Workers and Their Families: By Demographic Characteristics."

Gross average hourly earnings estimates total or actual earnings of workers before any deductions are made. Real earnings adjust earnings for inflation or price changes over time. Hourly earnings indexes adjust earnings for the effects of fluctuations in overtime premiums and seasonal employment.[1]

The gross average hourly earnings series reflects actual earnings of workers, including premium pay. They differ from wage rates, which are the amounts stipulated for a given unit of work or time. Gross average hourly earnings do not represent total labor costs per hour for the employer, for they exclude retroactive payments and irregular bonuses, various welfare benefits, and the employer's share of payroll taxes. Earnings for those employees not covered under the production worker and nonsupervisory-employee categories are not reflected in the estimates.

The real earnings data (expressed in 1977 dollars) indicate the changes in the purchasing power of money earnings as a result of changes in prices for consumer goods and services. These data cannot be used to measure changes in living standards as a whole, which are affected by other factors such as total family income, the extension and incidence of various social services and benefits, and the duration and extent of employment and unemployment.

Hourly earnings indexes are calculated from average hourly earnings data adjusted to exclude the effects of two types of changes that are unrelated to underlying wage-rate developments: fluctuations in overtime premiums in manufacturing (the only sector for which overtime data are available) and the effects of fluctuations and varying trends in employment activity (aggregate worker hours) in the proportion of workers in high-wage and low-wage industries. To adjust for varying trends in employment activity, fixed weights are assigned to each of the component industries. The weights are derived from the industries' base-period estimates of aggregate worker hours. To approximate straight-time average hourly earnings, gross average hourly earnings are adjusted by eliminating only premium pay for overtime at the rate of time and one-half. Thus, no adjustment is made for other premium payment provisions such as holiday work, late-shift work, and premium overtime rates other than at time and one-half.[2]

Analysts and newspersons sometimes use average hourly earnings statistics as if they were indicators of the income of a typical worker or income of an average family; however, average earnings do not measure the income of a typical single worker or family, as the Bureau of Labor Statistics points out. (In fact, a typical full-time employee or family does much better than the average.)

One reason for the difference is the way the number of employees are counted.[3] The number of employees is based on establishment data. Under this procedure, employers count an employee each time the person appears on a payroll. This means part-time workers are counted along with full-time workers, and people with more than one job are counted more than once (each time they appear on a payroll). The effect is to make earnings (of all workers) lower than earnings of a typical or average full-time employee (which is how the statistics are mistakenly interpreted sometimes).[4]

A much different view of earnings for a typical family is obtained when adjustments are made for the family status of the worker. For example, the earnings of husbands who are full-time, year-round workers tend to be substantially above the average earnings for all job holders. Income would be higher if adjustments were made for the number of wage earners in the family, particularly since both husband and wife are employed in many families. Another characteristic that affects income in a family with, say, three dependents, is that the average worker tends to be older, more skilled, and has more experience than average and thus tends to receive wages above the average of all job holders. Finally, two other factors that tend to pull down the average earnings for all workers are the entry into the labor force of the post-World War II baby-boom generation and women. Both groups tend to receive somewhat lower incomes than the typical head-of-family employee (say, with three dependents).

Data Available: Gross earnings and hours are available for over 450 industries, on a national basis.

Earnings and hours for manufacturing industries are available nationally for each state, as well as for over 200 areas.

Real earnings, and the hourly earnings indexes, are available for major industry groupings.

Measures of gross earnings are available monthly; the hourly earnings indexes are available quarterly.

Related Series: Two broader measures of earnings are average hourly compensation and the Employment Cost Index.[5]

Average hourly compensation measures per-hour changes in wages and salaries, plus costs to the employer of including supplementary benefits such as vacations, pensions, and social security. (The data include estimates for the self-employed.) Employee compensation does not represent total labor costs, which is more encompassing and includes factors such as the costs of recruiting and training and administrative expenses incurred in administering benefit programs.

The Employment Cost Index measures quarterly changes in wages, salaries, and compensation in the private nonfarm economy, free of employment shifts. The purpose of the index is to provide a comprehensive and timely measure of employer labor costs (covering wages, salaries and benefits), which is standardized so that it has a constant industrial, occupational, and geographic composition—somewhat like the fixed-weight market basket of commodities for the Consumer Price Index. The Employment Cost Index measures changes rather than the level of compensation. It is not a measure of the total cost of employing labor, which would include training expenses and retroactive pay.

On the spending side, the Bureau of Labor Statistics publishes expenditure studies for families and single consumers. Expenditure data are broken down by geographic areas of the country and family characteristics.[6]

Source of Data: The primary source of data is state employment security agencies, which collect data from cooperating employers monthly. Data relate to the payroll period, which includes the twelfth of the month (standard for all federal agencies collecting data on an establishment basis).

Data cover the fifty states and the District of Columbia and include full-time, part-time, temporary, and permanent workers; workers who are on paid leave (sick, holiday, vacation); and persons who worked only part of the specified pay period. Persons on the payroll of more than one establishment are counted each time they are reported. Persons in a nonpay status for the entire period due to layoff, strike, leave without pay, or similar reason, and self-employed and unpaid family workers are excluded.

When Series Become Available: The estimated release date for real earnings data is published near the beginning of the "Current Labor Statistics" section of the *Monthly Labor Review*. Earnings data are usually released around the third week (or beginning of the fourth week) of each month for the preceding month. For example, data released around April 23 cover March.

The estimated release date for gross average hourly and weekly earnings and the Hourly Earnings Index is published in the U.S. Department of Labor, Bureau of Labor Statistics, *Monthly Labor Review*, near the begininng of "Current Labor Statistics" under "Employment Situation." The information is usually released around the first Friday (sometimes the

second Friday) of each month for the preceding month. For example, data
released around April 3 cover March.

Publications: Current Data:

Council of Economic Advisers, *Economic Indicators*, Washington, D.C.:
U.S. Government Printing Office. Monthly.

U.S. Department of Labor, Bureau of Labor Statistics, *Current Wage Developments*. Monthly.

U.S. Department of Labor, Bureau of Labor Statistics, *Employment and Earnings*. Monthly.

U.S. Department of Labor, Bureau of Labor Statistics, *Monthly Labor Review*.

Publications: Historical Data:

Council of Economic Advisers, *Economic Report of the President*, Washington, D.C.: U.S. Government Printing Office. Annual. See statistical appendix.

U.S. Department of Labor, Bureau of Labor Statistics, *Supplement to Employment and Earnings: Revised Establishment Data*, August 1981. Annual.

U.S. Department of Labor, Bureau of Labor Statistics, *Employment and Earnings, 1909-1978*. 1979.

References:

Moore, Geoffrey, "Inflation and Statistics," *Contemporary Economic Problems 1980*, Washington, D.C.: American Enterprise Institute for Public Policy Research, 1980, pp. 167-192.

U.S. Department of Labor, Bureau of Labor Statistics, *BLS Handbook of Methods for Surveys and Studies*, Bulletin 1910, 1976.

U.S. Department of Labor, Bureau of Labor Statistics, *BLS Handbook of Methods, vol. 1*, Bulletin 2134-1, 1982.

Mail and Telephone Reference:

U.S. Department of Labor
Bureau of Labor Statistics
Publications Department
441 G. Street, N.W.
Washington, D.C.   20212
(202) 523-1913

Earnings of Workers and Their Families: By Demographic Characteristics

Issuing Agency: U.S. Department of Labor, Bureau of Labor Statistics, Office of Current Employment Analysis.

Coverage: In 1979, the Bureau of Labor Statistics, working through the Bureau of the Census, began to collect data on weekly earnings by demographic groups throughout the year, rather than just once a year (in May), as had been the case. The data were needed to keep track of differences in earnings between various population groups—men and women, whites and blacks, young and old, and so on. These data, however, were not available from the earnings data reported by establishments. To obtain current earnings of demographic groups at relatively little additional cost, the Current Population Survey (which is designed primarily to obtain information about the labor force, the employed, and the unemployed) was modified.

Those surveyed are asked, "How much does . . . USUALLY make per week at this job before deductions? Include any overtime pay, commissions or tips received." The response is for the worker's sole or principal job. The term *usually* is interpreted as perceived by the respondent; however, if the interviewer is asked for a definition, she or he is instructed to define the term as more than half the weeks worked during the past four or five months.

The data are collected for wages and salaries of workers sixteen years and older. The usual weekly earnings of a family (defined as two or more people residing together who are related by blood, marriage, or adoption) are obtained by aggregating the usual weekly earnings of all family members sixteen years and older who were employed as wage and salary workers during the reference work week. The statistics on families are not tabulated for families with no wage or salary workers or in which the person maintaining the family is either self-employed or in the armed forces.

Wage and salary workers are employed people who receive wages, salaries, commissions, tips, payment in kind, or piece rates. The group includes employees in both the private and public sectors but excludes self-employed persons whose businesses are incorporated.

The employed comprise all those who during the survey reference week (the calendar week Sunday through Saturday, which includes the twelfth of the month) did any work at all as paid employees in their own business, profession, or farm or who worked fifteen hours or more as unpaid workers in an enterprise operated by a member of the family; and all those who were not working but who had jobs or businesses from which they were temporarily absent because of illness, bad weather, a vacation, labor-management dispute, or personal reasons, whether or not they were paid by their work employers for the time off, or whether or not they were seeking other jobs.

Each person is counted only once (in contrast to the establishment survey in which a person is counted in every job). Those who held more than one job are counted in the job at which they worked the greatest number of hours during the survey reference week.

Data Available: Usual median weekly earnings are available quarterly for families: by number of workers and relationship of workers; by race and Hispanic origin; with unemployment by presence and relationship of worker(s) to the unemployed members. The employment status of persons is also reported by family relationship.

Median weekly earnings of *full*-time wage and salary workers are reported by sex and age; family relationship; race, Hispanic origin, and sex; occupation and sex. Median weekly earnings of *part*-time wage and salary workers are available by sex and age; family relationship; race, Hispanic origin, and sex.

The percentage change in current and in constant dollars of median weekly earnings for families and for full-time wage and salary workers is reported by selected characteristics.

Related Series: Once a year weekly earnings by demographic groups are available. Each May, all respondents in the Current Population Survey are asked supplemental questions that cover multiple jobholding, union representation, receipt of premium pay for work in excess of forty hours a week, work schedules, usual weekly earnings, and usual hourly earnings. The additional data obtained each May are published annually.

The new weekly earnings data for individuals that are available quarterly are similar to but not entirely comparable with the Current Population Survey of earnings data previously reported annually (in May). Differences are derived from slight changes in collection procedures, in the definition of wage and salary earners, and in processing procedures. The quarterly series, in contrast to the annual series, excludes self-employed workers because their business is incorporated. In addition, another change is that the earnings of nonrespondents, which had previously not been taken into account, are imputed to minimize any bias that might result from differences in the response rate among groups with very different earnings levels.

Source of Data: Data for usual weekly earnings of workers and their families are collected through the Current Population Survey. The survey is conducted each month and provides information on the labor force, the employed, and unemployed, including characteristics such as age, sex, race, Hispanic origin, family relationship, marital status, occupation, and industry attachment.

In order to obtain the quarterly data required on usual weekly earnings of wage workers and their families, the monthly survey was modified slightly. To minimize the burden on the respondents, the questions pertaining to earnings are asked of only one-fourth of the wage and salary workers in the monthly sample. (In the annual May survey, all respondents were asked the questions.) The results are averaged over the three months for publication on a quarterly basis.

Limitations: Earnings of workers and their families are published quarterly in response to the demand for demographically oriented data. One of the reasons for collecting such data is that the existing series were not appropriate measures of the income of a typical worker or family. A more-representative picture of worker and family income can be obtained by comparing earnings based on demographic characteristics.

When Series Become Available: Quarterly data for the usual weekly earnings of workers and their families become available two months after the quarter to which the data refer. For example, figures for the first quarter become available around the end of May, and figures for the second quarter become available around the end of August, and so on.

Publications: Current Data:

U.S. Department of Labor, Bureau of Labor Statistics, *News: Earnings of Workers and Their Families.* Quarterly.

U.S. Department of Labor, Bureau of Labor Statistics, *Employment and Earnings.* Monthly. See January, April, July, and October issues.

Publications: Historical Data:

U.S. Department of Labor, Bureau of Labor Statistics, *Employment and Earnings.* Monthly. See January, April, July, and October issues beginning with October 1980.

References:

U.S. Department of Labor, Bureau of Labor Statistics, *BLS Handbook of Methods, vol. 1*, Bulletin 2134-1, 1982.

U.S. Department of Labor, Bureau of Labor Statistics, *News: Earnings of Workers and Their Families.* Quarterly.

U.S. Department of Labor, Bureau of Labor Statistics, *Technical Description of the Quarterly Data on Weekly Earnings from the Current Population Survey*, Report 601, July 1980.

Mail and Telephone Reference:

U.S. Department of Labor
Bureau of Labor Statistics
Publications Department
441 G Street, N.W.
Washington, D.C.   20212
(202) 523-1913

Employment, Unemployment, Labor Force, and Participation Rate: Based on the Household Survey[7]

Issuing Agency: U.S. Department of Labor, Bureau of Labor Statistics, Division of Employment and Unemployment Analysis.

Coverage: Employment statistics for the United States are based on a survey that is conducted every month.[8] The survey is designed so that every civilian sixteen years or older who is not in an institution, such as a prison or mental hospital, is classified as employed, unemployed, or not in the labor force.

People are considered employed if they did any work at all for pay or profit during the survey week. This includes all part-time and temporary work, as well as regular full-time, year-round employment. Persons also are counted as employed if they have a job at which they did not work during the survey week because they were on vacation, ill, involved in an industrial dispute, prevented from working by bad weather, or taking time off for various personal reasons.

Each employed person is counted only once; those who had more than one job are counted in the job at which they worked the greatest number of hours during the survey week.

The data include citizens of foreign countries who are temporarily living in the United States but not on the premises of an embassy. Excluded are persons whose only activity consisted of work around their own homes (such as housework, painting, or repairing) or volunteer work for religious, charitable, and similar organizations.

Thus the civilian employed consist of all nonmilitary noninstitutional persons sixteen years old or over: (1) who did any work at all during the survey week as paid employees or in their own business, profession, or farm, or (2) who worked fifteen hours or more as unpaid workers in a family-owned enterprise, and (3) were not working but had jobs or businesses from which they were temporarily absent because of illness, bad weather, vacation, labor-management dispute, or personal reasons.[9]

Persons are unemployed if they have actively looked for work in the past four weeks, are currently available for work, and do not have a job.[10] Looking for work may consist of any of the following specific activities: registering at a public or private employment office, meeting with prospective employers, checking with friends or relatives, placing or answering advertisements; writing letters of application, or being on a union or professional register.

Two groups of people do not have to engage in a specific job-seeking activity to be counted as unemployed: persons waiting to start a new job

191

within thirty days and workers waiting to be recalled from layoff. In all other cases except temporary illness, the individual must be currently available for work.[11]

The total unemployment figure, therefore, measures more than the number of people who have lost their jobs. It includes persons who have quit their jobs to look for other employment, new workers looking for their first jobs, and experienced workers looking for jobs after an absence from the labor force (as, for example, a woman who returns to the labor force after her children have entered school).

Summarizing, the unemployed consist of: all persons who do not work at all during the survey week but made specific efforts to find a job within the previous four weeks, and who were available for work during the survey week (except for temporary illness); all persons who were not working and were waiting to be called back to a job from which they were laid off; and all persons who were not working and were waiting to report to a new job within thirty days.

The civilian labor force comprises all persons sixteen years old or over in the civilian noninstitutional population classified as employed or unemployed.[12]

The unemployment rate measures the total number of unemployed as a percentage of the civilian labor force.

Some people are classified as not in the labor force. Persons under sixteen years of age are automatically excluded from the official labor force measurement, as are all inmates of institutions, regardless of age. All other members of the noninstitutional population are ineligible for inclusion in the labor force. Those persons sixteen and over who have a job or are actively looking for one are classified as in the labor force. All others—those who have no job and are not looking for one—are counted as not in the labor force. Many who do not participate in the labor force are going to school. Family responsibilities keep others out of the labor force. Still others are afflicted with a physical or mental disability, which prevents them from participating in normal labor-force activities.

Summarizing, not in the labor force are people who are under sixteen years old, confined to jail, asylums, hospitals, or other institutions, and are not counted as part of the employed, unemployed, and labor force. Other people in the civilian noninstitutional labor force are eligible to participate but may choose not to. They are counted as not in the labor force.

The civilian labor force participation rate is defined as the ratio of the civilian labor force to the civilian noninstitutional population.[13]

Data Available: Comprehensive data collected for the labor force, employed, and unemployed cover a variety of characteristics, including age, sex, race, marital status, family relationship, occupation, and industry attachment.

Other special information is also available for the employed and unemployed. For example, data are available for the unemployed by reasons for unemployment, job-search method, and duration of unemployment; the employed by hours of work and full- or part-time status; persons not in the labor force by work history and job-seeking intentions.

Annual employment and unemployment data are provided by region and state.

Source of Data: Data based on household interviews are obtained from a sample survey of the population sixteen years of age and over. The survey, called the Current Population Survey (CPS), is conducted each month by the Bureau of the Census for the Bureau of Labor Statistics and provides comprehensive data on the labor force, the employed and the unemployed, including such characteristics as age, sex, race, family relationship, marital status, occupation, and industry attachment. The survey also provides data on the characteristics and past work experience of those not in the labor force. The information is collected by a special group of over 1,000 highly trained interviewers from a sample of about 65,000 households, representing 614 areas in 1,113 counties and independent cities, with coverage in fifty states and the District of Columbia. The data collected are based on the activity or status reported for the calendar week that includes the twelfth of the month.

The information is recorded on a special reporting form and later processed by computer at the Bureau of the Census in Washington, D.C. Each person is classified by computer according to the activities reported. Then the total numbers are weighted or adjusted to independent estimates. The weighting takes into account the age, sex, race, and urban-rural distribution of the population, so that these characteristics are reflected in the final estimates.

Limitations: Many aspects concerning the measurement of the unemployment rate have led economists and policymakers to criticize the official government indicator because it is thought to be biased upward or downward.[14] Additionally, some commentators point out that our economy may have changed enough structurally to cause the measured unemployment rate to reflect inaccurately changes in economy-wide business activity.[15]

The duration of unemployment is defined as the length of time workers remain unemployed. The rate of unemployment can rise even when the absolute number of workers becoming unemployed per week remains constant. Such an anomaly will occur whenever the average duration of unemployment increases because fewer workers then leave the ranks of the unemployed. Hence, an increase by a week or two in the average duration of unemployment may increase the unemployment rate by .5 percent.

Some policy analysts have suggested that for policy purposes a better statistic is the percentage of the unemployed labor force that remains out of work for a long period of time—say, more than six months. Even during a severe recession, most unemployed workers find jobs within fourteen weeks.

Additionally, not all unemployed persons are workers who were fired or laid off. About half of those reported as unemployed had either left their last job, had never worked before, or were reentering the labor force after an absence, for example, due to illness or pregnancy.

The labor-force participation rate indicates the percentage of available individuals of working age who are actually available to be counted in the labor force.

In the last few years, the overall participation rate in the labor force has been on the rise, a fact that has led to concurrent increases in both unemployment and employment. In other words, an increased labor-force participation rate can lead to more employment simultaneously with more unemployment. If we consider simply the unemployment rate, we draw a conclusion that may be false with respect to the entire economy-wide health index. Which is more important: the amount of employment or the amount of unemployment? The answer is not easy to give, but the question is important. Employment figures are just as important as the unemployment figures.

The survey methods used to collect data in the United States produce an upward bias in Bureau of Labor Statistics' unemployment statistics. The methods indeed have a built-in tendency to exaggerate the statistic. The main question asked of someone out of work is, "Are you looking for work?" An affirmative response is considered acceptable even if that person merely flips quickly through the local newspaper job-vacancy columns. In the United Kingdom, unemployed workers must physically go to an agency to report that they are unemployed. Thus, a U.S. unemployment rate of, say, 5 percent might be equivalent to a United Kingdom unemployment rate of 2.5 percent.

Looking for work is not the only criterion for someone to be counted as unemployed. The other two key elements concern whether an individual surveyed is not working and is available for work. A person may fulfill these two requirements by registering for work as part of the eligibility for certain types of welfare-assistance programs. For example, recipients of food stamps, Aid to Families with Dependent Children (AFDC), and several other smaller federal assistance programs are required to register for work as a condition of eligibility. By the terms of the 1971 and 1977 amendments to the food stamp and AFDC programs, certain recipients must register for employment with state-employment-service offices at the time of application and at least once every six months thereafter. Any welfare recipient who has registered for work can lose the welfare assistance by refusing to comply with employee-service directives, such as requests for testing and counseling. Only 6 percent of the food stamp registrants, however, were declared ineligible for benefits because of their failure to comply with work-registration provisions or with employee-service directives.

The result of the requirement that certain welfare recipients must register for work is an upward bias in measured unemployment statistics. In 1977, for example, over 2 million individuals registered for work because of the food stamp and AFDC programs. To determine the extent to which such registrations constitute an overcounting of unemployment, we must find out how many of the welfare recipients who register are unemployable or have no need or intention to work.

If large numbers of welfare recipients who now are counted in the official unemployment statistics have chosen not to work or are largely unemployable, the work-registration requirement will have permanently increased the measured rate of unemployment even though the number of persons actually seeking work may remain relatively constant. Consequently the unemployment data collected since the implementation of the work-registration programs in 1972 are not comparable to the data collected previously. More important, the current data collected are perhaps misleading for public-policy purposes because such decisions are now based on incorrect notions of what the unemployment figures represent.

The exclusion of certain groups from the definition of the labor force biases the unemployment index downward.

An example of some of these problems refers to the more than 124,755 Mariel boatlift refugees who entered Florida in late 1980. About 80,000 of those settled in Dade and Monroe counties. The Bureau of Labor Statistics indicated that Dade County's October unemployment rate was only 6.7 percent that year because the government did not count most Mariel refugees since they never had jobs in this country. The Department of Labor's monthly household surveys rely heavily on job history, including layoff and unemployment compensation figures. Of the 80,000 refugees who settled in Miami at that time, most of them were unemployed, but because they were not counted as part of the labor force, they were not counted as part of the unemployment figures. Ironically, the low jobless rate reported in Dade County in October 1980 led to a $20 million cut in Federal Comprehensive Employment Training Act funds.

According to the South Florida Employment and Training Consortium, the true jobless rate in Dade and Monroe counties was double what the Bureau of Labor Statistics quoted. Almost 80 percent of the Cuban and Haitian refugees living in Dade County were unemployed.

When Series Become Available: The release date is published in the U.S. Department of Labor, Bureau of Labor Statistics, *Monthly Labor Review* near the beginning of the "Current Labor Statistics" section. Employment and unemployment information is generally released on the first Friday (sometimes the second Friday) of each month for the preceding month. For example, data released around April 3 cover March.

Publications: Current Data:

Council of Economic Advisers, *Economic Indicators*, Washington, D.C.: U.S. Government Printing Office. Monthly.

U.S. Department of Labor, Bureau of Labor Statistics, *Employment and Earnings*. Monthly.

U.S. Department of Labor, Bureau of Labor Statistics, *Monthly Labor Review*.

Publications: Historical Data:

Council of Economic Advisers, *Economic Report of the President*, Washington, D.C.: U.S. Government Printing Office. Annual. See statistical appendix.

U.S. Department of Labor, Bureau of Labor Statistics, *Employment and Earnings*, March 1982. Usually the revised series appear in the January issue.

References:

U.S. Department of Labor, Bureau of Labor Statistics, *BLS Handbook of Methods for Surveys and Studies*, Bulletin 1910, 1976.

U.S. Department of Labor, Bureau of Labor Statistics, *BLS Handbook of Methods, vol. 1*, Bulletin 2134-1, 1982.

U.S. Department of Labor, Bureau of Labor Statistics, *How the Government Measures Unemployment*, Report 505, 1977.

U.S. Department of Labor, Bureau of Labor Statistics, *Special Labor Force Reports*.

The Current Population Survey is used also for a program of special inquiries to obtain detailed information from particular segments, or for particular characteristics of the population and labor force. Approximately eight to ten such special surveys are made each year. Reports on these special surveys, as well as supplemental information obtained through the regular survey, are first published in the *Monthly Labor Review*. Reprints of the articles, together with technical notes and additional tables, are published as *Special Labor Force Reports*.

Mail and Telephone Reference:

U.S. Department of Labor
Bureau of Labor Statistics
Publications Department
441 G Street, N.W.
Washington, D.C.   20212
(202) 523-1913

Employment by Industry: Based on the Establishment Survey[16]

Issuing Agency: U.S. Department of Labor, Bureau of Labor Statistics, Division of Employment Statistics.

Coverage: Employed persons are all persons who received pay (including holiday and sick pay) for any part of the payroll period including the twelfth of the month. Employed persons include both permanent and temporary employees and those who are working either full time or part time. Since proprietors, the self-employed, and unpaid family workers do not have the status of paid employees, they are not included. Domestic workers in households are excluded from the data for nonagricultural establishments. Persons holding more than one job (about 5 percent of all persons in the labor force) are counted in each establishment that reports them; thus, people holding more than one job are counted more than once.

Data Available: Comprehensive employment information is available for over 500 industries and for each of the fifty states and for most major metropolitan areas.

Employment data are also collected for groups of employees designated as production workers, construction workers, or nonsupervisory workers depending upon the industry.

Source of Data: Data based on establishment records are compiled each month from mail questionnaires by the Bureau of Labor Statistics, in cooperation with state agencies. The establishment survey is designed to provide industry information on nonagricultural wage and salary employment, average weekly hours, average hourly and weekly earnings for the nation, states, and metropolitan areas. The employment, hours, and earnings series are based on payroll reports from a sample of establishments employing over 30 million nonagricultural wage and salary workers. The data relate to all workers, full time or part time, who received pay during the payroll period that includes the twelfth of the month (which is standard for all federal agencies collecting data on an establishment basis). Persons on the payroll of more than one establishment are counted each time they are reported. Persons in a nonpay status for the entire period due to layoff, strike, leave without pay, or similar reason and self-employed and unpaid family workers are excluded.

Limitations: Total employment in nonagricultural establishments from the establishment survey (Current Employment Statistics—CES—program) is not directly comparable with the bureau's estimates of the number of persons

198

employed in nonagricultural industries, obtained from the monthly household survey (Current Population Survey—CPS). The establishment series excludes unpaid family workers, domestic servants in private homes, proprietors, and other self-employed persons, all of whom are covered by the household survey; the establishment series counts a person employed by two or more establishments at each place of employment, while the household survey counts only once and classifies the person according to single major activity; and certain persons on unpaid leave are counted as employed under the household survey but are not included in the employment count derived from the establishment series.

In addition to these differences in concept and scope, the surveys employ different collection and estimating techniques. Therefore, although each survey measures changes in employment, direct comparability should not be expected. Over time, however, the trends are similar.

When Series Become Available: The estimated release date is published in the U.S. Department of Labor, Bureau of Labor Statistics, *Monthly Labor Review* near the beginning of the "Current Labor Statistics" section. Employment information is generally released on the first Friday (sometimes the second Friday) of each month for the preceding month.

Publications: Current Data:

Council of Economic Advisers, *Economic Indicators*, Washington, D.C.: U.S. Government Printing Office. Monthly.

U.S. Department of Labor, Bureau of Labor Statistics, *Employment and Earnings*. Monthly.

U.S. Department of Labor, Bureau of Labor Statistics, *Employment and Earnings: States and Areas*. Annual.

U.S. Department of Labor, Bureau of Labor Statistics, *Employment and Earnings: United States*. Annual.

U.S. Department of Labor, Bureau of Labor Statistics, *Monthly Labor Review*. Monthly.

Publications: Historical Data:

Council of Economic Advisers, *Economic Report of the President*, Washington, D.C.: U.S. Government Printing Office. Annual. See statistical appendix.

U.S. Department of Labor, Bureau of Labor Statistics, *Supplement to Employment and Earnings: Revised Establishment Data*, August 1981. Annual.

U.S. Department of Labor, Bureau of Labor Statistics, *Employment and Earnings, 1909-1978*. 1979.

References:

U.S. Department of Labor, Bureau of Labor Statistics, *BLS Handbook of Methods, for Surveys and Studies*, Bulletin 1910, 1976.

U.S. Department of Labor, Bureau of Labor Statistics, *BLS Handbook of Methods, vol. 1*, Bulletin 2134-1, 1982.

Mail and Telephone Reference:

U.S. Department of Labor
Bureau of Labor Statistics
Publications Department
441 G Street, N.W.
Washington, D.C.   20212
(202) 523-1913

Notes

1. For purposes of comparisons, it is impossible to talk about earnings without incorporating measures of hours worked.

The work-week information relates to average hours paid for, which differ from scheduled hours or hours worked. Average weekly hours reflect the effects of such factors as absenteeism, labor turnover, part-time work, and strikes.

Overtime hours represent the portion of gross average weekly hours in excess of regular hours and for which overtime premiums were paid.

2. The U.S. Department of Labor, Bureau of Labor Statistics, does not publish the series on spendable weekly earnings any longer since it was extremely misleading (as the bureau pointed out).

3. To estimate average weekly hours (which is used directly or indirectly in compiling these statistics), the number of hours worked in a plant is divided by the number of production workers.

4. The following example illustrates the problem. "Consider the following hypothetical example: Joe Smith, a married worker with three dependents, earns $200 a week, working a full-time forty-hour week. Feeling the pinch of inflation, his wife decides to get a part-time job and earns $80 for a twenty-hour-week. The family income goes up to $280. But since two persons are working, the average earnings per worker goes down to $140. Furthermore, suppose Joe decides that $280 is not enough and does some moonlighting weekends with another employer, picking up $50 a week that way. The family's income is now $330, but since Joe is now listed on two payrolls and his wife on a third, the earnings of three workers are reported, and the average goes down to $110. Mr. and Mrs. Smith's attempt

to beat inflation has made the average earnings per worker completely unrepresentative." Geoffrey Moore, "Inflation and Statistics," *Contemporary Economic Problem*, American Enterprise Institute, 1980, pp. 184, 185.

5. Data for both of these series can be obtained from: U.S. Department of Labor, Bureau of Labor Statistics, *Employment and Earnings* (monthly), and U.S. Department of Labor, Bureau of Labor Statistics, *Monthly Labor Review*. A technical explanation of the series is available in the U.S. Department of Labor, Bureau of Labor Statistics, *Handbook of Methods for Surveys and Studies*, Bulletin 1910, 1976, and U.S. Department of Labor, Bureau of Labor Statistics, *BLS Handbook of Methods, vol. 1*, Bulletin 2134-1, 1982. Also see G. Donald Wood, "Estimation Procedures for the Employment Cost Index," *Monthly Labor Review*, May 1982, U.S. Department of Labor, Bureau of Labor Statistics, pp. 40-42.

6. The consumer-expenditure studies are published in articles in the U.S. Department of Labor, Bureau of Labor Statistics, *Monthly Labor Review*, and in bulletins and reports as they are completed.

7. Employment statistics are compiled from two major sources: household interviews and reports of employers. The household and establishment data supplement one another, each providing information the other cannot supply. Population characteristics, for example, are readily obtained only from the household survey, and detailed industrial classifications can be reliably derived only from establishment reports.

Data from the two sources differ from each other because of differences in definition and coverage, sources of information, methods of collection, and estimating procedures. Sampling variability and response errors are additional reasons for discrepancies.

8. Much of this section is taken from U.S. Department of Labor, Bureau of Labor Statistics, *How the Government Measures Unemployment*, Report 505, 1977.

9. In category 3, persons are counted as employed whether or not they were paid by their employers for the time off or whether or not they were seeking another job.

10. Unemployment statistics are intended to measure unutilized available labor resources rather than persons who are suffering a hardship.

11. Many countries base their estimates of unemployment on the number of people receiving unemployment insurance payments or the number of persons registered with government employment offices as available for work. These data are available in the United States, but are not used to measure unemployment because they exclude several important groups.

Statistics on the insured unemployed are collected as a by-product of the unemployment insurance program. Workers who lose their jobs and are covered by the program usually file claims, which serve as notice they are beginning a period of unemployment. The insured unemployment for a given week represents the number of workers who have filed claims during the previous week.

More than three-fourths of the civilian labor force are covered by unemployment insurance programs. The major groups not covered are domestic service workers, self-employed workers, and unpaid family workers. Insured-employment data also exclude unemployed workers who have exhausted their benefits, unemployed workers who have not yet earned benefit rights (new entrants or reentrants to the labor force), and disqualified workers whose unemployment is considered to have resulted from their own actions rather than from economic conditions (for example, a worker discharged for misconduct on the job).

Because of these shortcomings, the statistics on insured unemployment cannot be used effectively to measure the use of total labor resources. For a comprehensive analysis of the difference between total and insured unemployment figures, see Gloria Green, "Measuring Total and State Insured Unemployment," *Monthly Labor Review*, June 1971, U.S. Department of Labor, Bureau of Labor Statistics.

12. The survey actually covers all persons fourteen years old and over. Since 1967, however, data for fourteen and fifteen year olds have been excluded from the total count and have been published separately.

13. Four separate modifications in the Current Population Survey became effective with January 1983 data. (1) Persons in the armed forces stationed in the United States are included in the national labor force and employment totals and thus in the base for the overall unemployment rate. (2) All occupational detail in the CPS are coded according to the classification system developed for the 1980 decennial census, which evolved from the 1980 Standard Occupational Classification system (SOC). (3) In terms of racial classification, data are published for the black group instead of for the broader black and other category. (4) Revised first-stage ratio estimates based on the 1980 Census of Population and Housing have been introduced into the estimation procedures.

These changes affect the data in different ways. The first and third relate to data presentation, the second is one of classification, and the last one updates the estimating procedure. See John E. Bregger, "Labor Force Data From the CPS to Undergo Revision in January 1983," *Monthly Labor Review*, November 1982, U.S. Department of Labor, Bureau of Labor Statistics, pp. 3, 4.

14. This section is adapted from Roger LeRoy Miller and Arline Alchian Hoel, *Media Economics Source Book*, New York: West Publishing Co., 1982, pp. 82-89.

15. There are always some people in the economy who will be counted as unemployed. Consider the following example of how in a dynamic economy there are always some people in the process of changing jobs, and some will be caught in the survey who expect to report to a new job within thirty days. These people will be classified as unemployed. For example, some years ago an author of an economics textbook was part of the sample survey in the July to October period. He had finished his degree in July and had a contract to start teaching in September. "When he was interviewed in July, he was not looking for work and did not want to work. Accordingly, he was classified as 'not a part of the labor force.' In August, however, even though he still was not looking for work and did not want to work, he was scheduled to work within thirty days. In August, then using the definitions of the Bureau of Labor Statistics, he was counted as part of the Civilian Labor Force and as unemployed. In September, he was counted as employed." This example is taken from Richard B. McKenzie and Gordon Tullock, *Modern Political Economy*, New York: McGraw-Hill, 1978, p. 438.

16. Employment statistics are compiled from two major sources: household interviews and reports of employers. The household and establishment data supplement one another, each providing information the other cannot supply. Population characteristics, for example, are readily obtained only from the household survey, and detailed industrial classifications can be reliably derived only from establishment reports.

Data from the two sources differ from each other because of differences in definition and coverage, sources of information, methods of collection, and estimating procedures. Sampling variability and response errors are additional reasons for discrepancies.

5 Indicators of International Finance and Trade

Balance of Payments: Merchandise Trade Balance, Goods and Services Account, Current Account

Issuing Agency: U.S. Department of Commerce, Bureau of Economic Analysis, Balance of Payments Division.

Coverage and Limitations: The balance-of-payments accounts are a record of the value of a country's international transactions. The data are used for a variety of reasons. In addition to the measures of the balance of payments, which some view as summary measures, a set of detailed tables presents a more-comprehensive picture of a country's international transactions.

Three measures of the balance of payments are published: the merchandise trade balance, the goods and services account, and the current account.[1] No one number, however, can adequately describe the international position of the United States during any given period. The definition of an international deficit or suplus is an analytical one, and the appropriate focus changes as the circumstances and nature of the problem change. Moreover, useful analysis of a problem is almost impossible on the basis of balance-of-payments measures alone; additional data relating to international transactions are necessary.

The merchandise trade balance measures the difference between U.S. exports and imports of tangible items.[2]

The goods-and-services account is similar to the merchandise trade balance except that services and intangible items have been added. All unilateral transfers, as well as all capital transactions, official and private, are included. Also included are shipping, insurance, tourist expenditures, and income from foreign investments. The items are net in the sense that they represent the difference between what foreigners purchase here and Americans purchase abroad. The investment income aspect of the goods and services account indicates the difference between the income received by Americans from direct investments abroad and income received by foreigners from investments here. Direct investment involves Americans' putting up money capital to buy or start businesses in other countries. The goods and services account represents the net transfer of real resources to or from foreigners.[3]

The balance on current account covers goods, services, remittances, and current-account government grants (net government and private transfers). Thus, it includes extension of foreign aid (government transfer payments) by the United States to other countries, private gifts to those living in other countries, and military sales and expenditures abroad. With adjustments for errors and omissions and for valuation changes, the current-account balance mirrors changes in U.S. financial claims on foreigners.[4]

Data Available: The balance-of-payments accounts are published quarterly as memoranda items in detailed tables summarizing U.S. international transactions.

Data are available that provide details on U.S. international transactions with respect to the rest of the world in aggregate and with respect to selected individual countries (such as Canada and Japan) and groups of countries (such as Western Europe and Latin America). Major types of transactions covered are merchandise trade, travel, transportation, income on international investment, U.S. government military and other services, U.S. private services, private remittances, foreign-aid programs, short- and long-term private capital flows, and changes in foreign official assets in the United States and U.S. official reserve assets.

Related Series: International investment estimates measure the international investment of the United States. This work consists of the analysis of estimates of U.S. direct investment abroad; foreign direct investment in the United States; income flows associated with these investments; and other economic transactions of multinational enterprises, including their trade, employment, taxes, and plant and equipment expenditures.[5]

Source of Data: Major sources of data for international transactions are the U.S. Department of Commerce, Census Bureau and the U.S. Department of Commerce, Bureau of Economic Analysis, and the U.S. Treasury. Estimates are based on extensive surveys conducted for and compiled by these entities.

When Series Become Available: The estimated release dates for quarterly international financial statistics appear on the last page in the December issue of U.S. Department of Commerce, Bureau of Economic Analysis, *Survey of Current Business.* The merchandise trade balance is released with a lag of about four or five weeks; data on selected international transactions are released with a lag of about six to seven weeks; the summary of international transactions (which includes all balance-of-payments measures) is released with a lag of about two and a half months. For example, data for the first quarter are released about as follows: for merchandise trade balance, May 1; for selected international transactions, May 20; and for summary international transactions, June 18.

Publications: Current Data:

Council of Economic Advisers, *Economic Indicators,* Washington, D.C.: U.S. Government Printing Office. Monthly.

U.S. Department of Commerce, Bureau of Economic Analysis, *Survey of Current Business*. Monthly. (Data released quarterly.)

Publications: Historical Data:

Council of Economic Advisers, *Economic Report of the President,* Washington, D.C.: U.S. Government Printing Office. Annual. See statistical appendix.

U.S. Department of Commerce, Bureau of Economic Analysis, *Survey of Current Business*. Monthly.

Revised estimates of U.S. international transactions that incorporate new information) appear each year in the June issue of *Survey of Current Business*.

References:

Denison, Edward F., "International Transactions in Measures of the Nation's Production," *Survey of Current Business,* May 1981, U.S. Department of Commerce, Bureau of Economic Analysis, pp. 17-28.

"1977 Benchmark Survey of U.S. Direct Investment Abroad," *Survey of Current Business,* April 1981, U.S. Department of Commerce, Bureau of Economic Analysis, pp. 29-37.

"Report of the Advisory Committee on the Presentation of Balance of Payments Statistics," *Survey of Current Business,* June 1976, U.S. Department of Commerce, Bureau of Economic Analysis, pp. 18-27.

Mail and Telephone Reference:

U.S. Department of Commerce
Bureau of Economic Analysis
1401 K Street, N.W.
Washington, D.C.   20230
(202) 523-0777

The Bureau of Economic Analysis also provides on request a list, "BEA Contacts for Data Users." The list provides the names and telephone numbers of people to contact, by subject. The list is updated periodically.

Foreign Exchange Rates

Issuing Agency: International Monetary Fund (IMF).[6]

Coverage: The foreign-exchange rate is the price of foreign currency in terms of domestic currency, or vice-versa. For example, if the exchange rate for French francs is $.20, $.20 buys one franc. An alternative way of stating the exchange rate is that the value of the dollar is five francs; five francs are needed to purchase one dollar.

Exchange rates play a major role in the process of external adjustment to price and monetary developments in the economy. They are also widely used as conversion factors, so that economic time series expressed in different national currency units can be presented in a common unit of account to facilitate international comparisons.

The IMF is the basic source of data that are useful for analysis of exchange-rate developments and to provide conversion factors. The same time series, however, may not be appropriate for both purposes.[7]

Market-exchange rates are quotations in the different markets in which currencies are actually exchanged and reflect varying legal operational and institutional factors that may lead to different valuations of a country's currency. A currency that is freely usable and actively traded can be quoted in different markets, and the market-exchange rates quoted for the currency may vary. For currencies that are not freely usable (subject to restrictions), the market-rate quotations are likely to be affected by several factors, such as the nature of the restrictions on payments and transfers conducted through the exchange markets and the arrangements made for official settlements.[8]

Once the problems about the selection of the appropriate exchange rates have been resolved, decisions on the presentation of the data must be made. Two major considerations are the form in which the rate should be quoted (against which unit of account) and the period to which the data should refer (the end of period or an average for the period). On the basis of these considerations, a variety of different exchange-rate series (around twelve) can be generated for a currency.[9]

On the basis of established guidelines, the IMF determines which of these series to present in their regular publications. The effect of the guidelines is to reduce the number of series to be presented in the regular International Monetary Fund, *International Financial Statistics* publication from twelve to a maximum of four. The specific four series differ from country to country, depending on the specifics appropriate for each currency (such as the countries' practice of expressing currency in terms of a standard exchange rate). The page notes in the *International Financial Statistics* describe the details of the exchange-rate series used for each country.

Data Available: The IMF publishes twelve tables, one for each of the twelve exchange-rate series, showing for 143 countries eleven years of annual data from 1970 to 1980 for ten series and thirty-three years of annual data from 1948 to 1980 for the remaining two series.[10] It also provides seventeen years of monthly, quarterly, and annual data from 1964 to 1980 by country for 143 countries for the two most widely used standard time series (depending upon the form in which the rate is normally quoted).

Exchange rates are also available on a regular monthly and annual basis by country.[11]

Related Series: The IMF provides three types of exchange-rate statistics for major currencies: a time series on daily market quotations for the latest month, a series on three-month forward exchange rates, and a series on an index of effective exchange rate based on the fund's Multilateral Exchange Rate Model (MERM).[12]

Publications: Current Data:

International Financial Statistics, Washington, D.C.: International Monetary Fund. Monthly.

Publications: Historical Data:

International Financial Statistics Yearbook, Washington, D.C.: International Monetary Fund.
International Financial Statistics: Supplement on Exchange Rates, Washington, D.C.: International Monetary Fund, 1981.

Mail and Telephone Reference:

International Monetary Fund
Bureau of Statistics
700 19th Street, N.W.
Washington, D.C.   20431
(202) 477-3395

Special Drawing Rights (SDRs)

Issuing Agency: International Monetary Fund (IMF).

Coverage, Source, and When Available: Special drawing rights are international reserve assets created by the IMF to supplement existing reserves. They are valued on the basis of a basket of five currencies.[13] Allocations of the IMF's official SDRs are made only to countries that are members of the fund and have voluntarily agreed to use and accept SDRs according to procedures established by the fund (these member countries are called participants in SDRs). SDRs may also be acquired, held, or used by the fund itself and other official entities prescribed by the fund (these entities are called other holders of SDRs).

SDRs exist only on the books of the IMF. In other words, they are a bookkeeping entry in the accounts maintained by the IMF. No physical SDR, such as a metallic coin, piece of paper, or definitive security, is exchanged or traded when a transaction involving SDRs occurs.[14]

The value of the SDR is calculated daily by multiplying fixed-weight amounts of each of the five currencies in the SDR market basket by the daily exchange rate as shown in table 5-1.[15] The exchange rates, by which each of the five fixed amounts is multiplied to calculate the value of the SDR, are determined daily by traders at the Bank of England using the noon (London) exchange rates.[16]

Table 5-1
Illustration of the Calculation of the International Monetary Fund SDR Valuation for Tuesday, May 26, 1981

Currency	Currency Amount under Rule 0-1[a]	Exchange Rate[b]	U.S. Dollar Equivalent
Deutsche mark	0.46	2.3299	0.197433
French franc	0.74	5.5795	0.132628
Japanese yen	34.00	223.770	0.151942
Pound sterling	0.071	2.0694	0.146927
U.S. dollar	0.54	1.0000	0.540000
			1.168930

SDR1 = US$ 1.16893
US$1 = SDR 0.855483

Source: International Monetary Fund, "An Explanatory Note for Participants and Other Holders in the Special Drawing Rights Department," November 4, 1981, pp. 16, 17.

[a]Rule 0-1: The value of the special drawing shall be the sum of the values of the following amounts of the following currencies: U.S. dollar, 0.54; deutsche mark, 0.46; Japanese yen, 34; French franc, 0.74; and pound sterling, 0.071.

[b]Exchange rates in terms of currency units per U.S. dollar except for the pound sterling, which is expressed as U.S. dollars per pound.

Publications: Current Data:

International Monetary Fund, *International Financial Statistics*, Washington, D.C.: International Monetary Fund. Monthly.

Publications: Historical Data:

International Monetary Fund, *International Financial Statistics: Yearbook,* Washington, D.C.: International Monetary Fund. Annual.

References:

International Monetary Fund, Treasurer's Department, Operations Division for SDRs and Administered Accounts, "An Explanatory Note of Participants and Other Holders in the Special Drawing Rights Department," Washington, D.C.: International Monetary Fund, November 4, 1981.

Mail and Telephone Reference:

International Monetary Fund
Bureau of Statistics
700 19th Street, N.W.
Washington, D.C.   20431
(202) 477-3395

International Statistics:
Other International
Indicators

Issuing Agency: International Monetary Fund (IMF), Bureau of Statistics.

Coverage: The IMF, Bureau of Statistics, compiles for over 100 countries many international statistics on all aspects of international and domestic finance. These statistics are reported in a series of statistical publications by the fund.

International Financial Statistics is a monthly publication showing for most countries of the world (about 140) current data needed in the analysis of problems of international payments and of inflation and deflation. Included are data on exchange rates, international liquidity, money and banking, international trade, prices, production, government finance, and interest rates. Information is presented in country tables and in tables of area and world aggregates.

International Financial Statistics Yearbook contains available annual data for thirty years, beginning with 1952 for all countries appearing in the monthly publications.[17]

Balance of Payments Statistics consists of monthly issues and a two-part yearbook containing balance-of-payments statistics for over 110 countries.[18] The monthly issues contain aggregated presentations covering annual data and, where available, quarterly or semiannual data for eight or nine recent periods. Part 1 of the yearbook includes aggregated as well as detailed presentations and explanatory notes. Part 2 provides about seventy tables of data, featuring area and world totals of balance-of-payments components and aggregates.

Direction of Trade Statistics provides data on the distribution, by partner countries and by areas, of countries' exports and imports. It is published monthly, covering data for recent periods for about 135 countries and industrial countries as an area reported by themselves or their partners. It is also published annually in a yearbook giving seven years of data for about 150 countries and two sets of world and area summaries: world and area trade as seen by the reporting countries and as seen by partner countries to those transactions.

Government Finance Statistics Yearbook provides detailed data on revenue, grants, expenditure, lending, financing, and debt of central governments and indicates the amount represented by social security funds and extra budgetary operations. Also provided are summary data for state and local governments, information on the institutional units of government and the accounts through which they operate and lists of sources of information, nonfinancial public enterprises, and public financial institutions. Volume 6, published in August 1982, contains information for 124 countries with up to ten years of data extending through 1980 or 1981 for most countries.

Mail and Telephone Reference:

International Monetary Fund
Bureau of Statistics
700 19th Street, N.W.
Washington, D.C.   20431
(202) 477-3395

Notes

1. In June 1976, the following measures of the balance of payments were discontinued: official reserve-transactions balance, net liquidity balance, and balance on current account and long-term capital. For a detailed explanation of the reasons for the discontinuance, see "Report of the Advisory Committee on the Presentation of Balance of Payments Statistics," *Survey of Current Business,* June 1976, U.S. Department of Commerce, Bureau of Economic Analysis, pp. 21-26. A summary of the reasons follows:

The net liquidity balance and balance on current account and long-term capital encounter practical difficulties in trying to measure the concepts they are designed to portray. The net liquidity balance attempts to measure transactions that can be reversed in the short run and to distinguish between liquid and nonliquid short-term financial assets. In practice, however, the distinction cannot be made, and the categories used are too arbitrary to serve as distinct classification in the statistics.

The balance on current account and long-term capital was supposed to reflect enduring trends in international transactions but did not do so adequately. Capital flows, especially financial flows with foreign affiliates that are in this balance, are quite volatile. The original term to maturity, which the statistician uses, may not be the asset's current term to maturity when a transaction is made. Finally, long-term investment decisions may be made with short-term assets, and vice-versa.

When the official reserve-transactions balance was introduced in 1965, its primary purpose was to reflect the extent of official intervention in foreign-exchange markets to maintain relative values of currencies within narrow limits. This balance-of-payments measure was discontinued for three reasons. First, with the adoption of floating exchange rates and discretionary official intervention to maintain currencies' value, the usefulness of the measure declined markedly. Second, much of the increase in U.S. liabilities to foreign official agencies (particularly those of the aid exporting countries) is a result of those agencies' investment decisions rather than a reflection of their exchange-rate policies. Third, some analysts viewed the official reserve-transactions balance as an important element affecting the U.S. money supply. On the contrary, however, foreign monetary authorities tend to use international reserves they acquire to purchase U.S. Treasury obligations and interest-bearing bank deposits, and these transactions for the most part do not clearly affect the U.S. monetary base or basic money stock measures.

2. Transfers of goods and services under U.S. military grant programs are excluded.

The merchandise trade balance has been criticized as being too narrow to use as a summary measure of U.S. international transactions. Moreover, it has been said that it tends to emphasize excessively the distinction between goods and services that are of little economic significance.

3. A reconciliation table is published in U.S. Department of Commerce, Bureau of Economic Analysis, *Survey of Current Business,* which shows the relation between net export of goods and services in the national income and products accounts and the net exports of goods and services in the balance-of-payments accounts.

The balance on goods, services, and remittances, which is also published, includes pensions, remittances, and some other transfers. Private remittances typically fluctuate in some periods of natural disaster during which private assistance is provided to victims of the disaster or military activities. Some believe that the balance is useful since it focuses on the amount of government transfers and loans that with private capital flows would be needed to maintain an equilibrium with the other items in the balance. Third, some analysts believe that the balance is useful in comparing the financing problems of industrialized and developing countries since it separates government grants and loans as a source of funding.

4. According to some analysts, one weakness of the current account is that it draws a sharp distinction between U.S. government grants to foreigners and U.S. government capital transactions. Some feel that this distinction is more apparent than real since many government loans have a grant element (for example, a grace period, below market rates of interest, or provision for repayment in local currency), and to some extent the balance treats a difference of degree as though it were a difference in kind.

5. For example, see Russell B. Scholl, "International Investment Position of the United States: Developments in 1981," *Survey of Current Business,* August 1982, U.S. Department of Commerce, Bureau of Economic Analysis, pp. 42-46.

6. The Board of Governors of the Federal Reserve system also publishes foreign-exchange rates, as well as an index of the weighted-average exchange value of the U.S. dollar. For a description and back data,

see "Index of the Weighted-Average Exchange Value of the U.S. Dollar: Revision," *Federal Reserve Bulletin,* August 1978, p. 700. The Federal Reserve publishes exchange rates weekly in the statistical release, *Foreign Exchange Rates,* H.10 (512), and monthly in the statistical release, *Foreign Exchange Rates,* G.5 (405). Foreign-exchange rates are also published monthly in Board of Governors of the Federal Reserve System, *Federal Reserve Bulletin.* Historical data for exchange rates for selected countries can be found in Council of Economic Advisers, *Economic Report of the President,* Washington, D.C.: U.S. Government Printing Office, published annually.

7. For a more-comprehensive explanation, see *International Financial Statistics Supplement on Exchange Rates,* No. 1, Washington, D.C.: International Monetary Fund, 1981, pp. iii-viii. Most of this section is taken from this source.

Many of the conceptual issues about exchange rates concern the changes in the international monetary system during the 1970s, including the dissolution of the par-value system, widening the range within which rates were permitted to fluctuate, and finally the abandonment by some countries of par or central rates in favor of market-exchange rates. A further complicating factor is that the time of the switches from par or central rates to market-exchange rates varies from country to country.

8. The IMF requires each member to report to it on the exchange arrangements involving its currency. It is primarily by reference to these reports that the basis of the time series on market-exchange rates is determined.

9. Three principal categories of exchange-rate series are (for which twelve separate series are actually calculated): (1) series that market rates are reported in preference to fixed rates with narrow or wider margins for all dates for which data is available (six series); (2) series used for the calculation of reserves and monetary data (two series); and (3) series that are used as conversion factors for external trade and balance-of-payments data (four series). All twelve series for all 141 IMF members, plus the Netherlands, Antilles, and Switzerland, are available on tape.

10. *International Financial Statistics: Supplement on Exchange Rates,* No. 1, Washington, D.C.: International Monetary Fund, 1981.

11. *International Financial Statistics,* Washington, D.C.: International Monetary Fund, published monthly; *International Financial Statistics: Yearbook,* Washington, D.C.: International Monetary Fund.

12. The effective exchange rate is an index combining the exchange rate between the currency in question and seventeen other major currencies with weights derived from the MERM.

13. The five currencies, as of 1982, are the U.S. dollar, the deutsche mark, the French franc, the Japanese yen, and the British pound sterling.

Beginning on January 1, 1981, the SDR valuation basket consisted of the currencies of the five members having the largest exports of goods and services between 1975 and 1979.

14. In recent years, new instruments denominated in SDRs have become increasingly available on the private international financial markets. Transactions between private parties, however, do not involve entries on the books of the IMF.

15. The fixed weights reflect the relative importance of each of these currencies in international trade and finance, as based on the value of the exports of goods and services of the IMF member countries.

16. The daily value of the SDR in terms of dollars is announced each morning by the IMF in Washington, D.C., and in terms of the other four currencies in the afternoon. As a consequence of the SDR valuation procedure, the percentage value of each currency in the SDR can change daily.

17. The IMF also publishes a series of *International Financial Statistics* supplements on special topics. The supplements present more-detailed explanation of the underlying data and extensive historical data for the series in the publication. At the time of this writing, the following supplements have been published: *Supplement on Exchange Rates,* 1981, *Supplement on Prices Statistics,* 1982, *Supplement on Fund Accounts,* 1982, and *Supplement on Trade Statistics,* 1982.

18. The statistics are compiled in accordance with the Fund's *Balance of Payments Manual,* 4th ed., 1977.

6 Indicators of Government Influence

The Federal Deficit or Surplus as Measured by: The Federal Budget, the National Income Accounts, the Full Employment Budget

Issuing Agency: Office of Management and the Budget.

Coverage: When the federal government spends more than it receives in revenue, it runs a deficit; when it receives more than it spends, it runs a surplus; when expenditures equal receipts, the budget is in balance.

Some analysts focus a great deal of attention on the budget deficit (or surplus) as an indicator of the effect of government policy on economic activity. There are, however, several different ways in which the federal deficit or surplus can be measured, depending on the purpose for which the concept is used. One concept of measuring the federal deficit or surplus is based on the federal budget—the budget that the president submits to Congress at the beginning of each year. The second concept is based on the national income and product accounts, which measure the nation's final output of goods and services produced each year. The third concept is derived by assuming a high level of employment or full employment in the economy over the year.

Federal Budget Measurement: Early in each calendar year, the president transmits to Congress the federal budget (also known as the unified budget), which embodies his financial plan and indicates his priorities for the federal government. The budget is the culmination of many months of planning and analysis throughout the executive branch.[1]

The federal deficit or surplus is measured by the difference between total budget expenditures and receipts. Economic activity and the federal budget, however, are closely interrelated.[2] Implicit in the president's budget proposals are assumptions about economic activity. The budget reflects not only the president's financial plans but also assumptions or forecasts about future economic activity. Similarly, federal budget deficit or surplus then reflects both the effect of the president's proposals and the effects of the forecast of economic conditions. Typically the unified deficit, or deficit derived from the federal budget, is quoted as the deficit.[3]

The current-services estimates, compiled by the Office of Management and the Budget, show what federal outlays, receipts, and the budget authority would be if no policy changes were made. They provide a base against which the president's budget proposals and its effects can be compared. In effect, the current-services budget shows how the budget would come out if no changes were adopted by Congress during the current year. Estimates of the current-services budget are based on the same set of economic assumptions as the president's budget proposals.

This concept is useful because it helps to separate the effect on the budget of changes brought about by changes in economic activity from changes in the president's proposals (such as spending and taxing proposals). Changes in economic conditions significantly affect budget estimates because their effects on tax receipts, unemployment benefits, and other programs vary with different assumed levels of unemployment, inflation, and interest rates. Consequently, if different economic assumptions were used in the current-services budget and the president's budget, it would be impossible to distinguish between the effects of the different economic assumptions and the effects of the president's policy proposals.

The federal budget and the economy are interrelated. The sensitivity of budget estimates to economic conditions has become increasingly apparent in recent years.[4] For example, actual federal spending in 1980 was $48 billion higher than the original estimate in January 1979, in 1981, outlays were almost $45 billion above the original estimate in January 1980. In both cases, assumptions about economic conditions accounted for over half of the increase. If the Reagan administration in January 1982 had assumed that inflation and nominal gross national product growth was 2 percent higher during the calendar years 1982-1987, then the administration's deficit forecast would be $14.7 billion by 1987 instead of $53.2 billion.

As an additional indication of the sensitivity of the budget forecasts to underlying economic assumptions, every budget between fiscal 1975 and 1982, projected a balanced budget two years into the future with growing surpluses in the out-years. The point of which analysts should be aware is the extreme sensitivity of these estimates to underlying assumptions of economic conditions.

National Income and Product Accounts Measurement: For purposes of studying aggregate economic activity, the NIA, compiled by the U.S. Department of Commerce, Bureau of Economic Analysis, provide the most-useful measures of federal receipts and expenditures. There are major differences between the way receipts and expenditures are recorded in the budget and the federal sector of the NIA. Consequently the deficit and surplus as measured under these alternatives differ as well. Briefly, there are five major differences between the federal budget and the federal sectors of the NIA.[5] First the NIA measures the nation's current income from final production—and therefore does not include transactions such as loans, which are an exchange of existing assets and liabilities—rather than current income and production. Second, the contributions of government agencies to the retirement trust funds of their employees are not included in the budget totals. Third, the budget normally counts as receipts only income from taxation or similar sources that arises from the exercise of governmental power to compel payment. Money received in the course of business-type transactions is normally shown as an offset against outlays. For example, receipts from social-insurance programs operated by the Veterans Administration are netted against outlays in the budget. In the NIA, however, these insurance premiums are treated like social-insurance receipts, just as are receipts from compulsory government programs. Fourth, timing adjustments are necessary when there are differences in recording receipts and expenditures on a cash or accrual basis. For example, the budget records receipts at the time the cash is collected, regardless of when the income is earned, and outlays (except interest paid to the public) are recorded at the time the checks are issued. The NIA attempts to record most receipts from the business sector in the time period in which income is earned rather than when taxes are actually paid. Fifth, there are a number of miscellaneous adjustments for certain specialized items in the NIA, such as the purchase and sale of land and geographical exclusions. In addition, bonuses paid on the outer continental shelf aid leases have become a significant reconciliation item between the budget and the NIA.

Full Employment Government Budget Measurement: Some economists do not like to look only at the government's actual deficit or surplus. They do not think it is useful to look at the current levels of expenditures and taxes or the current budget deficit and surplus that results. For example, suppose the economy is at full employment and the budget is in balance. Then the economy goes into a recession and incomes fall. If government spending remains unchanged and revenues fall (since some taxes are based on income), a formerly balanced budget goes into deficit (since government spending exceed revenues). The budget deficit should not be regarded as an active stimulating governmental policy decision since it is the result of a recession, not a counter-recessionary move.

Some economists who focus on the deficit therefore make calculations to determine whether at full employment or high employment the government budget would be in a deficit or surplus position. The result is called the *full employment* or *high-employment government budget.* It is defined as what the federal budget surplus or deficit would be if the economy operated at full employment throughout the year.[6]

Data Available: Detailed explanations of federal spending programs and analyses of receipts are presented in *Budget of the U.S. Government.* In addition, detailed financial information including the effects of supplementals, recisions, proposals, and new legislative proposals are available for all agencies in the *Budget of the United States Government—Appendix.* Finally, the overall effects of spending and revenue, as reflected by summary measures such as the deficit or surplus, are available.

When Series Become Available: Budget documents that provide details of the proposed spending and revenue programs, as well as the effect on the federal deficit or surplus, become available around mid-January, when the president transmits the budget to Congress. When conditions warrant, the estimates are revised during the year.

Limitations: One of the reasons the measures do not indicate the true size of the federal government is because the government's accounting procedures keep numerous expenditures off budget. In other words, the scope of the federal government extends beyond its direct spending and receipts. The federal government's pervasive presence in the credit markets, for example, stems from three sources: activities of off-budget agencies, operation of government-sponsored enterprises, and provision of federally guaranteed loans.[7]

The key point is that none of these three major loan activities shows up directly in the federal budget. Congress does not directly vote on appropriations and expenditures for these activities. This point relates most importantly to off-budget agencies. For the most part, their deficits are financed by loans from the U.S. Treasury.

Some economists argue that an appropriate measure of the deficit requires several adjustments. First, the unified budget does not include borrowing of off-budget federal agencies. Second, the federal deficit is distorted by the effect of inflation. Third, a relevant measure of the deficit should reflect the net liabilities of the government—that is, assets minus liabilities measured at market value (not book value). These adjustments result in a measure of the federal government's real net liabilities. Such a concept, critics argue, more accurately reflects the drain of the federal sector on the credit markets.

Over the past twenty years, in fact, the real net liabilities of the federal government have declined. In contrast, the unified deficit has risen, suggesting two very different effects of the federal government on the private sector.[8]

Publications: Four sets of documents are prepared for each fiscal year by the Office of Management and the Budget to provide the financial information, in various levels of detail, for the budget of the U.S. government.[9]

The Budget of the United States Government contains the budget message of the president and presents an overview of the president's budget proposals. It includes explanations of spending programs in terms of national needs, agency missions, basic programs, and analyses of estimated receipts. It also contains a description of the budget system and summary tables on the budget as a whole.

United States Budget in Brief provides a more-concise, less-technical overview of the U.S. budget.

Budget of the United States Government—Appendix contains detailed information on the appropriations and funds that comprise the budget. It contains detailed information for each agency, including the proposed text of appropriation language, budget schedules for each account, new legislative proposals, explanations of the work to be performed, and the funds needed. Supplemental and recision proposals are presented separately. Information is also presented on certain activities where expenditures are not part of the budget totals.

Special Analyses are designed to highlight specified program areas or provide other significant presentations of the federal budget data. For example, it contains alternative views of the budget and economic and financial analyses of the budget covering government finances and operations as a whole.[10]

A separate publication, *The Economic Report of the President*, written by the Council of Economic Advisers, sets forth the economic basis for the key elements of the president's economic program, analyzes the effects of the administration's policies, and spells out the domestic and international economic implications.

Notes

1. The federal budget serves several purposes: it reflects the spending and taxing of the federal government; proposes an allocation of resources between the private and public sectors and within the public sector; sets forth the president's requests to Congress for appropriations action on existing and new programs and for changes in tax legislation; and is a report on how the government has spent its funds in the past several years.

No single budget concept can completely satisfy all of these purposes. The budget and related Treasury reports provide detailed information on the finances of the federal government and on the tax and spending programs proposed by the president.

For a practical guide to the congressional budget process and the federal budget, see Stanley E. Collender, *The Guide to the Federal Budget: Fiscal 1983 Edition*, Northeast-Midwest Institute, 1982. This edition of the book is based on the fiscal 1983 budget and describes the steps that determine it, explains their significance, and details the procedures under which they may (or may not) take place. The budget figures are discussed, tables are used as examples, and page numbers are cited as references from the presidential budget proposed for fiscal 1983. The book describes all of the budget documents compiled by the Office of Management and the Budget.

Office of Management and the Budget, *Budget of the United States Government, Fiscal Year 1983,* Washington, D.C.: U.S. Government Printing Office, 1982, pp. 7-1 to 7-18, and Office of Management and the Budget, *The United States Budget in Brief, Fiscal Year 1983,* Washington, D.C.: U.S. Government Printing Office, 1982, pp. 70-73.

2. For example, a rise in the unemployment rate affects both federal receipts and expenditures. Federal receipts derived from income taxes would fall off (or rise more slowly), and federal expenditures, as a result of increased unemployment outlays, would rise. The effect of the increased unemployment in this overly simplified example would be an increase in the federal budget deficit.

3. The deficit as measured by the federal or unified budget includes only the deficit arising from on-budget expenditures. The federal government, however, borrows to finance off-budget activities as well, and the effects do not show up in the unified deficit. Financial statements of off-budget agencies and the combined effect of their financing plans are available in the *Appendix* and *Budget*, respectively.

4. For more detail, see Office of Management and the Budget, *Budget of the United States Government, Fiscal Year 1983,* pp. 2-6 to 2-13.

5. For a more-detailed explanation, see Office of Management and the Budget, *Special Analyses: Budget of the United States Government, Fiscal Year 1982,* Washington, D.C.: U.S. Government Printing Office, 1981, pp. 66-69. For an easily understandable set of articles that describe budget deficits—measurement, causes, and implications—see Federal Reserve Bank of Atlanta, "The Deficit Puzzle," *Economic Review*, August 1982. The *Review* can be obtained free of charge by writing to the Federal Reserve Bank of Atlanta, P.O. Box 1731, Atlanta, GA   30301.

6. "In order to estimate the full employment budget, one needs to estimate potential real GNP, or the level of real gross national product at which the economy would be operating if all resources were fully utilized. The government estimates potential real GNP (corrected for inflation) by looking at (1) the working age population, (2) the ratio of the labor force to total population, (3) the ratio of total employment to total labor force, and (4) the ratio of real GNP to employment. . . .

"Once potential real GNP has been estimated, government analysts attempt to measure the full employment amount of tax revenues that would be collected if the economy were at full employment. . . . Of course, tax revenues are only one side of the government accounting coin. The other side involves expenditures. Here analysts must estimate the relationship between changes in employment and changes in government expenditures. . . .

"Critics of the full employment budget approach to an analysis of fiscal policy contend that inflation has not adequately been taken into account. Full employment budget estimates have assumed uniformly that there is no price gap corresponding to the GNP gap and the unemployment gap. In the 1970s and the early 1980s, such an assumption has proven to be unrealistic. Moreover, because of the progressive individual income tax, inflation has increased budget receipts automatically as income has risen with prices: Bracket creep or taxflation has occurred. Budget expenditures have tended to lag, on the other hand, with respect to rising prices. The full employment budget has, therefore, had an inherent bias toward restrictiveness.

"Nonetheless, an increasing number of government policy makers are starting to use the full employment budget again as a measure of the basic stance of fiscal policy. The full employment budget still allows the analyst to separate changes in budget conditions that are simply due to changes in economic activity from those that are due strictly to policy changes. Additionally, as the rate of inflation continues to fall in the 1980s, the major criticism of the full employment budget estimation procedure will wither away." Roger LeRoy Miller, *The Economics of Macro Issues*, 4th ed., New York: West Publishing Co., 1983, pp. 99-101.

7. The first major type of loan activity is the so-called off-budget agencies. All off-budget agencies are owned or controlled by the federal government. Examples of off-budget agencies are the Federal Financing Bank, the Pension Benefit Guaranty Program, and the Rural Electrification and Telephone Revolving Fund. By law, however, their transactions are excluded from the federal budget.

The second major federal involvement with the credit markets consists of government-sponsored enterprises that were originally established to perform specific credit functions but are now privately owned. Although the transactions of these enterprises are not included in the federal budget, they are subject to government supervision. Three of these agencies operate under the watch of the Farm Credit Administration: Bank for Cooperatives, Federal Intermediate Credit Banks, and Federal Land Banks. Three agencies support the housing market: the Federal National Mortgage Association (Fannie Mae), the Federal Home Loan Banks, and the Federal Home Loan Mortgage Corporation (Freddie Mae).

The third category consists of the so-called federally guaranteed mortgage pools or loans for which the federal government wholly or partly insures or guarantees payment of the loan principal and/or interest. Like the off-budget agencies and federally sponsored agencies, federal loan guarantees do not show up in the federal budget. The bulk of loan guarantees have been used to support housing; however, in recent years guarantees have been used increasingly for other purposes (for example, the loan guarantees involving New York City and Chrysler).

8. A further refinement in the broad measure of the deficit involves a distinction between explicit and implicit liabilities of the federal government. Over the past twenty years, implicit liabilities of the federal government—promises to pay that are not binding legal commitments (such as social-security retirement benefits and pension-fund liabilities)—grew rapidly. In fact, by some estimates, implicit liabilities of the federal government overshadow the explicit liabilities—legally binding commitments. Using a broad measure of government debt, one that makes adjustments to explicit debt and also takes into account implicit debt, the projected impact of the federal government can be much different than the narrow concepts suggest. As an example, the *Economic Report of the President*, February 1982, projected under the proposals presented that implicit liabilities in the 1980s would not increase as rapidly as over the past twenty years. The overall effect of the federal deficits in the 1980s would add only marginally to the burden of the debt.

For two easily understandable articles that deal with these issues, see Council of Economic Advisers, *Economic Report of the President*, February 1982, Washington, D.C.: U.S. Government Printing Office, pp. 102-108, and Brian Horrigan and Aris Protopapadakis, "Federal Deficits: A Faulty Gauge of Government's Impact on Financial Markets," *Business Review*, March-April 1982, Federal Reserve Bank of Philadelphia, pp. 3-16.

9. In fiscal 1983, an additional publication was added as a supplementary report to the budget documents, *Major Themes and Additional Budget Details*, which highlighted the way in which the 1983 budget implements major themes of the president's program and describes programmatic changes and their effects.

10. Prior to fiscal 1983, *Special Analyses* was published by Office of Management and the Budget as one document. In fiscal 1983, however, the analyses were published separately as a series of technical reports.

Appendix A:
Selected Sources of
Business and Financial
Information

The following list of selected sources of business and financial information is reproduced from *Investments* by William Sharpe. The sources include general information on business and financial developments, industry information, company information, securities-market information (such as investment advice), security price quotations, security price indexes and averages, data on foreign companies, data on money markets, and data on mutual funds.

I. General Information on Business and Financial Developments

Economic Data Handbooks

> Economic Statistics Bureau of Washington, D.C. *Handbook of Basic Economic Statistics.*
> Financial Times. *International Business & Company Yearbook.*
> Standard & Poor's *Statistical Service. Current Statistics.*
> U.S. Bureau of the Census. *Statistical Abstracts of the U.S.*
> *County & City Data Book.* Suppl. to *Statistical Abstracts of the U.S. Pocket Data Book.*
> U.S. Office of Business Economics. *Business Statistics.*

Daily Newspapers

> *American Banker.*
> *Daily Commercial News.*
> *Financial Times* (British).
> *Journal of Commerce.*
> *New York Times.*
> *Wall Street Journal*
> *Washington Post.*

William Sharpe, Investments, © 1981, 2nd ed., pp. 561-567. Reprinted with permission of Prentice-Hall, Inc., Englewood Cliffs, N.J. This book is also an excellent reference which integrates recent advances in the theory of finance with the institutional details of the securities markets, types of investment instruments, investment management, and international diversification. Moreover, the book is encyclopedic without excessive detail and analytical apparatus.

Weekly Newspapers

Barron's.
Commercial and Financial Chronical (twice weekly).
Financial Post (Canadian).
Money Manager.
National Observer.
Market Chronical.
Wall Street Transcript.
Weekly Bond Buyer.

Weekly Periodicals

Business Week (see especially "Finance" section).
Financial World.
Investment Dealers' Digest.
Japan Stock Journal.
California Business.
Weekly Business Statistics.
San Francisco Business.
Newsweek (especially "Business and Finance" section).
Time (especially "Business" or "Economy and Business" section).
U.S. News and World Report.
United States Investor.

Biweekly Periodicals

Chase Manhattan Bank. International Finance
Forbes

Monthly Periodicals

Business Conditions Digest.
Conference Board Record.
Conference Board Statistical Bulletin.
Dun's.
Economic Indicators.
Federal Reserve Bank Reviews: Monthly reviews are issued by all the
    Federal Reserve Banks.
Federal Reserve Bulletin.
Federal Reserve Monthly Chart Book.
Finance.
Financial Executive.
Fortune.
Donoghue's Money Fund Report.
Insitutional Investor (incorporates *Corporate Financing and Pensions*).

Management Science.
Market Value Index.
Nation's Business.
OTC Review.
Stock Market Magazine.
Survey of Current Business.
Bank letters: issued by various banks, e.g.: *Cleveland Trust Company; First National City Bank of New York; Morgan Guaranty; Chase Manhattan; Bank of America; Wells Fargo.*
Venture Capital.

Bimonthly Periodicals

Financial Analysts Journal.
Financial Planner.
Harvard Business Review.
Investment Strategy.

Quarterly Periodicals

Journal of Business.
Journal of Finance (five issues a year).
Journal of Financial and Quantitative Analysis (five issues a year).
Journal of Money, Credit and Banking.
Mergers and Acquisitions.
Business Starts.

Annual Economic Reviews

U.S. President. *Economic Report . . . together with the annual report of the Council of Economic Advisers.*
U.S. Bureau of Domestic Commerce. *U.S. Industrial Outlook.*
U.S. Congress. Economic Joint Committee. *The . . . Economic Report of the President; Hearings* (i.e., hearings held to consider the President's *Economic Report*).
U.S. Congress. Economic Joint Committee. *Joint Economic Report* (i.e., the Committee's report on their hearings on the President's *Economic Report*).
U.S. Office of Business Economics. *Business Statistics* (biennial; published as a supplement to the *Survey of Current Business*).

II. Industry Information

Business and Financial Journals and Periodicals
(see section I above)

Government Publications and Documents;
See Especially

U.S. Census Bureau. *Census of Manufacturers' Census of Services In-dustries* (every four to five years).
_____ . *Census of Retail Trade.*
_____ . *Census of Wholesale Trade.*
_____ . *Current Industrial Reports.*
U.S. Bureau of Domestic Commerce. *U.S. Industrial Outlook.*
U.S. Census Bureau. *Statistical Abstracts of the U.S.*
U.S. Office of Business Economics. *Business Statistics.*
U.S. Mines Bureau. Minerals Yearbook.
U.S. Census Bureau. *Annual Survey of Manufacturers.*
Survey of Current Business (monthly periodical).
Treasury Bulletin (monthly periodical).
Annual reports of regulatory commisions such as the F.P.C., F.T.C., I.C.C., and the S.E.C.

Reports of Investment and Business Services

Arnold Bernhard & Co.:
    Value Line Investment Survey.
    Value Line Options and Convertibles.
Moody's:
    Manuals.
    Bond Survey (weekly).
Howard & Company. *Going Public.*
Kidder, Peabody & Co., *Research Service.*
Smith Barney, Harris Upham & Co. *Research Service.*
Standard & Poor's:
    Investment Advisory Survey (weekly).
    Industry Surveys.
    Outlook.
    Statistical Service. *Current Statistics.*
Wells Fargo Bank. *Security Market Plane Report.*

Special Bibliographies (indexes to periodicals)

Business Periodicals Index.
Public Affairs Information Service. Bulletin.
Wall Street Journal Index.
F & S Index of Corporations and Industries (Domestic and International).
Predicasts (abstracts periodical articles that contain forecasts for vari-ous industries).
F & S Index of Corporate Change.
Disclosure Journal (index 10-K Reports, Annual Reports to Share-holders, Registration Statements).

Special Reports of Private Agencies

Audit Investment Research, Inc.
  Audit's Realty Trust Review.
  Real Estate Disclosure Review.
Creative Strategies Inc. *Industry Analysis Service.*
Retail Automation Report.
Stanford Research Institute. Long Range Planning Service. *Reports.*

Announcements of Mergers and Acquisitions
(monthly publication of the Conference Board)

Reports and Brochures of Brokerage and Banking Firms

Wall Street Transcript (weekly newspaper, most of whose contents are
  reprints of brokerage house reports).
Merrill Lynch Review.
M.A. Schapiro & Co.
Kidder Peabody & Co.:
  Economic Perspectives.
  Financial Perspectives.
  Money and Capital Markets.
  Portfolio Manager's Digest.
  Portfolio Strategy.
  Portfolio Managers Digest.
Bank of America:
  Daily Quotation Sheets: U.S. Government Securities, Federal Agencies
  Federally Guaranteed Tax Exempt Notes.
  Weekly Monetary Summary.
Bankers Trust. *Credit and Capital Markets.*
Siegel Trading Company. *Weekly Market Letter.*
Smith Barney, Harris Upham & Co. *Analysts Roundtable.*
Thomson and McKinnon Auchincloss Kohlmeyer:
  Commodity Letter.
  Technical Analysis.
Goldman, Sachs. *Risk, Return and Equity Valuation.*

Trade Association Publications (especially
annual review numbers)

Dow Jones Investor's Handbook.
Symbol Stock Guide, GTE.
Security Traders Handbook.

Trade Journals (especially annual statistical numbers)

III. Company Information

Corporation Reports

Annual reports to shareholders.
10-K reports.
Pospectuses.
Registration statements.
Disclosure Journal (indexes annual reports to shareholders, 10-K reports, registration statements).
Financial Stock Guide Service. *Directory of Obsolete Securities.*

Financial and Business Journals (see Section II above; the F & S Index of Corporations and Industries indexes most of these extensively by Standard Industrial Classification and by company name)

Publications of Brokerage and Banking Firms

Manuals

Moody's Manuals (Industrials; Transportation; Public Utilities; Banks and Finance; Municipals and Governments; O.T.C. Industrials).
Over-the-Counter Securities Handbook.
Penny Stock Handbook.
Standard and Poor's Standard Corporation Descriptions.
Standard and Poor's Stock Reports (American Stock Exchange; New York Stock Exchange; Over-the-Counter and Regional Exchanges).
Walker's Manual of Far Western Securities (Industrial & Financial).

Publications of Financial Services

Moody's:
  Bond Record.
  Bond Survey.
  Manuals (see Section III, above; note especially the semiweekly supplements and the blue sections in the center of annual volumes).
  Dividend Record.
  Handbook of Common Stocks.
  Stock Survey.
Standard and Poor's:
  Analysts Handbook (annual, with monthly supplements).
  Bond Guide.
  Called Bond Record.
  Commercial Paper Reports.
  Dividend Record.
  Earnings Forecaster.
  Fixed Income Investor.

Industry Surveys.

Outlook (incorporates Investment Advisory Survey).

Standard Convertible Bond Reports.

Standard Corporation Descriptions (note especially the daily supplements).

Stock Guide (also called the *Security Owner's Stock Guide*).

Statistical Service. *Current Statistics.*

Financial Dynamics (see also its *Debt Analysis Supplement*).

Vickers Guide to Insurance Company Porfolios (Common Stocks).

_____ . (Buying-Selling-Holdings of Common Stocks).

_____ . (Buying-Selling-Holdings of Stocks & Bonds).

United Business Service. *United Business & Investment Report.*

Arnold Bernhard & Co.:

    Value Line *OTC Special Situation.*

    Value Line Investment Survey.

R.H.M. Warrant and Stock Survey.

John S. Herold, Inc. *Over-the-Counter Growth Stocks.*

Kalb, Voorhis & Co. *KV Convertible Fact Finder.*

Quote (American; New York; Over-the-Counter).

IV. Securities Market Information: Investment Advice

Bond and Stock Ratings

    Moody's *Manuals* (Bonds).

    Moody's *Bond Record.*

    Standard and Poor's *Bond Guide.*

    Call Bond Record.

    Value Line Investment Survey. Commercial Paper Rating Guide.

    Value Line Options and Convertibles.

    Value Line OTC Special Situation Service.

Beta Factors

    Merrill Lynch, Pierce, Fenner & Smith, Inc. *Security Risk Evaluation.*

    Goldman, Sachs. *Risk, Return and Equity Valuation.*

    Wells Fargo Bank Security Market Plane Report.

    Value Line Investment Survey.

General Market Conditions and Outlook

    Moody's *Bond Survey.*

    Moody's *Stock Survey.*

    Standard and Poor's *Outlook.*

    United Business Service. *United Business and Investment Report.*

Publications of brokerage and banking firms (see Section II).
Wells Fargo Bank. *Market Performance Report.*

Recommendation and Appraisals of Securities

Wells Fargo Bank. *Security Report.*
Goldman, Sachs. *Risk, Return and Equity Valuation.*
Brokerage and banking house reports and brochures (see Section II).
Reports of financial reporting agencies and investment services, especially:
Smith Barney, Harris Upham & Co. *Research Service.*
Moody's *Bond Survey.*
Moody's *Stock Survey.*
Standard and Poor's *Outlook.*
Standard and Poor's *Fixed Income Investor.*
United Business Service. *United Business & Investment Report.*
Value Line Investment Survey.
Standard and Poor's *Investment Advisory Survey.*

V. Security Price Quotations

Daily Range and Close

Commercial and Financial Chronicle (Monday issue contains high and low, but not the close, for each day of the preceding week).
New York Times.
San Francisco Chronicle.
Wall Street Journal.
Standard & Poor's *Daily Stock Price Record.*

Weekly Range and Close

Barron's.
Financial Post (Canadian).

Monthly Range

Bank and Quotation Record.
Standard and Poor's *Daily Stock Price Record.*

Annual Range

Bank and Quotation Record (January issue has range for preceding year; other issues have range for current year to date).
Barron's (first issue in January has range for preceding year; other issues have range for current year to date).
Commercial and Financial Chronicle (Monday issue).

Dow Jones *Investor's Handbook* (annual).
Standard and Poor's:
  Standard Corporation Descriptions.
  Standard Convertible Bond Reports.
  Stock Reports (A.S.E.; N.Y.S.E.; O-T-C and Regional Exchanges).
  Stock Guide.
  Bond Guide.

Other Compendia of Price Quotations

Daily Stock Price Record (American Stock Exchange; New York Exchange;
  over-the-counter; each quarterly volume lists range for each stock for
  each day of the quarter).
National Bond Summary; National Stock Summary (list bid and asked prices
  on each O-T-C trade as reported to the National Quotation Bureau).

VI. Security Price Indexes and Averages

Daily and Financial Newspapers

Periodicals

  Barron's.
  CPI Detailed Index.
  Commercial and Financial Chronicle (Monday issue).
  Federal Reserve Bulletin.
  Survey of Current Business.
  Producer Prices and Price Indexes (formerly *Wholesale Prices Index*).

Special Services

Standard and Poor's:
  Outlook.
  Statistical Service. *Current Statistics.*
  Daily Stock Price Index.
Moody's:
  Manuals (blue section).
  Bond Survey.
  Stock Survey.

Other Compendia of Price Indexes and Averages

  Dow Jones Averages 1885-1970 (averages for each day since the series
    began).
  Wall Street Journal Index (pages at the back list Dow Jones averages for

for each day of the month covered in that volume of the index).
Fisher, L., and J.H. Lorie. *A Half Century of Returns on Stocks and
Bonds.*

VII. Data on Money Markets

Weekly Bond Buyer

Salomon Brothers

Analytical Record of Yields and Yield Spreads (looseleaf).
Comments on Credit (weekly).
Bond Market Roundup (weekly).
Annual Review of the Bond Market.
Preferred Stock Guide (annual).
Supply and Demand for Credit (annual).

Euromoney

VIII. Data on Mutual Funds

Institutional Investor (monthly periodical).
United Business Service. *United Mutal Fund Selector.*
Vickers Guide to Investment Company Portfolios.
Wiesenberger Investment Companies Service, Inc. *Investment Compa-
nies* (annual).
N-1R Reports (annual reports of mutual funds to SEC).
Investment Dealers' Digest. *Mutual Fund Directory.*
Johnson's Investment Company Charts.
Spectrum 1 & 2 Stock Holdings Summary; Bank Portfolios.
Spectrum 3 & 4 Bank Stock Holdings Summary; Bank Portfolios.
Investment Company Institute. *Mutual Fund Fact Book.*
Hirsch, Yale. *Mutual Funds Almanac.*
International Fund Year Book.
Investment Companies International Yearbook.
*Management Results. Mutual Funds and Closed-End Investment Com-
panies.*
Lipper Equity Analysis Report on Large Investment Companies.
Donoghue's Money Fund Report.

Appendix B:
Financial Statements

Business firms periodically (commonly every three or six months and annually) issue financial reports of their activities and current status. Reproduced below is a slightly simplified balance sheet reported for the United Mining Corporation for March 31, 1982 (see table B-1). A *balance sheet* presents a listing and cost valuation of a company's assets, liabilities, and ownership structure. *Assets* are the resources owned by the corporation. There are always claims held by other people against a business; these claims are called *liabilities*. The net value of these assets—that is, the value after liabilities are subtracted—is called *equity* or *net worth*.

The basic definition is:

$$\text{Assets} - \text{Liabilities} = \text{Equity},$$

which can be rewritten:

$$\text{Assets} = \text{Liabilities} + \text{Equity}.$$

The firm's balance sheet presents items classified as assets on the left side and liabilities and equity on the right side. What do the listed items mean?

Assets

Assets are divided into several categories and are grouped separately as either *current* or *long term*. Current assets are made up of:

Cash. The amount of money held, including checking accounts.

Accounts receivable. These are the past sales yet to be paid for by customers; charge accounts or credit extended to customers allowing them, usually, 30 days to pay.

Reserve for bad debts. Very likely some customers will fail to pay their debts. To express this fact and to estimate the expected amount of receivables that will become "bad," the accountants subtract an amount called a "reserve for bad debts" or "doubtful accounts." This is called a "reserve" because it expresses a "reservation" or "qualification" about the value of the receivables. Reserves in accounting statements do *not* represent collections of money or assets that have been reserved in the sense of being set

From *Exchange and Production, Competition, Coordination, and Control*, 3rd ed., by Armen A. Alchian and William R. Allen. © 1983 by Wadsworth, Inc. Reprinted by permission of Wadsworth Publishing Company, Belmont, California, 94002.

aside. In bookkeeping, the word *reserve* almost never denotes a setting aside of cash or actual reserving of assets. It is almost always used to express explicitly a reservation or adjustment in the stated value of some asset or liability.

Unbilled costs. The corporation is making some products to customer order; and, as gradually completed, the corporation records the incurred costs as claims accruing against the customer, for which a bill will be submitted upon completion and delivery to the customer.

Inventories. The corporation refines ores. This is the value of ore removed from its mines and not yet sold, plus any other unsold products. In general, this records values or products or raw materials on hand.

Prepaid expenses. The corporation has paid in advance for some goods and services yet to be obtained—just as when you prepay a magazine subscription, you would record that asset as a prepaid expense in your personal balance sheet.

Marketable securities. These are typically U.S. government bonds or notes payable in the near future, common stocks of other companies, or bonds of other companies. In all cases, these securities are saleable on bond or stock exchanges.

Long-term assets are made up of the following:

Investments. This corporation owns some stock of another company. Usually, the particular investment is identified in footnotes that accompany the balance sheet.

Table B-1
United Mining Corporation Balance Sheet, March 31, 1982
(in thousands of dollars)

Assets		Liabilities	
Current		Current	
Cash	$1,929	Accounts payable	$11,923
Accounts receivable	4,669	Notes payable	2,358
Reserve for bad debts	−600	Accrued liabilities,	
Unbilled costs	13,335	future production	10,200
Inventories	7,515	Current liabilities	24,481
Prepaid expenses	756	Long Term	
Marketable securities	5,577	Long-term debt	48,623
Current assets	33,181	Minority interest	3,974
Long Term		Long-term Liabilities	52,597
Investments	9,334	Equity	
Government contracts	18,244	Preferred, convertible stock,	
Plant and equipment	69,877	10,000 shares (5%, $100)	1,000
Less reserve for depreciation	−7,000	Common stock (20¢ par)	
Other	538	5,175,000 issued	1,035
Goodwill	100	Capital surplus	28,658
Long-term assets	91,093	Retained earnings	18,538
			47,196
Total assets	124,274	Liability + Equity	124,274

Plant and equipment. This is the original amount paid for the physical property—mines, mills, smelters, and the like—of the corporation. Sometimes this is the *cost of replacing it*, especially if there have been drastic changes in costs of this equipment since purchase.

Reserve for depreciation. The property, plant, and equipment have been used and partly worn out. An estimate of the portion of the plant so consumed is called depreciation or reserve for depreciation. Subtracting depreciation from the initial price gives the "book" value of equipment. (See above: *Reserve for bad debts.*)

Other assets. These can be almost any kind of asset—mines, land, buildings, claims against others, and the like. Usually footnotes to the balance sheet will give clues.

Goodwill. Patents and trademarks are often given some small or token estimate of value and called goodwill. Sometimes the continued success of a company is reflected in certain intangibles, for example, its greater income, because it is known to supply good, reliable products.

Liabilities

Liabilities are conventionally categorized into *current* and *long-term* liabilities, with the former usually representing claims that must be paid within a year.

Accounts payable. The corporation has purchased goods and equipment for which it must yet pay. The amount still due is recorded.

Notes payable. The corporation has borrowed, and the amount due is shown. This item may also include any long-term debt that will fall due within a year.

Accrued liabilities. At the present moment (the end of the month), the corporation has accrued obligations to pay taxes or wages. For example, if wages are paid on the fifteenth of the month, then at the end of the month it will owe about half a month's wages, to be paid in two weeks.

Long-term debt. The corporation has issued bonds to borrow money. In the present instance, these will run until about 1995. Bonds are the paper record of indebtedness of the firm to the bondholders.

Minority interest. The corporation is the primary owner of a subsidiary company, the entire value of which has been recorded among the assets. However, because this corporation is not the sole owner, it has recorded here the ownership rights of the other owners. This recorded *minority interest* offsets part of the value shown on the asset side. Usually every balance sheet has footnotes giving further details. A footnote in this report would tell us that the subsidiary company, which has a recorded value of about $14,700,000, is all included in this corporation's reported property, plant, and equipment ($69,877,000) on the asset side. $3,974,000 of that belongs to other people—the subsidiary company's other owners, the *minority interest.*

Equity or Ownership

Many firms include many different items under *Equity.*

Preferred, convertible stock. Preferred stock is a term for what is simply a debt of the company, probably issued by the firm to borrow investment funds. It is called *preferred* stock because its holders, in the event of bankruptcy, have a preferred claim against the company, prior to that of the common stock holders. This might have been called bonds of $100 denominations paying 5% per year—except that preferred stock often differs from a bond in that if the $5 "interest" or "dividend" on the stock is not paid, its holder cannot institute legal foreclosure proceedings against the company. The holder simply has preference to the earnings, if any, for payment of interest before any dividends can be paid to the common stock holders. Sometimes the preferred stock is "cumulative," which means that if any arrears of unpaid dividends accumulate, the common stock holders cannot take any dividends until they are paid. And, as here, the preferred stock may be *convertible:* The preferred stock holder has the option to exchange (convert) it into common stock at a preset exchange rate. In the present instance, the exchange rate is 10 common for one preferred stock (information usually given in a footnote to the balance sheet). Thus the present preferred convertible stock has a par of $100 with 5%; it pays $5 preferred dividends each year (if earned) and may be converted to 10 shares of common stock.

A person who buys a share of preferred, convertible stock for $100 has some hope that the common stock will rise above $10 a share; converting to 10 shares will then give the holder more than $100. As the price of a common share approaches $10 in the stock market, the selling price of preferred convertible stock will rise above $100, reflecting both the current value of the preferred "dividends" due and the present values of further future possible rises in the common stock price. A purchaser of *convertible* preferred common stock is in fact a partial common stock holder or owner. A purchaser of nonconvertible preferred stock is simply a creditor of the company.

Finally, some preferred stocks (and bonds) are "callable"; that is, the company has the option to pay them off prior to their due date. A $100 callable preferred stock will usually be callable at some price slightly above $100, but the premium diminishes as the due date approaches. The owner of a callable, convertible, cumulative, preferred stock (of $100 par value, at

5%, convertible at $10, and callable at $105 within five years) will collect $5 a year in dividends, if earned; $105 may be offered for the stock, which the holder must take or convert to common stock (10 shares because at $10 per share they will equal the $100 par value of the convertible preferred share). As you can see, all sorts of terms are possible in a "preferred stock."

The remaining three items show the equity, the ownership rights of the stockholders, which usually is expressed in three parts: *common stock, additional paid-in capital,* and *retained earnings* (sometimes the last two are combined and called simply *capital surplus*). We already know that equity, by definition, equals the difference between assets and liabilities (including preferred stock as a liability). In the present instance, if we subtract the liabilities (current plus long term) from the assets ($124,274,000 − $77,078,000), we get $47,196,000, which is the *book value* of the commonstock holders' equity. How was it attained? Initially, when the stock was issued, $29,693,000 (= $28,658,000 + $1,035,000) was paid into the company. The figure recorded for legal and tax purposes is $1,035,000 as the *initial par value* and $28,658,000 as the *additional amount paid* originally for that stock. This division is of no economic significance and reflects some technically legal quirks. We mention it here to avoid any impression that the par value reflects some currently relevant economic value.

What happened to that $29,693,000? It was invested and spent (along with proceeds of loans) for property, wages, equipment, and the like, and at the moment the results of that activity are shown as assets on one side and as incurred obligations on the other.

Retained earnings. The corporation has *invested* $18,538,000 of its earnings to purchase new equipment and facilities. It may also have paid out some of the earnings as dividends to common stock holders, but we can't tell from the balance sheet data. If it had losses, they will reduce this figure.

Such is what the balance sheet record of this corporation indicates. If we divide the recorded *book value* of the ownership, $47,196,000 (= $1,035,000 + $28,658,000 + $18,538,000), by the 5,175,000 shares outstanding, it comes to about $9.12 a share.

It is tempting to conclude that a share of common stock is worth about $10; but don't yield to that temptation. . . . Why? Because the figures in the balance sheet's asset column are the historical outlays for the equipment (adjusted for depreciation). They do not tell us what the company will do in the future. How do we know that the mine—which *cost,* say, $1,000,000 to find and develop—is not going to yield $100,000,000 in receipts, or maybe nothing?

None of this is revealed by the balance-sheet asset records—unless the corporation directors decide to make a prognosis of that future receipt stream, discount it into a present value, and record it under "goodwill" or "profits." But they don't do this, simply because they know how unreliable that is. Instead, they issue a report of operations and events along with their balance sheets. For example, this corporation once reported: "The outlook for widespread civilian and military use of uranium improved greatly during the past year. The capability of the industry in the free-world countries, based on currently known or reserve information, is estimated to be about 20,000 tons annually, in the face of a projected annual amount demanded of 40,000 tons, excluding military purchases." But the directors did not foresee the rejection of a proposal to build another nuclear-powered aircraft carrier or the current fear of nuclear hazards. All the directors could do was report what was then known and make some clearly labeled forecasts, which other people can accept, reject, or revise at their own risk.

The recorded book values measure only the past costs of accumulating the assets—adjusted by a formal depreciation method. They are *not* measures of what the assets would sell for now if disposed of piecemeal because the company was to be liquidated. Nor is it a measure of the value of the company's future net receipts from its business operations. The present value of its future earnings may be far above the costs of the assets it uses. An excess of stock price over book value is an indication of profitable prospects; it is not an indication of deception of the stockholders. Nor is a stock price below the book value any evidence that it is a safe investment in the sense that if worse came to worse the company could sell off its assets and collect enough to pay each stockholder the book value. The book value is a measure neither of the piecemeal disposal value nor the value of the going enterprise as a whole. It is instead merely a formalized means of indicating the past dollar measure of costs of the owned assets, adjusted for depreciation by some formal method that often bears little if any relation to the future earnings prospects or the decrease in current market demand for those assets.

At the time the balance sheet situation is disclosed the company also issues its *Income Statement*, a statement of its receipts and expenditures during the year ending at the date of the balance sheet (see table B-2). It reported net earnings of $.08 per share of common stock for the year ending March 31, 1982. That is less than 1% per year on the value of a share of stock, hardly a return competitive with yields available on secure bonds or on common stocks (around 12%). Why the difference? The current earnings may grow to large earnings in the future. It is the present value of all those future earnings that is reflected in the stock price.

The present value of the stock of a company with expectations of rapidly rising future earnings will be high relative to current reported earnings. Stocks should not be compared by looking at only their current earnings. A company with negative earnings this year but with superb prospects of large positive earnings in the future could be worth more than one with positive

Table B-2
United Mining Corporation Income Statement, Year Ended March 31, 1982

Sales		$83,261,000
Costs and Expenses		
Costs of goods sold (labor, materials, power)	$67,929,000	
Depreciation of equipment and depletion of ore	4,599,000	
Selling and administrative	6,079,000	
Interest on debt	4,105,000	
		82,712,000
Operating net income		534,000
Share belonging to minority interest		111,000
Federal Income Tax		25
Net earnings		422,075
Earnings per share		$.08

earnings this year but no prospects for future earnings growth. The ratio of stock price to *current* earnings is a highly misleading basis for comparing two stocks—although many people naively use that ratio.

Appendix C:
The Standard
Industrial Classification

The Standard Industrial Classification (SIC) is an important tool developed to promote the comparability of statistics describing various facets of the U.S. economy.[1] The SIC defines industries in accordance with the composition and structure of the economy and covers the entire field of economic activities. It is revised periodically to reflect the changing industrial composition of the economy.

Much of the usefulness of statistics presented by industry is that they can be compared with other types of data for the same industries. This is possible because federal and state agencies follow as closely as possible a single system to define and classify industries in the U.S. economy: the SIC. The SIC is also widely used by individual business firms for classification of their customers and suppliers in market research, nongovernment research and business organizations, and trade and professional associations that compile statistics supplementing those provided by federal agencies.

Three general principles were followed in developing the SIC: the classification should conform to the existing structure of American industry; each establishment is to be classified according to its primary activity; and to be recognized as an industry, the group of establishments constituting the proposed classification must be statistically significant in the number of persons employed, the volume of business done, and other measures of economic activity.

Since there are thousands of products and activities, the SIC provides for grouping them into both broad and narrow categories to make the

Table C-1
Titles of Standard Industrial Classification Divisions

Division	Title
A	Agriculture, forestry, and fishing
B	Mining
C	Construction
D	Manufacturing
E	Transportation, communication, electric, gas, and sanitary services
F	Wholesale trade
G	Retail trade
H	Finance, insurance, and real estate
I	Services (including agricultural services)
J	Public administration
K	Nonclassifiable establishments

industrial statistics useful for those interested in different levels of detail. The structure of the classification makes it possible to tabulate, analyze, and publish establishment data on a division (the broadest category), a two-digit, a three-digit, or a four-digit (the narrowest category) industry-code basis.[2]

The broadest level grouping divides the economy into eleven divisions, as shown in table C-1. At the two-digit level, all products and services are combined into eighty-four major groups. Thus, in the Manufacturing Division, establishments engaged in manufacturing or processing foods and beverages for human consumption and certain related products, such as manufactured ice, chewing gum, vegetable and animal fats and oils, and prepared feeds for animals and fowls are combined into major group 20 (figure C-1).

Division D. Manufacturing.

Major Group 20. Food and kindred products: This major group includes establishments manufacturing or processing foods and beverages for human consumption, and certain related products, such as manufactured ice, chewing gum, vegetable and animal fats and oils, and prepared feeds for animals and fowls.

Group   Industry
No.   No.

201   MEAT PRODUCTS
          2011   Meat Packing Plants

Establishments primarily engaged in the slaughtering, for their own account or on a contract basis for the trade, of cattle, hogs, sheep, lambs, and calves for meat to be sold or to be used on the same premises in canning and curing, and in making sausage, lard, and other products. Establishments primarily engaged in killing, dressing, and packing poultry, rabbits, and other small game are classified in Industry 2016; and those primarily engaged in killing and processing horses and other nonfood animals are classified in Industry 2047. Establishments primarily engaged in manufacturing sausages and meat specialties from purchased meats are classified in Industry 2013; and establishments primarily engaged in canning meat for baby food are classified in Industry 2032.

Abattoirs, on own account or for the trade: except nonfood animals
Bacon, slab and sliced: *mitse*
Beef, *mitse*
Blood meal
Canned meats, except baby foods: *mitse*
Cured meats, *mitse*
Hames and picnics, *mitse*
Hides, cured or uncured: *mitse*
Lamb, *mitse*
Lard, *mitse*

Meat extracts, *mitse*
Meat, *mitse*
Meat packing plants
Mutton, *mitse*
Pork, *mitse*
Sausages, *mitse*
Slaughtering plants: except nonfood animals
Variety meats (fresh edible organs), *mitse*
Veal, *mitse*

Source: Office of Management and the Budget, *Standard Industrial Classification Manual,* 1972, p. 59.

Figure C-1. Example of the Standard Industrial Classification. Division D. Manufacturing; Major Group 20. Food and kindred products; Group 201. Meat products; Industry 2011. Meat packing plants.

The three-digit level provides several hundred categories. In Food and Kindred Products (major group 20), the SIC provides nine groups of industries: 201, meat products; 202, dairy products; 203; canned and preserved fruits and vegetables; 204, grain mill products; 205, bakery products; 206, sugar and confectionary products; 207, fats and oils; 208, beverages; and 209, miscellaneous food preparations and kindred products.

Thousands of products and activities are distinguished at the four-digit level. For example, in group 201, meat products, four industries are defined: 2011, meat-packing plants; 2013, sausages and other prepared meat products; 2016, poultry dressing plants; and 2017, poultry and egg processing.

Notes

1. Office of Management and Budget, *Standard Industrial Classification Manual*, 1972, pp. 3-13.

2. An establishment is defined as an economic unit generally at a single physical location where business is conducted or where services or industrial operations are performed (for example, a factory, mill, store, hotel, movie theater, mine, farm, ranch, bank, railroad depot, airline terminal, sales office, warehouse, or central administrative office). An establishment is not necessarily identical with the enterprise or company, which may consist of one or more establishments. Also, it is to be distinguished from subunits, departments, or divisions. For more detail, see ibid., p. 10.

Appendix D:
Value Added and
Gross National Product

Gross national product (GNP) measures the value of final output. It ignores intermediate goods because to include them would be to double count. An example can clarify this point. The example will be to determine the value added at each stage of production. Value added is the amount of value added to a product by each stage of its production. Table D-1 shows the difference between total dollar value of all sales and value added in the production of a doughnut. The sum of the values added is equal to the sale price to the final consumer. It is the 15¢ that is used to measure GNP, not the 32¢. If the 32¢ is used, that would be double counting, for it would include the total dollar value of all of the intermediate sales that took place prior to the doughnut's being sold to its final consumer. Such a double counting would grossly exaggerate GNP if it were done for all of the goods and services sold.

In principle and in practice, the GNP in the United States can be calculated by adding up the value added by all industries for any given year. This is done in table D-2 for the year 1975. Notice that the only way to measure the value added of government output from these data is by assuming that value added is equal to the wages and salaries of government workers.

There is no market measure of the value added by government since most goods and services provided by government are not sold in the marketplace at a market clearing price.

From Roger LeRoy Miller, *Economics Today*, 4th ed., New York: Harper and Row, 1982, pp. 187, 188,

Table D-1

Sales Value and Value Added in Cents per Doughnut at Each Stage of Production

(1) Stage of Production	*(2)* Dollar Value of Sales	*(3)* Value Added
Stage 1: Fertilizer and seed	$.01 ⎤	$.01
Stage 2: Growing wheat	.02 ⎟	.01
Stage 3: Flour milling	.04 ⎟	.02
Stage 4: Doughnut baking	.10 ⎟	.06
Stage 5: Doughnut retailing	.15 ⎦	.05
Total dollar value of all sales	$.32	Total value added $.15

Stage 1: A farmer purchases a penny's worth of fertilizer and seed that are used as factors of production in growing wheat.

Stage 2: The farmer grows the wheat, harvests it, and sells it to a miller for 2¢. Thus, we see that the farmer has added 1¢ worth of value. That 1¢ represents income paid in the form of rent, wages, interest, and profit by the farmer.

Stage 3: The flour miller purchases the wheat for 2¢, and adds 2¢ to the value added; that is, there is 2¢ for him as income to be paid as rent, wages, interest, and profit. He sells the ground wheat flour to a doughnut-baking company.

Stage 4: The baking company buys the flour for 4¢ and adds 6¢ as the value added. It then sells the doughnut to the final retailer.

Stage 5: The doughnut retailer sells fresh, hot doughnuts at 15¢ apiece, thus creating additional value of 5¢.

We see that the total dollar value of sales resulting from the production of one doughnut was 32¢, but the total value added was 15¢, which is exactly equal to the retail price. The total value added is equal to the sum of all income payments, including payments to rent, wages, interest, and profit.

Table D-2

Value Added by Selected Industries in United States, 1975

Industry	Value Added (billions of dollars per year)
Agriculture, forestry, and fisheries	55
Mining	38
Manufacturing	346
Construction	67
Transportation	57
Wholesale and retail trade	272
Communication	38
Electricity, gas, and sanitation	37
Finance, insurance, and real estate	209
Other services	182
Government	201
Rest of the world	11
Gross national product	1,513

Source: Survey of Current Business, July 1976.

Glossary

Absolute or nominal prices The prices that people pay today for goods and services in terms of today's dollars or current dollars.

After-tax profits Profits after all federal and state taxes have been accounted for.

Assets The economic resources owned by the organization. They include current assets, such as cash, accounts-receivable inventories, and marketable securities, and fixed assets, such as land, buildings, and machinery.

Automatic transfer system (ATS) accounts A transaction-type account in which the depositor has a checking account, where interest is not earned, and a time-deposit account, where interest is earned. Whenever the balance in the checking account is insufficient to cover checks written, there is an automatic transfer from the interest-earning time, or savings, account.

Balance of payments The value of all transactions between two nations (usually for one year), such as goods, services, or financial assets.

Balance of trade The value of goods and services bought and sold in the world market.

Balance on current account Goods and services account plus the extension of foreign aid (government gifts) by the United States to other countries, private gifts to those living in other countries, and military expenditures.

Balance sheet Presents a company's financial position at a particular point in time, such as the end of the year. Indicates the company's assets, liabilities, and equity.

Bankers acceptance A draft or order to pay a specified amount at a specified time, drawn on individuals and businesses. When the party on whom the draft is drawn, usually a bank, acknowledges the obligation to pay at maturity, usually by writing *accepted* across the draft, the draft becomes an acceptance.

Bond A type of security that is an evidence of a debt owed by the issuing company or government to the receiver. Typically it states that a specified payment will be made at periodic intervals and that a certain principal will be paid off at a specified date.

Business fluctuations The ups and downs in overall business activity, as evidenced by changes in national income, employment, and prices.

Business transfer payments Payments to persons for which the latter do not perform current services. Included are liability payments for personal injury, corporate gifts to nonprofit institutions, and bad debts incurred by consumers.

Capacity-Utilization rates   Designed to measure the extent to which a firm is realizing its potential output rate with the existing stock of capital in a given time frame. The capacity-utilization rate is expressed as a percentage of the actual output to the potential output.

Capital-consumption adjustment   For corporations, the tax-return-based capital-consumption allowances less capital-consumption allowances that are based on estimates of uniform service lives, straight-line depreciation, and replacement cost.

Capital-consumption allowances   Consists of depreciation charges and accidental damage to fixed business capital.

Capital expenditures   Two major components: plant and structures; and machinery and equipment. The distinction is not always clear-cut between the two categories; however, a useful guideline is that plant and structures are not movable (such as factories, warehouses, stores, pipelines), and machinery and equipment are movable (such as automobiles, trucks, computers, furniture, fixtures).

Central bank   A banker's bank, usually an official institution that also serves as each country's Treasury's bank. Central banks regulate commercial banks.

Certificate of deposit (CD)   A receipt for funds deposited in a bank for a specified period of time at a stated rate of interest. The receipt or certificate indicates the amount of money deposited, the rate of interest to be paid, and the principal amount due on the maturity date.

Coincident Indicators Index   A composite index that turns upward and downward with the national economy as a whole.

Commercial paper   An unsecured short-term promissory note sold by financially strong, highly rated businesses on a discount basis to investors.

Common stock   A security that indicates the real ownership in a corporation. It is not a legal obligation for the firm and does not have a maturity. It has the last claim on dividends each year and assets in the event of firm liquidation.

Compensation of employees   The income accruing to employees as remuneration for their work. It is the sum of wages and salaries and supplements to wages and salaries.

Constant dollars   Dollars expressed in terms of real purchasing power using a particular year as the base or standard of comparison.

Consumer credit   Includes all short- and intermediate-term credit extended through regular business channels to finance the purchase of commodities and services for personal consumption or to refinance debts incurred for these purposes.

Consumer price index (CPI)   An index of the prices of a fixed market basket of goods and services people buy for day-to-day living—food, clothing, and shelter and fees to doctors, lawyers, transportation fares, and so on. Prior to 1978 only one index, the Index for Urban Wage and Clerical Workers (CPI-W), was published, which represented the buying habits of 40 percent of the population. Since 1978 the Index for All Urban Consumers (CPI-U) has also been published, which reflects the buying habits of 80 percent of the population, including professional workers, the self-employed, wage earners and clerical workers, the poor, the unemployed, and retired persons.

Corporate profits The income of corporations organized for profit and of mutual financial institutions that accrues to residents.

Cost-push theory of inflation A theory that attempts to explain the rise in prices by input costs' pushing up the prices of final products. These major explanations are used in the cost-push inflation theory: union power, big-business monopoly power, and higher raw-materials prices.

Currency In the United States, the medium that consists of paper bills and coins.

Current assets The company's cash and assets that can be readily converted to cash; usually consists of cash, marketable securities, accounts receivable, and inventories.

Current liabilities A company's debts that must be paid off within one year; usually shown separately on the balance sheet and include short-term notes payable, accounts payable, income taxes, and payroll and other accruables.

Cyclical unemployment Unemployment resulting from business recessions that occur when aggregate (total) demand is insufficient to create full employment.

Debenture A type of bond backed only by the general credit of a corporation rather than by a specific lien on particular assets of the corporation.

Deficit or surplus The differences between receipts and expenditures. When expenditures exceed receipts, the difference is negative and called a deficit. When receipts exceed expenditures, the difference is positive and called a surplus.

Deflated (inflation corrected) prices Absolute or nominal profits adjusted for a rise in the average level of prices.

Demand deposits Checking-account balances. Funds can be withdrawn or transferred on demand.

Demand-pull theory of inflation A theory that attempts to explain the rise in prices by demand's pulling up prices. When total demand in the economy is rising and the available supply of goods is limited, demand pulls prices up. Goods and services may be in short supply either because the economy is fully utilized or because the economy cannot grow fast enough to meet the growing economy-wide demand.

Depreciation   Reduction in the value of capital goods over a one-year period due to physical wear and tear and also to obsolescence.

Discount rate   The rate that the Federal Reserve charges depository institutions for borrowed reserves.

Disposable personal income (DPI)   Personal income after personal income taxes have been paid.

Durable consumer goods   Goods used by consumers that have a life span of more than three years; that is, goods that endure and can give utility over a longer period of time.

Duration of unemployment   The length of time workers remain unemployed.

Employed   All people who worked for pay or profit during the survey week or who had a job but did not work because they were on vacation, ill, involved in an industrial dispute, prevented from working by bad weather, or taking time off for various personal reasons.

Employment cost index   Measures quarterly charges in wages, salaries, and compensation in the private nonfarm economy, free of employment shifts.

Equity   The owners' or stockholders' investment in the organization. Equity arises from direct investment by the owners, such as purchasing stock, and from profits retained in the organization.

Equity capital   Capital raised by a firm by the sale of common stock.

Equity financing   The issuance of stock as a long-term source of funds. Equity financing offers the firm flexibility since dividend payments are optional and there is no maturity date on stock, but it also extends voting rights and control to more owners.

Eurodollars   Deposit liabilities, denominated in dollars, in banks located outside the United States.

Expansion   A business fluctuation in which overall business activity is rising at a more-rapid rate than previously or at a more-rapid rate than the overall historical trend for the nation.

Expenditure approach   A way of computing national income by adding up the dollar value of current market prices of all final goods and services; to be contrasted with the income approach.

Federal financing bank (FFB)   An off-budget agency that provides most of the financing for off-budget agencies and for certain on-budget agencies. The FFB was originally designed to act as an intermediary by buying securities those agencies issued and paying for them with funds borrowed from the Treasury.

Federal funds   Normally federal funds transactions are not secured by anything other than the promise of the borrower to repay. Accordingly, federal funds transactions take place only among credit-worthy institutions. The crucial feature of these transactions is that they are settled in immediately available funds; the funds are available the same day the transaction takes place. Most federal funds transactions involve overnight loans or overnight money (funds lent out one day and repaid the following morning).

Final sales The portion of current gross national product sold to ultimate users. Final sales are derived by subtracting the change in business inventories from gross national product (since inventories are not yet in the hands of the ultimate consumers).

Fixed assets The company's assets that cannot be readily converted into cash, consisting primarily of the company's investment in property, plant, and equipment. Fixed assets are usually the primary income-producing assets, generally have long lives, and normally represent the company's largest investments.

Fixed exchange rates A system of exchange rates that requires intervention by the world's central banks to fix the value of each nation's exchange rate in terms of every other nation's exchange rate.

Flexible or freely floating exchange rates Foreign-exchange rates that are allowed to fluctuate in the markets in response to changes in supply and demand.

Foreign-exchange rate The rate of exchange or price of foreign currency in terms of the domestic currency. For example, if the foreign exchange rate for pounds is $2, $2 is needed to buy one pound. Alternatively the value of $1 is one-half of a pound; one-half of a pound is needed to buy $1.

Forward exchange rate The exchange rate at which people agree to buy and sell foreign currencies today for payment and delivery in the future.

Frictional unemployment Unemployment associated with frictions in the system that may occur because of the imperfect job-market information that exists. Since workers do not know about all job vacancies that may be suitable, they must search for appropriate job offers. This takes time, and so they remain frictionally unemployed.

Full employment government budget An indication of what the federal government budget deficit or surplus would be if the economy were operating at full employment throughout the year.

Futures exchange rate The exchange rate at which futures contracts are bought and sold. Futures contracts are agreements standardized with respect to amount, delivery location, and procedures. Like forward contracts, they provide for payment and delivery on future dates; however, they are made and traded only on the floor of organized future exchanges. Unlike forward contracts, futures contracts rarely result in actual delivery. Most are settled by buying or selling offsetting contracts before the last day of trading.

Gold standard A monetary standard under which gold coins circulated is the medium of exchange. Alternatively gold could be warehoused and the gold warehouse receipts circulate as the medium of exchange.

Goods-and-services trade balance   Merchandise trade balance plus services and intangible items.

Government purchases of goods and services   The compensation of government employees and purchases from business and from abroad.

Government-sponsored enterprises   Government-sponsored enterprises originally set up to perform specific credit functions but now privately owned. The transactions of the enterprises are not in the federal budget but are subject to government supervision.

Gross National Product (GNP)   The total money value of the nation's final product or output produced during the year.

Gross National Product (GNP) Implicit Price Deflator   An index of the average price level of all final goods and services.

Gross private domestic investment   The creation of capital goods, such as factories and machines, that can yield production and hence consumption in the future. Also included are changes in business inventories and repairs made to machines or buildings. In sum, it is investment before depreciation.

Income approach   A way of measuring national income by adding up all components of national income, including wages, interest, rent, and profits.

Indirect business taxes   All business taxes except the tax on corporate profits. Sales and business property taxes are included.

Industrial Production Index   A comprehensive measure of the physical output in the manufacturing, gas, and electric utilities.

Inflation   A sustained rise in the (weighted) average of all prices or a sustained fall in the purchasing power of the dollar.

Installment credit   All consumer credit that is to be repaid in two or more payments. The four major categories of installment credit are automobile credit, revolving credit, mobile-home credit, and other.

Interest   A payment for the use of money. It is a payment for the current use of resources rather than in the future.

International Monetary Fund   An international exchange policing agency, which was supposed to discourage the payments of debts with paper currency rather than with gold or else to urge a country to reduce its exchange rate, if it were using highly inflated currency as not commensurate with its gold holdings.

Inventory valuation adjustment (IVA)   The change in the business-inventories component of GNP, which is measured as the change in the physical volume of inventories valued in prices of the current period, less the change in the value of inventories reported by business (book value).

Labor force   The total population less inmates of institutions, persons under sixteen years of age, and people not in the labor force (for example, people engaged in own housework, school, retired, voluntarily idle, unable to work because of mental or physical illness).

Labor-force participation rate   The percentage of noninstitutionalized working-age individuals who are employed or seeking employment.

Labor force—people not in the labor force   People who are under sixteen years old and confined to jail, asylums, hospitals, or other institutions are not counted as part of the employed, unemployed, and labor force. Other people in the civilian noninstitutional labor force are eligible to participate but may choose not to. They are counted as not in the labor force.

Lagging Indicators Index   A composite index that tends to turn upward after the economy starts to expand and downward after the economy starts to weaken.

Leading Indicators Index   A composite index that tends to turn upward before economic expansions and downward before the economy weakens.

Liabilities   The debts owed by an organization to its creditors. Included are current liabilities, such as notes payable, trade accounts payable, income taxes, and accrued payrolls; and long-term liabilities, such as loans due in future years.

Merchandise trade balance   The difference between the export and import of tangible trade items.

Monetary base or high-powered money   Nonmarket-interest-bearing government debt. In the United States the base consists of the currency issued by the Federal Reserve and U.S. Treasury and deposits held by depository institutions at Federal Reserve banks.

Monetary theory of inflation   A theory that attempts to explain the rise in prices by too many dollars chasing too few goods and services. When individuals in the aggregate find they are holding cash in greater balance than desired, they will spend the excess on goods, services, and financial assets, hence bidding up the prices of these items.

Money supply   A generic term used to denote the amount of money in circulation. There are numerous specific definitions of the money supply. The narrowest is simply currency in the hands of the public plus nonbank travelers' checks, plus transactions accounts of depository institutions. This has been labeled the M1 money supply by the Federal Reserve System.

Mortgage   A loan on a house.

National banks   Banks that are issued their charter by the federal government. National banks must become members of the Federal Reserve system.

National income   The income that originates in the production of goods and services attributable to labor and property supplied by residents of the United States. Thus, it measures the factor costs of goods and services produced.

National income accounting A measurement system used to estimate national income and its components. This is one approach to measuring an economy's aggregate performance.

Near monies Assets that are almost money. They have a high degree of liquidity; they can be easily converted into money without loss in value. Time deposits and short-term U.S. government securities are examples.

Negotiable orders of withdrawal (NOW) accounts A checking-type account typically offered by savings and loan associations and savings banks. This is a so-called transaction-type account in which interest is earned on the balance in the account, but the check (NOWs) can be written on the account.

Net investment Gross private domestic investment minus an estimate of the wear and tear on the existing capital stock. Net investment therefore measures the change in capital stock over a one-year period.

Net national product (NNP) GNP minus depreciation.

New plant and equipment expenditures These expenditures refer to all costs (both replacement and expansion) chargeable to fixed-asset accounts and for which depreciation accounts are ordinarily maintained. The estimates cover expenditures to replace or to add to existing facilities and to provide new facilities and for exploration and development of properties.

Nondurable consumer goods Goods used by consumers that are used up within three years.

Off-budget agencies Entities owned and controlled by the federal government, such as the Federal Financing Bank; however, by law, their expenditures are excluded from the federal budget.

Personal-consumption expenditures Goods and services purchased by individuals, operating expenses of nonprofit institutions serving individuals, and the value of food, fuel, clothing, rent of dwellings, and financial services received by individuals during the year.

Personal-consumption expenditures implicit price deflator An index of the average level of consumer expenditures on final goods and services.

Personal income (PI) The amount of income that households actually receive before they pay personal income taxes.

Personal outlays The sum of personal-consumption expenditures, interest paid by consumers to business, and personal transfer payments to foreigners (net).

Personal saving Disposable personal income less personal outlays.

Prime Rate Interest rate charged by banks for money lent to businesses with high-credit credentials.

Producer Price Index (PPI) An index of the prices of a fixed market basket of goods sold in primary markets by producers of commodities in all stages of processing, formerly known as the Wholesale Price Index.

Productivity Measures the constant-dollar value of final goods and services produced within a given time period per hour of labor input.

Proprietors' income The income, including income in kind, of proprietorships and partnerships and of producers' cooperatives.

Public or national debt The total value of all outstanding federal government securities.

Real after-tax profits After-tax profits adjusted for a rise in the average of level of prices.

Recession A period of time during which the rate of growth of business activity is consistently less than its long-term trend, or is negative.

Relative or real prices The price of any item expressed in terms of the price of another commodity or relative to the average of all other prices in the economy.

Rental income The income of persons from the rental of real property, except the income of persons primarily engaged in the real-estate business; the imputed net rental income of owner-occupants of non-farm dwellings; and the royalties received by persons from patents, copyrights, and rights to natural resources.

Repurchase agreements Immediately available funds are acquired through repurchase agreements by selling securities and at the same time agreeing to buy them back, or repurchase them, at a later date. Usually repurchase agreements are made for one day; however, they can also be made for longer periods of time.

Reserve requirements The requirements that depository institutions keep a specified percentage of their deposits on reserve either in the form of vault currency or reserves at district Federal Reserve banks.

Reserves—borrowed Reserves borrowed by a depository institution from the district Federal Reserve bank.

Reserves—legal Deposits held at Federal Reserve banks and vault cash of depository institutions.

Reserves—nonborrowed Reserves held by depository institutions that have not been borrowed from the Federal Reserve.

Reserves—required The minimum amount of legal reserves—cash plus deposits at Federal Reserve banks—that a depository institution must maintain to back its deposits.

Retail trade Establishments engaged in selling merchandise for personal or household consumption and rendering services incidental to the sale of the goods.

Retained earnings   Those earnings that a corporation saves, or retains, for use in investment in other productive activities; earnings that are not distributed to stockholders.

Revenue   The resources, primarily cash, coming into an organization as a result of goods sold or services rendered. Revenue also includes interest earned on bank accounts or bonds, and cash dividends received from investments.

Seasonal unemployment   Unemployment due to seasonality in demand or in possible supply of any particular good or service.

Services   Things purchased by consumers that do not have physical characteristics. Examples of services are those purchased from doctors, lawyers, dentists, repair personnel, housecleaners, educators, retailers, and wholesalers.

Special drawing rights (SDRs)   International reserve assets created by the International Monetary Fund to supplement existing reserves.

Spot-exchange rate   The current exchange rate at which a foreign currency is bought for currency delivered on the same day (today).

State banks   Banks issued their charter by a state government.

Standard metropolitan statistical area   Includes a city or cities of specified population which constitute the central city and the county or counties in which it is located. SMSAs are designated by the Office of Management and Budget through the Federal Committee on Standard Metropolitan Statistical Areas.

Structural unemployment   Unemployment resulting from fundamental changes in the structure of the economy. Structural unemployment occurs, for example, when the demand for a product falls drastically so that workers specializing in the production of that product find themselves out of work.

Supplements to wages and salaries   Employer contributions for social insurance and of other labor income.

Technological unemployment   Unemployment caused by technological changes reducing labor demands in specific tasks.

Time deposits   Savings-account balances and certificates of deposit held in commercial banks and thrift institutions. The bank or thrift institution can require notice of intent to withdraw from a time-deposit account but does not normally do so.

Unemployed   A person is considered unemployed if that person (1) did not work at all during the week that the survey of the unemployed and employed was made, (2) was looking for work, (3) was waiting to be called back to a job from which he or she was laid off, (4) was waiting to start a new job within the next month and was not in school, or (5) was temporarily ill and otherwise would have been looking for a job.

Wages and salaries Monetary remuneration of employees, including the compensation of corporate officers; commissions, tips, and bonuses; and receipts in kind that represent income to the recipients.

Wholesale trade Establishments or places of business primarily engaged in selling merchandise to retailers; to industrial, commercial, institutional, farm, or professional business users or to other wholesalers; or acting as agents or brokers in buying merchandise for or selling merchandise to such persons or companies.

Index

About the Authors

Arline Alchian Hoel received the Ph.D. in economics in 1973. From 1973 to 1977 she worked as an economist at the Federal Reserve Bank of New York, and from 1978 to 1979 as an economist at Southeast Banking Corporation, Miami. Her teaching areas are price theory, monetary theory, and macroeconomics; since 1979, Dr. Hoel has been affiliated with the Law and Economics Center at the University of Miami.

Kenneth W. Clarkson received the Ph.D. in economics in 1971 and has taught at the universities of California, Virginia and Miami. Currently, he is a professor of economics and the director of the Law and Economics Center at the University of Miami, where he teaches price theory, public policy legislation, and quantitative economic evidence to law students. He has published more than fifty books, monographs, articles, and other publications on government efficiency, the accuracy of government economic statistics, the impact of government regulation, contract law, and public policy. Recently, Dr. Clarkson was the Associate Director for Human Resources, Veterans, and Labor for the U.S. Office of Management and Budget.

Roger LeRoy Miller received the Ph.D. in economics in 1968 and has taught at the University of Washington and the University of Miami. He co-founded the Law and Economics Center at the University of Miami School of Law in 1974, and has been its associate and interim director at various times since then. In addition to teaching economic analysis of legal cases, price theory, and monetary theory, he has lectured frequently to journalists throughout the country, presenting them with innovative ways to understand and report on economic news. Since 1970 he has written over fifty books in the areas of statistics, economics, business law, consumer economics, personal finance and political science.

Edwin L. Dale, Jr. was an economic reporter in Washington, D.C. for the *New York Herald Tribune* from 1951 to 1955 and for *The New York Times* from 1955 through 1976. In 1977 he was on the staff of the Subcommittee on Economic Stabilization of the House Banking Committee until he joined the U.S. Office of Management and Budget in 1981 as Assistant Director for Public Affairs.